COTTON TOP

REMEMBER ME

ELBERT ALBERSON

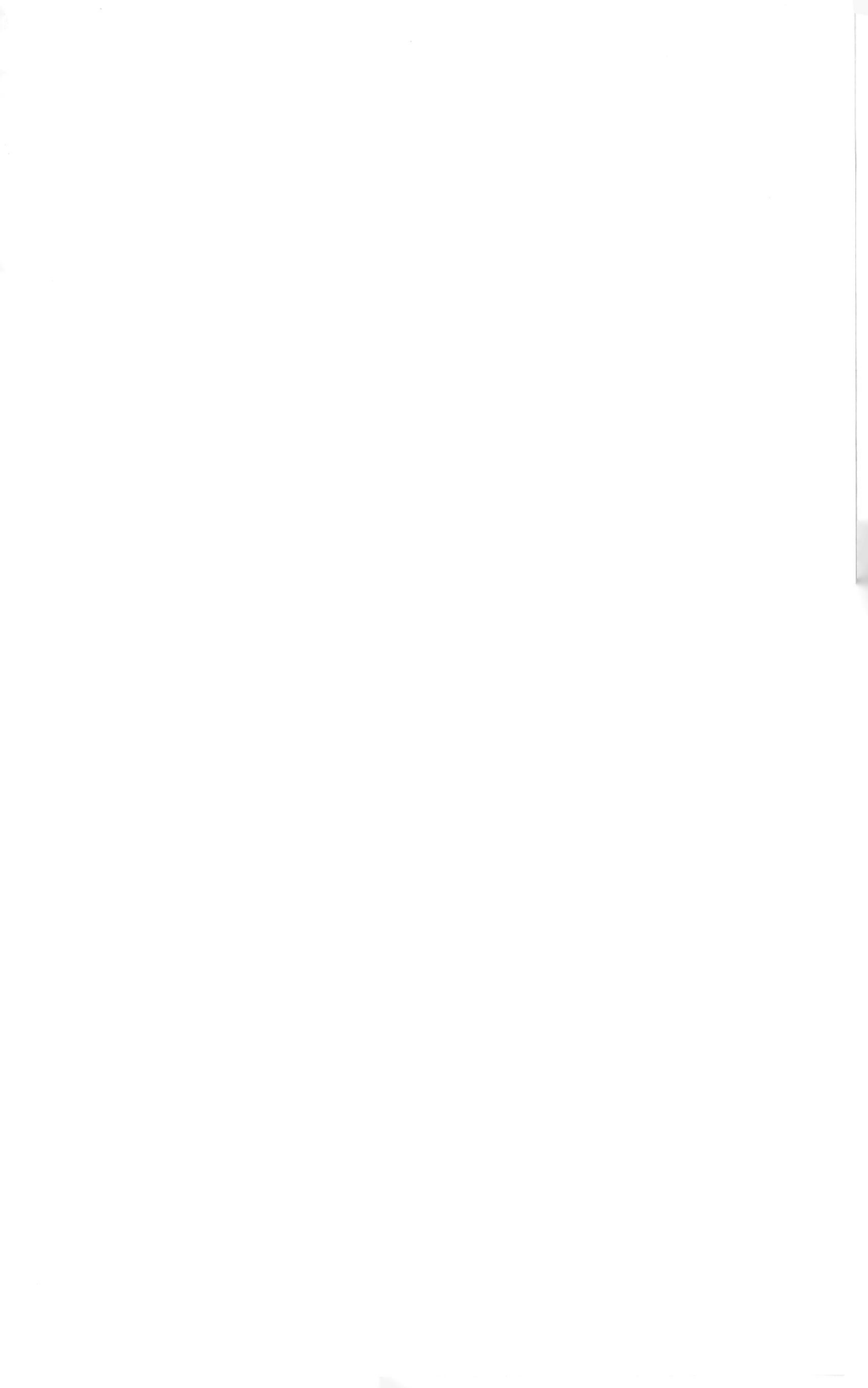

CONTENTS

Acknowledgments i

1 1941 thru 1945   Pg 1
2 1946 thru 1954   Pg 8
3 1955 thru 1959   Pg 40
4 1960 thru 1962   Pg 82
5 1963 thru 1964   Pg 124
6 1965 thru 1968   Pg 162
7 1969 thru 1973   Pg 187
8 1974 thru 2013   Pg 236

ACKNOWLEDGEMENTS

THIS BOOK CONTAINS MEMORIES OF YEARS PAST AND THE PEOPLE IN MY LIFE THAT WERE THE INSPIRATION TO WRITE IT ALL DOWN THANK YOU FOR BEING THERE WITH ME, THANK YOU FOR JUST BEING YOU.

CHAPTER 1   1941 through 1941

REMEMBER ME

September 26, 1941, this was the day that the Lord hath made. And while he was doing it, he made Elbert Elijah Alberson Junior. He didn't know it at the time but he would be allowed to live as full a life as can be lived. He was born at the St Joseph Hospital down town Memphis, Tennessee. His mother counted all his fingers and toes and took him home as a perfect little fellow. I understand he was a big baby and too pretty to be a boy. He heard that for years to come from the ladies at church, the beauty shop, the neighbors and others. When he was a year old there was a Health Contest in Memphis to see who had the healthiest baby. Well, you guessed it, and he has a picture and ribbon to prove it.

His first home was at 277 and a half Manassas Street. This was a duplex that sit high up off the street. There were concrete steps leading up to it from the street level. There were so many steps that there was a landing so you could rest on your way up. There were wide shoulders on each side of the steps that made a great slide for him and the little girl next door. I don't know about her, but he got fussed at for wearing the seat of his shorts out, sliding down the concrete slide. This is where he

ELBERT ALBERSON

lived until I was 5 years old.

His house was only a short distance from Poplar Ave and a long way to Jackson Ave. Manassas Street was fairly close to downtown or up town, anyway you wanted to look at it. He must have had a lot of company, because there are many family pictures of others that come to visit, and film must have been cheap for all the pictures in the family album.

1941 PERTINENT DATA

The average income was $1,770. A new car was $850. A new house was $4075. A house payment was approxioximately $40 a month. Bread was .08 cents a loaf. Gasoline was .12 cents a gallon. Milk was .54 cents a quart. The President was Franklin Roosevelt and Life Expectancy was 62.9 years. This was at the start of World War II and right after the depression of 1933.

DOWNTOWN MEMPHIS, TENNESSEE

Back in those days, there were no Malls, as we know them today. Everybody went to town to shop back then. People shopped at Department Stores like Goldsmiths, Lowenstein's, Gerber's, Woolworths, Kresses, and Tom McCann's shoe store. They would parade or walk all the way down main street on one side of the street then cross over, and walk all the way back up the other side of the street, shopping. Elbert's parents would often eat lunch at a restaurant across the street from the Train Station because some friend of the family worked there. She was a waitress and old friend of the family. The big Stores were class, the window displays made you want to buy everything that was on display. The sights, sounds and smells in the air were all terrific. The Planters Peanut Shop could be smelled from four blocks away.

The street cars sometimes called trolleys or street cars, because they had these big booms that rubbed on the wires overhead and that made them go, not gasoline. Sparks would fly occasionally from the overhead wires. If the power went out, the trolley stopped. As a little boy he remembered riding the trolleys that ran on rails, like trains. Brittlin's was a big restaurant they always had a buffet and it was the first one he had ever seen.

4

COTTON TOP

MEMORIAL PARK CEMETERY

Talking about pictures, there were a lot of pictures that were taken at Memorial Park. Memorial Park was the place his family went on Sunday afternoon, to visit grave sites of all their relatives, lined up in a row, and even had those Brass Plates with names already on them as to say, "This is where you will be put one day." Then they walked over to the picture taking areas in front of the Water Fall, the Wishing Well and the Caves lined with crystals. These were pictures mostly of the 1930's and 1940's. The 1950's brought a more affluent society and they went other places on Sundays than the Cemetery.

GERMAN SHEPPARD DOG

Elbert was asked to take the trash out one time onto a porch and it was night time. No sooner did he get onto the back porch, when the door closed behind him and it slammed shut because of the wind. The noise of the door slamming woke up a big White German Sheppard that lived next door and he is now pawing at the screen and showing his big white teeth and slobber is going everywhere. This five year old turned to get back into the house and found the door had locked when it shut. That did it, it was time to scream and cry. And he did with Gusto. Never did he go out that door in the dark again.

RUN AWAY FROM HOME

Elbert run away from home at the age of five one time. He made it about two blocks away when he heard them calling his name. He knew it was time to hide, as they were getting close. He climbed into a big tractor tire to hide. He could almost get his entire body into it but not all of it. Besides an Ice Cream man was watching the whole thing and squealed on him. His uncle was coming up the street and he seen the ice cream salesman, and ask about him. He smiled and pointed at Elbert hiding in the tire.

His uncle asked Elbert, "What are you doing?"

"I am running away from home."

"Where are you going?"

"I am going to join the Circus."

"Do you have any money?"

"I have a nickel."

5

"Well that isn't enough to join the circus."

"I know." A nickel wouldn't even buy me an ice cream."

His uncle Troy smiled and bought him an ice cream and hand in hand, they went walking up the sidewalk back home.

PEDAL CAR

One day, his dad brought home a pedal car and two cans of paint. Little cans one bright red and another bright Blue. They spread newspaper on the floor in the living room and painted that car, just his dad and him.

THE COAL PILE

In the back yard there was a giant pile of coal. And one day Elbert and the girl next door stacked up that coal and played out there long enough that we were filthy and covered in soot. A lot of people used coal fired furnaces, especially in the older houses near downtown. So it was common to see coal trucks on the street and often you would see them dumping coal down a chute in a basement window. Only the newer houses had natural gas or fuel oil steam heat radiators in each room.

ICE MAN

Elbert would be told when the ice man was expected and it was his job to watch for him. The ice man would pull up to the curb and throw back his big tarp that covered the ice and look up at our house for the sign in the window that told him how much ice to bring into the house. They had an ice box, not a refrigerator. He wore a big leather apron and he had this big piece of leather with a handle on each end that he carried the ice in. Sometimes they would get a 5, 10, or 15 pound block of ice. It was Elbert's job to put the number in the window when he heard him coming up the street.

NICKNAMES

His aunt Lillian had several nick names for him. Sometimes she called me, "Cotton Top" and sometimes "June Bug." Now you're thinking, how does he remember all these things? The answer is, kids pay more attention to what adults say than you think and they listen to the adults tell these stories a hundred times and they see the family pictures. They are black and white but they still like to look at them till this day.

EARLY WORLD WAR II YEARS

If you ever seen the movie, The Sting. The era and the clothes people wore the streets, the store fronts, the houses and cars, looked identical to the time when Elbert lived on Manassas. In a lot of the family pictures, the men are wearing Fedora's, a big tall wide Brim hat. All the cars on the street are from the 1930's. Since this is in the early 1940's and you don't see new cars of that period, its plain to see, people didn't get a new car every two years or so, like they do today. They drove them for some time because you can see some had lost Hub Caps and there were dents that originated long before the picture was taken. There were only a small number of cars made in 1942. None were made in 1943, 1944, and 1945.   The assembly lines were busy building planes, trucks, jeeps and tanks. The men were off to war and the women worked in the plants, many women doing men's jobs. Elbert met one of these ladies one time   when he was growing up. She was winding armatures for generators. It seemed so out of place for a woman to be doing a man's job. At his young age, he thought all women were at home looking after children and a home. But it was explained to him, where she got her training.

In the family picture album's there are many pictures, black and white of different family members in their uniforms. Mostly, Army and Navy uniforms, this was in the days of World War II. These were the days when you had to have stamps to buy sugar, tires, gasoline, and many other items, that were in short supply during the war. They were rationed because of the short supply available at home.

It was common for women to work at many jobs that had been men's jobs before the war. But now you heard of Ruby the Riveter. There were many women that come into the job market while the men were gone to war. They even welded, wearing goggles and gloves.

SOUNDS, SIGHTS, AND SMELLS OF MEMPHIS

It was common to see Blimps going over while outside in the yard. Probably from the Navy base in Millington, you could see streaks in the sky and learned it was caused by an airplane very high up in the sky. On quiet nights, you could hear Whippier Wills and other night birds and frogs. Lying on the front porch of their house, in the early evening, after the sun went down and the dew started to fall, the concrete porch would still be warm from the sun and you would try to get as much skin on the warm surface of the concrete to stay warm as the night air would be chilly. Off in the distance you could hear the coal burning steam trains getting wound up and blowing their whistles. In the day time you could occasionally see one in the distance with black smoke streaming out behind it, coming and going to Memphis Grand Central Station. When he stayed at his Grand Mothers house on the week end, they were close enough to the station downtown to hear them start off, Choo Choo Choot Choot Wooooo Wooooo.

There was a train trestle a block from his Grand Mothers house and he would walk to the park and play under the trestle. Elbert and his brothers would pick up slate that fell off the trains and rub it on the sidewalk to shape it into arrow heads then made Bows and Arrows. One day some older boys come along and took them from them and made them, start running. These boys started shooting their own arrows at them and if any of them had of hit them, it would have killed them. The arrows were falling all around them. They just knew they were going to get killed.

When they heard a train coming, they would put a penny on the rails and let the train mash it for them. That penny would be the size of a quarter after that. They put nails on the track also and made arrow heads out of them.

There were thick bushes all along the railroad tracks and you could see where people had made a path, so they often went exploring and found where Hobo's slept during the night and there were empty whisky bottles everywhere. Sometimes the trains went by fast and there were times they just poked along. They thought about hopping a train and ride it off to California, to see Roy Rogers and Dale Evans. But we were too scared to do that.

Every industry that manufactured something produced smoke into the air and each factory had distinct odors coming from it. Some wasn't so bad but others were terrible. Buckeye, on Jackson Ave, had an odor that would coat your nose linings and lungs and you could smell that

COTTON TOP

odor for days if you ever got a good whiff of it. Even the downtown district had its own smell. And the Mississippi River at times had an odor, usually of mud and blue gumbo clay.

CHAPTER 2   1946 through 1954

1374 ISABELLE STREET

Sometime in1946, Elbert and his parents moved to 1374 Isabelle Street, in the Highland Heights area of Memphis, Tennessee. This was a brand new neighborhood and the streets were still dirt and mud when it rained. For the most part, almost everybody on this street had children, so we had plenty of other kids to play with. The street behind them was Salem Avenue and that street was the city limits at that time. Most of these houses were built by Wallace Johnson and after the housing boom passed.   He started the Holiday Inn Motel Chain.

SHORTY AND THE CHAIN GANG

The street at the end of Isabelle was Bayliss street and they were in the process of widening it.   So every day Elbert rode his tricycle down there to Richard and Nancy Lowe's yard to watch the workers.   Elbert was fascinated by this huge bull dozer pushing dirt around every day and the guy driving the bull dozer was named Shorty. He was called Shorty because he was so short. Well back in them days, they used convict labor from the prison camp a lot and there was a chain gang there every day. He used to watch them, they wore black and white striped suits and they had a chain and ball on one leg. The ball seemed to be as big as a bowling ball and was real heavy. Every time they wanted to walk somewhere, they had to pick up the ball and carry it to where they were going.

Well, one day, this big giant of a black man, reached down and picked up his heavy ball by the chain and walked to a big stump and sit down. He reached down and picked up a fruit jar of ice water and leaned back chugging down the cold water. He never came back to the upright position he kept leaning further backwards until he fell off the stump, STONE COLD DEAD. He just lay there until somebody noticed he was laying there. Elbert didn't know until the next day he was dead, because he took off running for home and he was guessing, but he knew he had just seen his first dead man.

The next day, he realized he had left his tricycle in all the excitement and went back to get it. Guess what? Shorty, the man that was his idol, had run over it with the bull dozer. He never rode a tricycle again after that.

HUSKY DOGS

Once in a while, every now and then, on his way home from school, he would walk down Graham to Bayliss street and on to his house. Well about two blocks down Bayliss on the left, was a house with a fenced in yard that has three big red fuzzy Husky dogs. They would come running at you and throw themselves at you against the fence trying to get to them. Slobber would fly and the girls would scream and everybody hurried past that house for fear those dogs would get to them.

Well, one day, it was in the newspaper that the people that lived in that house had a little girl and one day she opened the back screen door and the dogs jumped her, and needless to say she did not survive. He didn't remember her age, but he walked by that house afterwards and there was no dogs ever there again after that. This was a terrible story, but true.

COLLIE DOG

The people that lived behind Elbert had a big Collie dog. The boy that lived there was Bubba Grace. This Collie was the biggest Collie in the world. Yes, he was pretty, but he could eat a 1952 Chevy for lunch. Well, there wasn't but one boy in the neighborhood that aggravated Elbert to death and he had never seen before. His name was Clayton. His bike was solid chrome and the pipe was octagon shaped, not round like everybody else's. Clayton would ride it around the block and do or say something to make Elbert chase him. Well, he made Elbert mad about something and Elbert was going to take a short cut through the Collie's kingdom to cut the boy off. Well, he almost made it. He bit Elbert on the calf of his leg and a wad of fat was poking out. Elbert just poked it back in, and put some of that clear tape, mother used to wrap presents. She never knew it, until he started limping when it got infected. He decided then, He would never have a dog that he couldn't kick across the goal post of life.

BROKE ARM

He was standing up in the swing, in his neighbor's yard, and was pumping it for everything he could, to get the height to jump out of the swing into a big metal wash tub. Well, he missed the tub and his arm came down on the side of the tub and broke my arm pretty bad. While it didn't hurt much, it sure looked funny and kind of scary. He walked home and came in the back door of his house and walked up behind his Mother in the hall, sitting on a stool talking on the phone. He said: "Mother." She ignored him and never looked up. He stood there a minute or so and said it again, "Mother." She never looked at him, just said: "Can't you see I am on the phone, now go on outside and play." He just stood there another minute or so, then reached over her with his arm inches from her eyes, she screamed and fell off the stool. He remembered her saying to somebody, "Oh no Bubba has broke his arm, I have to go." Then it was off to the hospital, they went.

TONSILS HAD TO COME OUT

He remembered going to St Joseph Hospital downtown. The place was dark and scary. It smelled of alcohol. And all the nurses were Nuns. They put him to sleep with ether. He remembered dreaming he was falling into a well that had no bottom. Then when he awoke, his throat was so sore, he couldn't talk. But what bothered him the most was the fact somebody took his underwear while he was asleep. He woke up

12

naked.

BROKE WATER PIPE

His mother was sitting in the hall again, on that stool she liked talking to somebody, and he had something he wanted to ask her or tell her. So he was waiting for her to hang up. He was standing in front of her this time, actually in the bathroom and sitting on the john listening to her talk to whomever it was and yet, not paying any attention either. Well the sink in the bathroom had two chrome legs that held it up and he was unconsciously turning one of the legs, not noticing that it was raising the sink higher and higher until, Wham Whooossssssshhhhhh. The water pipe broke and water started squirting everywhere neither had a clue as what to do. Elbert jumped up and ran next door to the neighbor and guess what? He was a plumber and had just got home from work. Wasn't that luck. And he fixed it. But wasn't his mother lucky to have Elbert, to run find a plumber?

45 CALIBER BULLET

One day Richard Lowe, Francis Perry, and Elbert, were walking along on the sidewalk, when Richard noticed something in the dirt and grass. He picked it up, and said: "It's a bullet." They all handled it and on the end of the bullet, it was stamped 45 Caliber. It was almost brand new, so clean and shiny. They passed it back and forth between them playing with it, until someone mentioned, throwing it down on the sidewalk to make it go off. Oh yeah, that's the thing to do. So they all took turns throwing it down on the concrete sidewalk, trying to make it go off. Nothing happened. So Richard reared back and led off with his left leg high in the air like the pitcher for the Memphis Chicks Ball Club. He came forward with all his strength, slamming the bullet onto the concrete. For a split second, they heard Richards mother calling him to come home for lunch. The word lunch, they didn't hear because the bullet went BOOM, it went off. Big eyed, they all had a smile on their face, and was about to yell, because the noise scared them to death. Richard reached for his face and eye. Blood started pouring from between his fingers and face. His mother come running and his mother snatched him up and ran with him to their house. Francis and Elbert run home scared to death. Elbert walked back to Richard's house and

13

ELBERT ALBERSON

knocked on the screen door. His sister came to the door and all he could think of to ask was. "Is he dead yet." Richard's mother said, they were going to the hospital and they left.

Later, Elbert and Francis sat on the front porch and watched for Richard to come home from the hospital. When he came home and got out of the car, he had a patch of gauze and a metal cup with little air holes all over it taped to his face, over his eye. The bullet had hit the bone at the side of his eye, and glanced away from him. It could have glanced into his eye and he would have been dead. As it was, he survived and is presently living just south of Dallas, Texas.

FRANCIS PERRY

Francis Perry lived directly behind our house on Salem, the next street over. Francis was Elbert's age, and they became good friends and were raised there with the other neighborhood boys. One side of Salem Street was the city limits and the other side was, Shelby County. Francis dad was a pipe fitter/welder and was an avid lover of motorcycles, and Midget Race cars. He had a big shop in his back yard and all the tools to do most anything. Francis didn't really seem to be interested in all that, but Elbert was. Elbert loved to pilfer around his dad's shop and tinker with his tools. Especially the drill press and the welding torches, Elbert drilled holes into any and everything he could find. Now to a kid anything lying around could really be scrap material, wood, or metal. And it could just as well be a very important piece that belonged on a race car or a motorcycle. Not knowing the difference. You guessed it. Elbert drilled holes in several things, Mr. Perry didn't want holes drilled into.

He had all kinds of welding stuff, Torches and arc welders. Francis and Elbert could turn on the torches and use the striker to light it and it would shoot flames out and they would heat up metal until it was cherry red and then burn their names in a piece of wood.

Mr. Perry, had an antique Motorcycle, he was in the process of restoring. It was called a Mustang it had solid wheels and was the size of a Harley Sportster. It had a Big Motor like a Harley 74, Police Motorcycle. Well, Francis and Elbert had looked at it for months. They had sat on it. And they started it up it with the kick starter several

COTTON TOP

times. They would sit on it and race the motor. You guessed it; Francis put it in gear one day and slowly rode it around in the back yard. Then, Elbert got on it and rode it around the back yard. Yep, they looked at each other and said with their eyes, let's ride it up the street and back. So, Francis slowly eased it out of the back yard and into the street. He went up the street a ways and returned. So, Elbert took a turn. Then Francis went around the block and seemed to be gone a long time, but soon returned. Well, Elbert couldn't let him out do him, smiling. So, he took it and went out of the yard and was on my way back when this happened.

Well, they had just built a new grocery store on Highland Avenue and were having the grand opening. And as normal anytime new buildings go up, sand gets all over the road and makes it slippery. As Elbert approached this new grocery store and the sandy area, he was following a 1955 Chevy being driven by a little old lady. She turned into the parking lot okay, but she stopped and shifted into low gear before rolling on into the parking lot. Well he just knew she would turn into the lot and just roll on into the parking lot, no sweat. He thought he would just pass her with no problem. She would be out of the way when he got to her.

Wrong!!!! All of a sudden, she stopped and when she did, he rammed her from behind. When he hit his brakes, the sand on the road, caused him to slide instead of stop and he hit her. He flew over the handle bars and landed on the trunk of her car, then slid off the trunk, onto the road. He wasn't hurt, not even a scratch and not a scratch on her car. But, the front forks of the motorcycle, was bent at an odd angle. He told her he was fine and he jumped on the bike and took off for home. When he got there, Francis and Elbert didn't have time to fix anything, so they put it back where his dad had parked it and piled other things against it, so his dad wouldn't see the damage, until they had time to fix it, if they could.

Wrong again. His dad found it, that night. The next day being Sunday, Elbert was dressed to go to church, when Francis came to his back door and told him his dad wanted to see him right now. So, Elbert took off, in his Sunday clothes and climbed over the

15

back fence to see Mr. Perry. Francis told him, his dad had found the damage. So there Elbert stood, in their kitchen, in my Sunday going to church suit and tie to see Mr. Perry. He was eating breakfast in a tee shirt and his underwear.   He looked up at me, and cocked one eye and said: "Son, you have torn up and drilled holes in everything in my shop, how about staying out of my shop. The only thing you haven't torn up is my race car. Elbert said, "Yes sir," a lot. Then Mr. Perry smiled at Elbert and said, "If you don't mind, don't mess with my race car and you can go with us to the races next Saturday, if you want. " Elbert smiled and said: "Yes sir" again. Then, he sent Elbert on his way, to go to church. Mr. and Mrs. Perry are both gone now, and Elbert just learned, Francis and his brother Mike have both passed recently.

WRINGER WASHING MACHINE

Growing up, Elbert often helped his Mother wash clothes and then feed them, piece by piece, back through the wringer on top. The water squeezed out and fell back into the washer. She would feed the pieces in and he would catch them, when they come out the other side.

Well, one day, the phone rang and his mother went to answer it. After awhile, he decided to go around to the front and feed a piece into the wringer and then hurry around back to catch it, when it came out. He was having a big time helping his mother, while she was on the phone. He had done a couple of pieces and all went well. So, while he was feeding another piece into the wringer it suddenly, grabbed his finger and started to pull his hand into the wringer. When it had his finger, it also had a piece of clothing and it didn't hurt, so he just kept trying to pull it out. But when it got to his elbow, it started to hurt and then it dawned on him, the rest of him was headed through the wringer. He laughs about it now.

But, he decided it was time to yell. He yelled to mother, but it must not have sounded serious enough, because she didn't come and he could hear her still talking on the phone. Well, when it got almost up to his armpit, he really yelled and here she came running. She knew just what to do and quickly unlatched the wringer and his arm was immediately free. She started rubbing it, to get the circulation going again, and she made him try bending his elbow and all my fingers worked.

He wasn't scared at all now, but now, she is all upset, hugging him and crying. It sure scared her, more than it did him. He later learned, that there had been several people, that had got their arm caught in the wringer of a washing machine and had serious damage to occur. He always assumed it was a different kind of wringer because it really never hurt as he remembered it.

THE FIRST CAR HE EVER BUILT

Living in a neighborhood with new houses being built all around them, the neighborhood was growing every day. There was an abundance of scrap material that the carpenters building a new house, just threw away or burned, to keep warm. So every now and then, Elbert and his buddies would gather an arm full and drag it home to make something out of it. They started out making a boat that they floated down the gutter along side of the street, when it rained.

But one day, they decided to build them a car. There was a grocery store close by, that threw out wooden crates that apples and oranges, were delivered in. So, now, they had plenty of wood. They took apart a good wagon, to get axles, and wheels. They used a round piece of wood out of a neighbor's fence for an exhaust pipe and cans for head lights and tail lights. They pushed it over and over until they wrecked many times. But they just repaired it and had a real good time. I think they got the idea, from Mr. Perry's race car, or from watching the Spanky cartoons on TV.

THE DUG OUT FORT

Now, in secret, Elbert, Richard Lowe, and Francis Perry, built a fort across the street from Richard's house. This was in a wooded area, between the street and the brick wall that went around the National Cemetery, and you couldn't see their fort from the street. They dug a hole, big enough for four kids to crawl into. Then they covered that, with small trees, limbs and brush, to hide the hole. This is where they played Cowboys and Indians and War with the Germans and Japanese. And, it was their Elephant trap, when we were playing Tarzan of the Jungle.

One day, Richard's sister, Nancy Lowe, came sneaking around, spying on them. When she found their Fort, she insisted on coming into their Fort. They told her, she had to know the pass word, and couldn't come in. But, you know how women are, she conned her way in. Anyway, under duress, they let her in and wouldn't you know it, she made fun of it and they told her to go home. She then wouldn't leave, so they held her down and rubbed mud all over her and she took off for home. Yelling all the way, saying, I'm going to tell and she did, too. Richard was the only one to get a spanking, though.

Treadwell School

When Elbert started to school, Treadwell was the closest, to their house. He used to walk to school and at the time, it seemed a long way. But recently, it was measured and it wasn't as far as Elbert thought, probably two miles. He went to Treadwell school, for the first, second and third grade.

He has several memories of things that happened while he went to that school, one being the "Squirrel." One day, while on his way home, he was walking down this long sidewalk, and way up ahead of him, he seen this squirrel, fall to the sidewalk out of a tree, with a thud, and it just lay there. Boy, he took off running, to see the squirrel. When he got to it, it was just laying there and not moving. He thought, it must be dead, so he set my book satchel down and opened the top flap with the two buckles.   He opened it and picked up the squirrel. Never, ever do that, did you hear me? Never, pick up a squirrel, they don't like it. And, that might be an understatement. He almost had the squirrel, into the top of that book satchel, when it came to, or it might have been playing possum. It might have been that it didn't want to be stuffed into the darkness of that satchel, or it might have been scared?

No, it was mad. The squirrel latched onto him with all his sharp teeth and claws, and Elbert jumped up screaming, hollering and, shaking his arm up and down, trying to get rid of that squirrel. Then, the lord stepped in, and saved him by making the squirrel, let him go, and live long enough to tell this story.   Elbert had to promise, to never do that again. The squirrel went one way and Elbert grabbed his book satchel and took off for home, to see about the scratches and to see where the blood was coming from.

THE SHEEP AND THE BOY SCOUT LEADER

Another favorite spot to walk by was the short red brick fenced in area next to a house that the man was a Boy Scout Leader. He kept sheep in his side yard fenced in by that brick wall. This wasn't but a block from Treadwell at the corner of Macon road within sight of Leawood Baptist Church.

THE BRIDGE

He remembered getting a paddling one time, along with some other boys, one day on the play ground. They were playing in the ditch, under the bridge looking up the girls dresses and the teacher, tore their tails up. He didn't remember, if it was the first, second or third grade. He wasn't sure why they got a paddling. Boys are dumb, you know.

ARMORED TRUCK

Occasionally, Elbert would ride the city bus, home from Treadwell School. He would get on it, in front of the school and ride the bus, to the bus turnaround on Jackson Ave, right at the gate of the National Cemetery and the foot of the Jackson Avenue viaduct. Then, he would transfer to a bus that stopped at the end of the street he lived on, Isabelle Street.

Well, one day, he had to stay after school for some reason. He was in the third grade. The teacher finally let him go, so he ran to the corner and he could see the bus on the other side of the intersection. He could tell the driver had shut the door and when the light changed, he knew, he would drive off and leave him.

Well, the crossing guards, had them long poles with the red flag and would not let him cross the street at the light where the bus was, so he went back about three cars that was parked there and darted across the street. Well, wouldn't you know it, but, an armored car was coming to the school, to pick up money from the cafeteria, at that time of day. And he didn't see it coming. The next thing he remembered was, trying to get up, and his legs wouldn't work. The truck had run over his legs between the crotch and knees. Somebody called an ambulance and some lady kept telling him to not move. He looked up, and seen the bus crossing the intersection, leaving him. But, he got to ride in an ambulance, to the hospital. After, an overnight stay, he went home and nothing was broken.

But, he had bruises that looked like the tire tread design on his legs for months. The driver told his parents, he had come from nowhere and something told him, to not hit his air brakes, if he had, he would have ripped his legs off. The driver just let the truck roll over him and it was the best thing he could have done.

ISABELLE STREET

Life at 1374 Isabelle Street, in the 1950's was totally different from today. Elbert remembers opening a big box of washing powder for his mother, and low and behold, there was a towel in there.   Sometimes, it would be a hand towel and sometimes a wash cloth. There was another Brand of something that had a saucer another had a cup. He remembers, getting a drinking glass sometimes.

It was common, to go to several friends house and find Jewel Tea Bowl's with mashed potatoes, peas or corn. He thought everybody in the neighborhood had the same towels and the same style dishes. At the gas station, you got things for buying so much gas. You know, the Cereal boxes were always full to the very top too, not half full, like today. And don't forget about the carnival glass dishes, setting around the house. This was dishes you won at the Cotton Carnival or the Fair at the Fair Grounds.

Do you remember Red wax lips? Wax bottles, with colored water in it. Putting cardboard or playing cards in the spokes of the wheels on my bike, to make it sound like a motorcycle. He would ride his bike to the Western Auto Store and look at the accessories you could buy for your bike. Red reflectors, rubber handles with the glass jewel, or with streamers, white wall tires. They even had a motorized Bike called a Whizzer that had a motor on it. You had to start pedaling real fast and the motor would take over, and give you a ride at a pretty good clip. Elbert cut many yards of grass, trying to save up to buy one, until he learned, his Mother said: "That wasn't ever going to happen."

As a kid, he noticed the similarity between grocery stores and gas stations. Both were customer   oriented in a big way. The grocery stores give you free bags to carry your groceries. They bag them for you, and offer to carry them to your car. And they still do today, sixty years later.

But, Gas Stations are another story. They used be so glad, you stopped in. It seemed like they were, waiting for you to pull in. When you did, they come running to you. They filled it up with gas, checked your oil, the air in your tires, your windshield wipers, fan belt, battery, radiator, and brake fluid.

And while they were doing all that, for free, I might add. You could get out and stretch your legs, get a free drink of ice cold water from the water fountain. And even get a free map also. One of the City, you were in, and one for a State. Sometimes, they even had one of the United States, all for free.

But not today, today nothing is free. Most stations don't even have a water faucet, much less a water fountain. Customer Satisfaction is a thing of the past. Greed is the Motto today. Yes, things were better in the good old days. A kid with a flat tire on his bike could push it to the local gas station, and most of them, would patch your inner tube and not even charge the kid. Adults had time or made time, for kids back then. Today, 65 years later, adults don't even see you, if you fell off your bike and skinned your knee, much less, pick you up and take you home.

Things change all the time, though. Some things change for the better and some for the worse.   Some things change because of necessity and sometimes for greed. Today they change for no more reason than the personal gain of some people. Companies have suffered a great loss in customer loyalty. They have also suffered a loss in revenue. But it happened so slow, that by the time the company realized what had happened, it was too late. Now, they have several problems, all caused by the guy they promoted and give a big raise, without looking at the long term results, if they made the change this young whippier snapper wants to make as he makes a name for himself, at the company's expense.

A lot of the problems, we have today, with the economy, could have been avoided, if we had recognized the greedy, personal gain ladder climbers and the unethical, political people in the past.

TELEVISION AND RADIO

There used to be a big up right radio that Elbert's mother and father bought before he could walk that he grew up listening to that radio. He remembered pulling up on it, learning to walk and pulling it over on him. His brothers did the same thing when they were learning to walk. At night, they used to listen to "The Green Hornet." "Fibber Mc Gee and Molly," "The Shadow" "Only the shadow knowssssss," the announcer would say.

The first Television he remembers was at Robert Wright's house across the street from his house. One night, Robert invited him and his brother, to come and watch the Monday Night Fights. That was boxing. He probably watched a hundred Monday night fights and very popular fighters but he was a kid. It was all exciting to him. Robert and his dad, knew the fighters names, and seem to know who was going to win before they even fought.

After awhile, Mother bought them a TV. Then, he found out about Howdy Doody Time, it became the show he liked to watch. Then later, it became Gene Autry and his horse Champion. He was a singing cowboy like Roy Rogers, Dale Evans, Trigger and Bullet. But both cleaned up the west, of outlaws and rustlers. Roy's side kick was Gabby Hayes. Gabby was an older man, with a big grey beard and no teeth causing him to talk funny, and constantly was heard to say, "Dag Nab it."

Then as he got older, he started watching the Ed Sullivan Show. There, they got to see our local boys making it big out in California. Like Elvis, Johnny Cash. Then there was the Ozzie and Harriet Show, America's most perfect family. And Father knows Best show. There was the Lone Ranger and Tonto with his horse "Silver," and he used silver bullets in his guns for the bad guys.

As his brothers and he grew up they had chores that had to be done, before Mother returned from work. This consisted of running the dust mop, running the vacuum, dusting everything, and washing the dishes. Its mentionable this point because it was Wayne's time to wash dishes. Wayne being the middle of three brothers so they all jumped on their chores and then went out to play and await the arrival of Mother. Well, one day they missed Wayne and went looking for him. Elbert and Neal, found Wayne, sitting in the middle of the living room floor, and he had set up an assembly line to wash dishes in the living room floor, so he could watch TV at the same time. The only problem was he paused a lot to watch the good guys chase the bad guys and it was taking longer than he expected. Well, you guessed it. Mother came home earlier than expected and caught Wayne in the middle of the living room floor with dish pans everywhere.

COOKING

Elbert's Mother had to be at work at five o'clock in the morning. She was the Manager of the Cafeteria at school. It was his job, to get Wayne and Neal, his brothers up every morning and fix them breakfast for several years. He reminded his Mother, it was about time for Wayne to learn how to cook, and Wayne did for awhile. Elbert ended up graduating to where he now fixed supper. One night he had cooked some Streak of Lean Salt Meat, corn, peas, and mashed potatoes. He had the table set and ready when mother came home from work.

His Mother had three jobs. She started her day at five am, then, had to be at Goldsmith department store until nine pm, five days a week and she sold Avon on the weekends and holidays.

She was delighted and we all sit down to eat. The first thing he put into his mouth was the salt meat, and he almost choked on the strong taste of salt. He had forgot, to wash it first, and it was terrible. He tried to act like nothing was wrong, but Wayne and Neal, made a big deal out of it by holding their throat and rolling out of their chairs into the floor, saying: "Bubba, that is what they called him," is trying to kill us. His Mother laughed and said: "Don't eat the meat." Everything else was fine, she said.

PAINTING THE HOUSE, INSIDE AND OUT

When Elbert got to be about fifteen years old, he began to notice different things. One was the appearance of their house. It needed painting. He had watched other people paint, and he decided, he could do that. So, he talked his mother into buying him some paint and a brush, and he went to work. School was out for the summer, so he had the time to do it. He borrowed a ladder, from the next door neighbor and jumped on it. Well, things went pretty well and he got a lot of it painted, but eventually got to the ladder part, and he just couldn't do it.

So, he had tried and did a lot, and as it worked out, the man his mother hired to finish the job, didn't charge her but for just finishing what he had started. It worked out that, he had really helped a lot.

His Mother was so impressed, at what he could do, she let him paint the inside of the house, and he was able to finish that also. One time he painted the living room, a rose color, and later he painted it a Dark Green.

So, years later, when he was home on leave from the Air Force. He was actually in transit from Savannah, Georgia, on his way to Japan. He was home for 41 days. And wouldn't you know it, his Mother remembered he could paint and ask him to paint the outside of her house that was now, rental property, while he was home. He told her, he would and borrowed that same ladder from the neighbor, as from years ago.

At the time, mother was renting the house to a girl he went to school with and her husband. So he painted and painted and visited with her. She was a year younger than him and most of the time, they were at work. But one day, when he got there, he noticed her car was there. He painted for a while and she came to the back door and asked him to come help her, so he put the brush down and hurried inside. She was in bed and said: "She was sick and felt faint." She closed her eyes and just lay there and he was trying to figure out, what in the devil should he do? He got a wash rag and wet it and put it on her forehead and tried to get her to say something. After a while, she came around and said: "she fainted." It scared the devil out of him. He didn't have a clue what to do and was on the verge of panicking. But, she came around and said: "She was okay now. "

After a while, he went back outside and the paint brush was ruined because the paint had dried in it. The gallon of paint, he had forgotten to put the lid on it and the paint had a skim of dried paint that he scraped out and saved the rest.

IRONING

After washing clothes, their mother didn't have a clothes dryer while they were kids. They hung their clean wet clothes out on the clothes line and let them dry by the sun and air. That could be a pretty funny thing, in the winter time, when the clothes would dry stiff from the cold. You had to be careful not to break a sleeve off and clothes pins were hard to remove frozen to the line.

When they were dry, they would bring them in the house and we sprinkled them with water, to get them damp again and roll each piece up in a ball and place in a dish pan. The sprinkler, was a coke bottle with a stopper, that had small holes in it, to let the water come out.

When the dish pan was full, they put it in the refrigerator for a while to let the items get totally damp. Then, everybody ironed their own clothes. That came about, because Elbert liked creases in his trousers and the neck of his shirts, done just so and so. So, when he got picky, from then on he had to do his own ironing. And since he was doing his, he was expected to finish whatever else was in that pan, before putting the ironing board away.

SEWING, KNITTING, AND CROCHETIN

His Mother took classes at Goldsmith and made some beautiful things, while he was growing up. She used to sit and crochet and knit while he and his brothers, would do home work or watch TV. She knitted a blue dress out of ribbon. She was a knock out in that dress. She made a black beaded hand bag that she was offered big money for it for years, but she wouldn't sell it for anything. She made doilies for the coffee table and end tables, that were elaborate and out of this world. She would, wash them and starch them and wad up newspaper to form them a certain way as they dried. It may be old fashioned now, but he still has some of them still out, in his house, to be enjoyed. People still admire the workmanship that goes into that kind of sewing. He never thought much about it until he just wrote this down about her, but her interest into making things, might have been part of the reasons, he has always been interested in making things.

1954 PONTIAC

He had a neighbor, a few houses up the street that had a Pontiac Car. One night he and his brothers were sitting on the front porch, enjoying the night air and the coolness. It was unusually clear and you couldn't begin to count the stars. You could see an occasional falling star in the night sky and the lightning bugs flying, his brothers chasing them and putting them in a jar. He learned, you couldn't keep them very long as they would die. So after awhile and surely before they went to bed, they would release them to be caught again on other nights.

Well, they noticed this car coming by their house, had a light on the hood of their car, and it was red. It slowed and turned in the driveway of the house two doors up the street. They walked over to see the light and it was a light, inside a red plastic head of and Indian Chief. He later learned it was an option and this car had that option. They thought that was the coolest thing. They went to Western Auto and found they had several kinds you could buy and put on your car.   But they were expensive.   In the year of 2010, they stopped making the Pontiac Automobile.

KAISER FRASIER

You could buy a Kaiser or you could buy a Fraser car. Both were ugly, big, wide, long, and heavy.   Elbert's Mother had a friend that had a Kaiser. Elbert and his brothers used to make fun of that car, and his mother made them keep their mouth shut when they went to visit. Oh, well, they stopped making both of these cars, and it had to be, because they were so ugly.

CROSLEY

The man, that developed the neighborhood, where they lived, would ride by from time to time. And he was, a big fat man. Elbert laughed behind his back because he was so huge and he drove the smallest car made in America, a Crosley. Oh, they don't make that car anymore either, probably, because it was so ugly.

BACK IN THE FIFTY'S

Every boy or man, that wore long pants, could look at a car on the road and tell you what year it was. What make and model, it was. What size engine was under the hood, what rear end ratio was in it and by little details, could tell you, if it had a two barrel carburetor or a four barrel carburetor.

The young sporty people drove convertibles, or a coupe. The married folks drove four door cars. The teen age boy had a hot rod. Then, in 1955, here come cars with V8 motors and the drag racing started. Then in 1960's, here come the Muscle cars, with the big block motors, two four barrel carburetors, and three two barrel carburetors, right off the assembly line. Now drag racing got out of hand on the streets, so the auto makers backed off and begin to tone it down some.

Now, those that had hot rods in the past, were getting married and having babies, and their money started going to making a living and supporting a family. Change was in the wind.

LINCOLN

His Aunt Nancy had a big black Lincoln. Some called her Ruthy, her middle name was Ruth. One day, she came to visit. Well, somebody had run over a cat and killed it. Elbert and his brothers found it and decided it would be funny, to tie it, to the bumper of her car. Then when she left, she wouldn't know it and people following her would see it. So they tied it to the bumper and slipped it under the car, where she wouldn't see it. When she left, they were all peeking around the house from the back yard and laughed as she drove off dragging that cat. Later, they all cried, as they got a whipping for doing that. They never did know how they found out who did it.

JAMES R. GRAGG SCHOOL

Well, it is time to go to the fourth grade, and he had to change schools as it was a new school hat had opened closer to home. It was called James R. Gragg school. He hated it. He didn't know anybody and it looked like a prison, all grey and concrete. He only remembered one thing about that school. He only went there for two years, and there was a little girl there, that was a first grader that wore glasses. She was cute as a button, but nothing else rang a bell about his time there.

EADS, TENNESSEE

His Mother was raised hard, in a big family in the country, on a farm outside of Macon, Tennessee. She remembered her days growing up and the values she learned, and she had it on her mind she wanted her children to learn those values and to experience living in the country.

So, one day, Elbert and his brothers learned, they were moving to the country. His Mother and Daddy had already found a place and they rented our nice new house out to a red headed lady friend of theirs.

He had heard how years ago, children went to one room schools, with a big pot belly stove, for heat, and they walked, or rode horses to school and that everybody had a garden to grow vegetables etc.

Well, the summer before for starting, the sixth grade, they moved to Eads, Tennessee. Their address used to be, 1374 Isabelle Street and then became, something or other rural route something or another. The house was what some called a shot gun house. They called it that because you could look in the front door, and see right through the house, and out the back door. There was no bathroom in the house, now mind you. They didn't even have running water. They had an outhouse, just like in the movies. Now, at night, you didn't want to go out in the cold and dark, so you used the enamel pot with the lid, it had to be emptied the next day, when you could see where you were walking.

They had a Cistern, not a well. A cistern, collected water off the roof, in a simple gutter system and ran in to the cistern. Then, to get it out, they had a bucket on a chain that they had to draw it up. In the summer time, they kept some water in a Cedar bucket, on the back porch, and drank out of a dipper. Inside the cistern, was not a deep dirt hole it was a deep cement lined hole.

On baths days, well, in the winter, they brought the bathtub in from the back porch, and put it in the kitchen and filled it with water, heated on a wood stove. They had two stoves. One was a wood stove, and one was an electric stove. In the summer time, they parked the car parallel to the road and put the tub behind the car. They filled it with water and let the sun heat it, when it was just right they took their bath, outside in the yard.

Now, Elbert has some school friends that will read this and say, that isn't true, Mrs. Alberson did not do that. Well, guess again. No, just Elbert and his brothers bathed outside.

That winter, was the 100 year winter, for snow. The most, they had ever seen in the Memphis area, in Elbert's lifetime. He remembered it well, his Daddy's car froze to the ground, and he couldn't go to work in Memphis, for two days. Elbert and his brothers chased rabbits, because they could see their tracks and they tried to catch them and sell them for a quarter to the little store downtown, Eads, Tennessee. That little store, was where the old men, would hang out, sitting around a pot belly stove. Right by the door was a table full of dead rabbits for sale, still wearing their furry hide. That is where they got the idea, to go rabbit hunting. But, they never did catch up to one. They were not even sure if they could have knocked a rabbit in the head, with the hammer they toted, around either.

Town was only about a hundred yards from their house. Elbert went to the store to buy bread etc, and the post office to get mail. The post office was a small room with one wall of little doors and you had to know the combination to open the little door to get your mail. There was a train track with a small depot, the train usually didn't stop in Eads, but if you wanted to ride the train, they would sell you a ticket and the train would stop and pick you up.

That winter, the snow was two feet deep in places and a foot deep everywhere else. Elbert met the neighbor's boy and rode with him on his horse to school about half the time, like summer. And the school bus in the winter. There was this boy, on the bus, that was a cripple boy and he had crutches. Nobody liked him and he didn't like anybody else. He would stick out those crutches and trip you, or bang you on the chins.

The school was not a one room school, but it was a two room school. There were some in the 4th the 5th and the 6th grade in his room alone, taught by one teacher. There was no talking, she carried a music baton and she would hit you on the arm if you talked. Elbert didn't know why, but he made better grades that year, than he did before or after the sixth grade.

They stayed in Eads, for that one full year. By that time, they all had their fill of country life. It was an experience that has given Elbert and his brothers a taste of how it was, when their parents were coming up. He had heard about getting a corn cob doll for Christmas. And now I believe it. One last story or two and we will get back to Memphis.

Their closest neighbor was an older man and woman, that had no kids, and wasn't real friendly when they first moved there, but they kind of grew on the boys and they become fun to be around. Mainly, because he would make them flutes out of some kind of stalk and if it ever quit working, he would make them another.

Every now and then, when Elbert got home from school, there would be a note and 75 cents, for him to walk to the highway and catch the Greyhound Bus at the Pure Oil Station. He would then ride it to Memphis and get off at the Bus station. His dad, worked across the street at Gold's Battery and Radiator. Elbert would go and wait for him to get off work and they would all eat supper with his grandmother. Her name was Sallie they called her Big Mamma, because she was so little.

Well, on one of these bus trips into Memphis wouldn't you know it Elbert had to make water. Yeah, he had to pee. You guessed it the bus driver would not stop and let him pee on the side of the road. The driver said: "Just go on back there in the back." Well, he was about to bust you know how a little boy, dances one foot to the other? Well, he went to the very back of the bus and did his business. Then he came back to the very first seat on the right next to the door, to ride the rest of the way, to Memphis. After a few minutes, the driver hit his brakes, and Elbert noticed something move in the isle. He looked and water was running down the center Isle and spilling down the steps and running outside under the door. When looked up, the driver's eyes met his, but he never said a word. He knew what it was and where it came from. Hey He is just a little kid.

The whole episode of Eads, Tennessee, was an effort of his mother, for her children to know how it was when she grew up and some people still live like that today. And you know what? Right here in Southeast Georgia, there are some houses without indoor plumbing, even today. And it really isn't the end of the world.

One last memory of Eads, Tennessee, was the late night rides, going home after visiting relatives in Memphis. They had a 1941 Chevrolet four door and they would ride the two lane black top roads and listen to the clickity clickity click, as their tires would run over the tar strips between the concrete slabs in the road. Their Mother would sing Hymns and they would sing along with her and today Elbert catches himself singing those same hymns and the words to a song called "Farther Along." In the winter time, Elbert and his brothers would sit in the floor in the back seat because the exhaust pipe ran just beneath the floor and the floor was the warmest place to be.

Elbert went to Eads recently, and at the turn off of Highway 64, it's hard to tell where you are at. But, when you get to the house they lived in, it's all caved in and over grown. It is not the same. But, he could visualize it, like it was and think about the sounds and the smells. It brought back memories of a long time ago. Sometimes, he wonders just why, the Lord has let him live so long, he feel s so unworthy. The Lord has let him enjoy the wonder of this world, in its entire splendor. Elbert hope's he has made as many people happy, as they have made him.

BOY SCOUTS

The Methodist Church at the corner of Bayliss and Highland, across from the National Cemetery, sponsored Boy Scout Troup # 61. Elbert had to be eleven to join the Boy Scouts and he was a scout for three years. His highest rank was Life Scout. He later joined, the Explorers, they met on Jackson Avenue, near the Jackson Theatre. He had to ride the bus to those meetings.

There was a lady, that donated a 100 foot yacht to their Explorer Lodge, and they had a few meetings on it. It was docked downtown on the river front Marina with many others. They learned, all about boats, boating and river navigation and knot tying. He wasn't in this group, very long, as other interest begin to pull him away.

While in the Boy Scouts, there were had many camping trips and he really liked sleeping and eating outdoors. He remembered it rained cats and dogs one time and everything they had, got wet and they all ended up in the back of a van the leader drove. They learned fast though, what to do on their future camping trips. He remembered one day on their way to a camping trip, they had to go to John Harrington's house to get something. It was a key to a gate, as they camped on some of his land. John's dad, came out the back door of his house and seen us off.

Elbert had two daughters, Lynn and Leigh that were cub scouts and Girl Scouts. He supported them and to this day they keep a lot of memorabilia just like he did.

1950' VISITING DADDY AT BIG MAMMA'S ON WEEKENDS

Sometimes Elbert and his brothers went to see their Daddy on the weekends. He lived occasionally, with their grandmother, Big Mamma, and even when he didn't, they would always see him there, as he would come by and spend time with them.

LAMAR THEATER

Elbert and his brothers usually went home on Sunday afternoon, so if they went to the picture show, they usually went on a Saturday, in time to stay for a double feature with their cousins Sandra and Johnnie Girl. Their Daddy would walk with them up Lamar Avenue about two blocks, to the Lamar Theater. After they got older, they would walk by themselves.

MR. LUCKS, HAMBURGERS

They like to go at lunch time, so they could go to Mr. Lucks Hamburger Place, across the street from the theater. If it was full, you just waited until a seat became available. Then, you got to tell him what you wanted and watch him cook it.

He was an older man, thin and tall. He always wore one of those white paper hats, a white tee shirt and a white apron, over white trousers. He had a big grill and would cook several hamburgers at a time. He started with a little round ball of meat, about the size of a golf ball. He then pitched it onto the grill and slow cooked it until done. He would mash it, and mash it, and mash it again, until it was real thin and about the size of a bun. He then took his big knife and sliced onions and pickles so thin you could read a paper through them. Then he salted and peppered the burger and put it on the bun. You put mustard and ketchup on it, if you wanted it. The hamburger was 10 cents and the coke, was a nickel. If you wanted two burgers, and a coke, it was 25 cents, and the show, he put on, was free. There was no sign outside on his place you had to know it was there to go there. It wasn't air conditioned and it was a memorable place that you eat cheap and he was a nice man.

REEVES DRUG STORE

Across the street from the Lamar Theater and next door to Mr. Lucks hamburger place, was Reeves Drug Store. They had a soda fountain to die for. Elbert always said if he ever got rich he was going to go in there and order one of every soda and sundae they could make and top it off with a Banana Split.

One time he had a sore throat, and his grandmother, sent him and his brothers to Reeves Drug Store, to the Pharmacist. The Pharmacist smiled and said for them to come on back behind the counter and he took one of those flat wooden sticks, pressed his tongue down and told him to say ah. He said, "Yes, your tonsils need to come out, but I have just the thing to make it better." He then took a fat cotton swab and dipped it into the mercurochrome bottle and swabbed their throat and tonsils. Then, he sent Elbert and his brothers on their way and Elbert learned shortly after that he was going to have his tonsils out.

Up front across from the soda fountain, along the far wall, was wooden booths, where you sat with your friends and or girl friends and carved hearts with your initials in it. It was there for years and had many initials carved in it. Some you recognized, and some you didn't. The floor had ceramic tile, black and white, little round tiles. And scattered around the room, were some small round tables with those bent iron back chairs. Years later, he went out of business and Elbert's uncle J.T, bought those booths.   Elbert would have given anything for them, but they are long gone somewhere. They would have looked really good on his screened in porch, been a great conversation piece and brought back a lot of memories.

LAMAR THEATER

Well, let's go across the street to the Movies. There, we will see a double feature. Maybe Lash La Rue, Billy the Kid, Roy Rogers and Trigger, or a Tarzan movie. Elbert also liked, James Dean, Bud Abbot, and Lou Costello, Dean Martin and Jerry Lewis.

Sometimes, he had Pop Corn and a Coke, and sometimes it was Pop Corn and Necco Wafers. The Necco Wafers would last a whole double feature. It was air conditioned and he got used to it, when he came outside, after a double feature, the bright sun and the afternoon heat would jar his senses. He watched for the light to change and traffic to stop, before crossing Lamar Avenue and walked back to big mama's house, on the shady side of the street.

When he got to Big Mamma's house, it was time to watch the Ed Sullivan Show and eat supper.   Sometimes, Aunt Bertha's boy friend "Monk" would come by and take them for a ride usually, to get an ice cream. Sometimes, he would take them, all the way to the Ice Cream Palace, across the street, from the Casino, at the Fairgrounds. They had two big White Polar Bears out front. Monks, real name was Wilfred, but everybody called him Monk. He drove a big truck, and delivered cars to the dealerships, all over the United States and every time he came to see Bertha, he had a different kind of car. All the kids really liked to ride in the jeeps.

BAKERY

About two blocks further out Lamar Avenue, was a bakery that was out of this world. You could smell the baking going on for blocks. Sometimes, they had enough money to go get an Éclair that was full of a white cream or a lemon cream. And the shell was paper thin and would crush on you and it would run all over the place.

OLD TIMEY GROCERY

Across Lamar Avenue, from Big Mammas, was an old style grocer that bought most of what he sold, from farmers. There was no grocery chain to speak of. He had live chickens and biddies you could raise your own, and buy feed for them there Rabbits too. You name it and he had it. It was great to be able to go to his store and buy stuff that was in a garden earlier in the day especially Cantaloupes and Watermelons. Big Mamma always kept them for the kids and she liked them too.   It was what we know of today, as a farmers market. But it too, is lost to memories, due to regulations and laws for this and that. Those laws were passed supposedly for health reasons, but they really were to benefit some business man, that bribed somebody to pass a law.

Staying with Big Mamma was always an experience with great memories. The street cars, or Busses, as some called them, ran all night and the bus stop was probably 50 feet from the window, where Elbert slept. There had no air conditioning then and he could hear the traffic all night long from the open window even with the fan running. The busses stopping and starting up again and way off in the distance, you could hear the trains leaving Central Station, downtown Memphis, heading north , south , east and west. Yes he had thoughts of hopping a train and riding in the wind, where ever it went.   But he also seen, a movie about HOBO's, and the life they lived, free to go anywhere they wanted , when they wanted, until they got caught and beat up, by the railroad police. He didn't like that part, so he decided he wouldn't do that.

MIGHTY MISSISSIPPI RIVER

The Mississippi river ran right by downtown Memphis. Elbert used to stand and watch the big river boats on the river and thought that might be fun, working on a river boat. They go all the way to the ocean. They even go up river to Ohio, St Louis, man that had to be fun. Then he read about the Sultana, back during the war between the states when the Civil War was over, the river boat, Sultana, a Paddle Wheeler, had just past Memphis, headed up river taking soldiers, back home to the North. When her boiler blew up, from the strain of being overloaded and going against strong currents fifteen hundred were on board, and only a little over a hundred survived.

Memphis, is high up on a bluff along the Mississippi River, and doesn't flood, like the Arkansas side of the river. When he was a child, he would go over to Arkansas to eat catfish. There used to be several places. One such place, stood out in his mind, it was right on the side of the highway and they pulled over on the hot dusty, gravel parking lot. They had to sit there, in the car, for a minute, or so, to let the dust settle. They then got out and went inside. The place was small, but long. They went to a table on the right and all of a sudden, he seen the biggest fat lady in the world. This lady was bed ridden, because she couldn't walk or stand. Her bed was about 10 feet away from their table, and their Mother evidently knew her from years past as they talked and had a great visit. Their Mother took Elbert and his brothers over to her to say hi and for her to get a good look at her boys. They were scared to death, Elbert just knew she might want to hug him and squeeze him like a grape, but she didn't. They ate there several other times, and she was very nice. The last time they went there, she had died.

As they left that fish place, you could see the cotton fields that went out of sight. You would see black folks picking cotton or chopping cotton and sometimes if they were close enough, you could hear them singing as they worked. Every now and then, you would see sometimes eight or ten little one or two room houses painted with whitewash, or a chalky red and each would have an outhouse, a clothes line and a shallow well. Those were share cropper houses, where they lived. The further you went west, the flatter the land got. You could tell where the Mississippi river went when it flooded from the winter snow melting up north and running down all the way to the Gulf of Mexico. A lot of land at the river's edge flooded and then receded and left that muddy stain on everything.

They had flooding in Memphis, but most of that come from the Wolf River and the Lucihatchi River bottom land. And in town, if it flooded, it was due to the sewer system not being able to handle excessive rains.

SHAKEY GROUND

The first time Elbert felt the ground shake, he thought it was funny and hesitated to say anything, for fear nobody would believe him. It didn't happen often and he can't remember but once or twice, but it did move at times. He was, an adult, before he ever heard of the Madrid Fault that runs close to Memphis. He had, never heard of any serious damage, but that is not to say, it hasn't ever occurred, one time or another. Memphis is, on a Bluff, it makes you wonder, if the fault lies under the Mississippi River.

STORM SHELTERS

When visiting relatives down in Mississippi, he learned it was common, to have a storm shelter. Elbert heard of Tornado's that went around Memphis, because Memphis was built high up on a Bluff   bad weather went around to the north towards Dyersburg or south down into Mississippi. Very seldom, did they have a tornado in Memphis. People that have storm shelters also use them to store can goods, canned from their gardens. The temperature stays a constant cool temperature year around.

JEWEL TEA MAN

He didn't know how often it was, it could have been once a month, but the JEWEL TEA man came and brought mother, coffee, spices and what have you. They accumulated, ice tea pitchers, plates, cups and saucers. Mother eventually, had a complete set of dishes. At one time, they had one of everything made by the Jewel Tea Company.

Today, if you go into many antique stores you can always find several pieces for sale and they have become very expensive and collector's items. He has, several pieces, and they sit in prominent places, like the cubby hole somewhere, or in the pantry, or the utility room.

INSURANCE MAN

He didn't know what kind of insurance it was but the Insurance man came on a regular basis. He was a tall older man and he also made and sold ceramics. One day he came with a large ceramic flower pot that looked like a pipe a man would smoke. Mother, had it for years and sometime or another she give it to someone or it got broke.

Elbert's grandmother was big on Burial policies. And, it was a good thing for a while. She had five children and she had a policy on each of them, herself, and each of the grandchildren. She paid them up and put them in the cedar chest to be used if and when necessary. However, through the years, the company was merged, or bought, or went out of business. Memphis Funeral Home was the people selling the policies for the company and they honored the policy only to the extent of $250.

However, the policy stated a funeral service to include visitation, the hearse, a Limo for the family, opening and closing the grave, and two motorcycle cops with blue lights flashing lights. Now wasn't that nice. She paid about some small amount a week for years on each policy. Eleven policies all total.

MUSIC MAN

This salesman came with his pretty pictures and talked Elbert's Mother into him taking Accordion lessons. He said he didn't want to and said so. He said he was interested in Piano lessons but the salesman said he should take Accordion lesson first and piano would be easy but they won. He took probably ten lessons and that wound that up. Everybody learned Elbert had no musical aptitude. And that was the best kept secret from all his friends. He never told anyone, his brothers did, they told everybody that would listen.

BLUE SPRINGS, MISSISSIPPI

One Friday afternoon Elbert and his brothers were informed they were going on a little trip, to visit some relatives. These were relatives the boys had never met before. Their mother had in years past, but not the boys. This was the side of the family my mother's mother came from. Elbert never knew his mother's mother as she died before he was born. She was very pretty and played the piano beautifully. She got cancer in her right arm and it had to be amputated which ended the piano playing. She later died as a result of cancer.

His Mother and all three boys all piled in the car and took off down the highway and into Mississippi. They went through New Albany, Mississippi and turned left onto a grey rock gravel road for several miles, then right onto a dirt road for several miles. They came to a crossroad and this lone little store. They continued on through the intersection for about a mile then turned right into the drive way to this little white farm house with chickens in the yard.

As they drove up, people began to come out to greet them and this began his first real experience of coming to the country. His Uncle Henderson was an older man and a big man. His Aunt Ruth was a little short older grey haired lady and pleasingly plump. She was the boss with her squinty little eyes, she hustled everyone into the house for supper. Also present was Claudine, Marilyn and Diggy. Diggy was a nick name. Everybody went into this big kitchen, with one big long table and benches down each side, and a chair at each end. Elbert and his brothers had never seen so much food. Uncle Henderson, said grace, and everyone began to dig in. As a bowl got empty, Aunt Ruth went to the stove and got some more and refilled it. When everyone had finished, we handed our dishes to Aunt Claudia and she started washing dishes. Then Aunt Ruth left the rest of the food on the table and covered it all with a sheet.

Then, everyone went into the living room and sit around the fireplace and of course Elbert, Wayne and Neal, sit quietly and listened to the older people talk. Eventually, everyone went to bed and Elbert slept in the softest bed he had ever slept in. He learned it was a feather mattress and feather pillows. He was sleeping so well, when he begin to hear someone moving around in the kitchen. He looked around and it was still dark. A few minutes later, he was told to get up and went into the kitchen, to breakfast. He learned, in the country, you got up and eat a big log rolling breakfast, before daylight, so by daylight, the chickens are fed and the eggs are gathered and the cows are milked, and the milk can is put out by the road, to be picked up by the milk man. And you can be bailing hay, as the sun comes up. It makes for a long day.

That first morning, he learned he was to go with the men folk they all piled into the back of a pickup truck and off they went to a field somewhere. They stopped in this field and everybody went to their respective jobs, but Elbert. Elbert was told to just sit on the tractor and steer it, and don't touch anything. He figured he could do that and he did. The tractor was barely moving and was pulling a big trailer. As he went by hay bales, coming out the back of a combine, the guys would pick one up and pitch it onto the trailer, and the boys on the trailer, would stack it neatly.

Well, this went on until about lunch time and everybody stopped and somebody was selected to go to that little store I told you about earlier and get us something to eat. At the store, one of the guys bought a big piece of baloney and a big piece of hoop cheese and a box of crackers and an orange crush for everybody.

When they got back, everybody had a pocket knife and they begin to slice the baloney into half in slices and the cheese into quarter inch slices and put the pieces between two crackers and that became lunch and of course chased it all down with the orange crush drink.

Elbert kept looking at that tractor and wanting to drive it bad. The wheels in his head were churning, looking for an excuse to go get on it and drive it somewhere, when he heard one of the boys say, they need to rake more hay in rows and they needed the rake. Well, he was looking at the rake about a hundred yards away and he jumped up and volunteered to take the tractor down to the rake, if they wanted him to. Somebody said fine go ahead, and he got on it got it cranked and in gear and started off down the hill. He pulled the gas lever all the way down and the tractor took off like a bullet and he seen up ahead he was going to have to turn right, or run into a big ditch. He was so busy trying to step on the brakes He didn't think to let up on the gas. By his right foot, were the brake pedals, both of them and in his excitement at the last minute he stood up on the brake pedals hard. His foot, slipped off the left one and onto the right brake and the tractor spun around to the right and stopped and choked down. The other guys come running and said, boy, you can drive that thing, and you put it right where we needed it to hook up to the hay rake. They thought he had done all that on purpose and the truth was he was out of control all the way down the hill even when he turned and stopped. The only explanation, he had was it wasn't his time to die and the Lord stopped the tractor.

The next morning, after breakfast, Aunt Ruth poured the milk from the cow into a butter churn. This was a tall wooden octagon shaped thing with a tick poking out a hole in the top. She sat there in a chair and pulled and pushed that stick up and down for what seemed like hours. And then she lifted the stick up and out of this thing, and there was a big blob of butter on the end. She had just made butter.

About that time, somebody yelled for him to come outside. There were two boys out there, and they had come to get him and Wayne, to go to their house and ride the big John Deere tractor. He said great and they took off running towards their house. To get there, they went through these woods, along a path, for about a hundred yards to their house. This patch of woods had a name and it was the snake pit. That was, another reason for them to run, instead of walk. Everybody knows a snake can't bite you if you're running.

Man, this was a big tractor. But these boys knew just how to start it and there they went. They were taking turns and it was time for Elbert to stop and let his brother Wayne drive it. They were circling the house, going round and round. As Elbert came around the house, he didn't stop and let Wayne have a turn and Wayne was fighting mad. Elbert thought it was funny. As he came around the house again, Wayne had a pump BB gun and he said: "You had better stop or I will shoot you." Elbert laughed even harder and kept going. Did I mention, they didn't have any shirt's on. Well, about that time, Elbert heard the BB gun go off and he felt the sting of a BB hit him in the back. Elbert reached behind him and felt where the BB had hit him and when he brought his hand back around where he could see it, it had blood on it. He stopped the tractor and climbed down and took off running through the snake pit to find help. He had been shot by his own brother, and if he lived, he was going to beat the snot out of him. When he ran into the house, they held him and looked at the damage. The BB had just broken the skin and it was just under the skin. They squeezed the BB out and handed it to him. They then, put some salve on it and made him take a nap.

    I failed to mention Diggy. Diggy was a special child. She had the mind of a child until the day she died, as an adult. She was cool and they enjoyed talking with her. She laughed at everything they said or done. This was the start of a visit to the country every summer. They had some really good times there, but as with everything else, times changed and something else took its place. Elbert could see them all, right now, as he thinks of their mannerisms and the way they talked. He wished he could go see them this afternoon. May we will all meet one day in heaven, let's hope so.

CHAPTER 3   1955 THROUGH 1959

KINGSBURY SCHOOL

Well, let us get on back to Memphis and get moved back into Elbert's house on Isabelle Street.   He has to start the seventh grade any day now. His mother just got the job, of Cafeteria Manager for the school he will be going to, Kingsbury Middle School. Heaven only knows what the days ahead are going to be like.

The 7th grade is where things started to pick up and change from the traditional classroom education. The first day of school and he learned today, he is going to go class to class and sign up for each course. He had never done that before which meant he would have to first find the class room he wanted, then line up outside each class room, to sign up for that class. Well, this is his first day at Kingsbury and he don't know, hardly anybody. He was doing pretty good when all of a sudden this guy says, "Hey kid you're in the wrong line. " He looked up at this guy and noticed he is one of those guys that already shaved.

When he grows up, he will have a heavy beard, because he looked like, he had been shaving for years. Elbert wondered if maybe this guy had maybe failed a couple of years. The reason he noticed that was because, it would probably be another ten years it seemed before he would shave. Elbert had no facial hair, none on his arms and legs and well, not much anywhere else either. These big guys would one day be the football team. They got a kick out of teasing him and he later learned the big guy was John Ratcliff. John and Elbert became very good friends and they even double dated to the prom together in his brother's brand new white Buick convertible.

The seventh grade was as high as Kingsbury School went that year, but as he graduated to the next grade the school then taught that grade and this followed suit, all the way to the 12th grade. In other words, the school, grew just like him, and became one of the greatest schools in Memphis.

1959, this became the year, of the first graduating class. And he was one of the first people to ever graduate, from that school. The standard had been set by the greatest people he knew. That was and includes the Principle and Staff of his school. A staff that cared for each and every student and had the highest hopes for the brightest future possible, he sure wished he had just known and cared enough for myself, as much as they cared for him.

10TH CLASS REUNION

His mother wanted to go as much as he did since she was the Cafeteria Manager of the school he went to, she knew all the students and some, better than he did.

After the reunion was over and later that night, Elbert and Janice, his wife went to Corky Ireland's new home and the first thing he spotted was a baby Grand Piano. He remember going to Corky's house many times, to get him to fool around and hang out, but his mother made him practice the piano until Elbert thought his fingers would fall off.

HARRY "CORKY "IRELAND

The last time he heard Corky play, was in his home in 1969. Corky played every song, anyone ask him to play, and without any music to go by, and it was astonishing. Elbert asked him how he could do that and told him, that was how he paid his way through college, playing in Bars, and night clubs. That is determination and called: "Where there is a will, there is a way." Corky didn't know it then, but he inspired Elbert to go back home to Jacksonville, Florida and get his College Degree. Elbert registered for college at night and went three nights a week from 5:45 to10:15, for four and a half years, straight through the summers, for fear if he stopped for the summers, he might not go back and finish. Thank you for the inspiration, Corky, he did it.

BUTCH Mc CARTER

One day Elbert seen Butch McCarter fiddling with his desk, and out came a bolt and nut that held the arm in the upright position. Butch then put a pencil in the hole and said: "Now, when the class changes, and the next person who sits here, leans or sits on the arm of this desk, the pencil will break, and it will scare them to death, that they broke the desk. " Butch was laughing, the whole time he is doing this. Elbert was nodding his head with a devilish smile, thinking this is going to be fun. He suggested they do several more for the fun of it. They agreed to do more, the rest of the day. Boy, they planned to get some laughs out of this. Well, they did, and they got the reaction they had hoped for. But now, there are about 20 Desk all over the school with the arms hanging down and the bolts missing.

You guessed it, Mr. Crothers, called Elbert and Butch in and grilled them and they each got three licks with his famous paddle, made right there in the school shop class. Then, they had to stay after school and fix every broke desk in the school. Which took several days?

SCHOOL PRINCIPLE

Mr. John Crothers, was the principle of all principles, he could look at you and tell what you were thinking. He would stand in the hall and watch the students change classes, and he would rock up on the balls of his feet, bounce a couple of times and you knew, that he knew, yesterday, you were not sick, when you didn't show up for school. You could read it in his eyes, that he knew you were playing possum. And you knew in your heart, he wasn't saying anything this time, but one day, he would let you know, he knew. Elbert used to catch himself, sometimes just standing and watching what is going on around him, and even rocking up on the ball of his feet, like he used to do.

A HORSE SHOE NAIL

Attending his 50th Class Reunion, Elbert was looking forward to seeing Mr. John Crothers. But, he was not there, as he had passed in 1992. However, he had left a special gift to each of there that night. Each received an envelope with a horse shoe nail and a poem in it. This was written by George Herbert 1593-1633.

For want of a nail: a shoe was lost
For want of a shoe: a horse was lost
For want of a horse: a rider was lost
For want of a rider: a message was lost
For want of a message: a battle was lost
For want of a battle: a kingdom was lost

All for the want of: A Horse Shoe Nail. Thanks go to Mr. Crothers and the people that put together, their 50th Class Reunion.

TEACHERS

Mr. and Mrs. McAlpin, he lovingly referred to them as, Mr. Mack and Mrs. Mack. Used team work on him and he said he was the better for it, to this day.

Mr. Vinson wanted him to be an architect so bad. He didn't really know why, but he didn't want to be responsible for designing a bridge or a building that might fall, and kill people. Being a draftsman was one thing, and he enjoyed that a lot more. He wished, Mr. Vinson could have known, that he did well for himself and he was one of the biggest reasons. Advanced Drafting, Elbert has used a thousand times. Before he build a new room, house, garage, car port, church, deck, he first drew a blueprint to go by, and use to determine a material list and just how he would build it. First things must come first, like a foundation, then floor, then walls, then roof. You can't build it any other way.

In wood shop, he built a stool to stand on to change a light bulb or whatever. He used it yesterday. That stool, is 55 years old, built by a kid, in school, and he used it yesterday. He will assure you, his wood shop teacher was good, thank you Mr. Mack, for a job well done.

Mr. Morrow was his art teacher. Elbert wished he could tell Mr.

Morrow, how he has used what he taught him so many times. Art, is a class, he really took for granted and never thought he would ever use any part of it. But it taught him about detail, presentation, color, the use of color, imagination. These were important to him as a manager of a large corporation and enhanced his presentations of materials, reports, and projects.

One day in Art Class, as Elbert was leaving the room, he walked by someone that was drawing a Horse's Head. He thought he could draw, but her picture of a horse head, humbled him. It looked like, if you touched it, it would bite you. That was, just how good it was. He hoped she went on to use her talent. He wished he knew her name, but he didn't. He has used Art, a thousand times picking out new furniture, or the color roofing he wanted, or the color of the brick in his new home.

Every class he took, he took because he had to, to get credit, which was required for graduation. He took classes, that he has never ever used, i.e. Spanish. The Mexicans in America today, can't even speak Spanish, because they speak 200 different dialects depending on which side of the river or mountain , they come from. But Wood shop, he has used, even professionally and to maintain his home or shop. With the use of tools and safety around tools he has built two story buildings and houses, and he learned to read and draw blueprints from Mr. Vinson, in high school.

Now English, He didn't so well, as you can see, by his punctuation, for instance. But those other classes were more fun at the time. Today, as a published author of eight novels, he will tell you he wished he had studied English more than he did.

Social Studies, Government, American history, taught by Mr. Bill Wicker, is something he took and passed, but had no idea, how important it was at the time, to understand, how our government operated. And right now, in 2013, our government is in the biggest mess since the 1930's. Now is the time to understand what happened, why it happened, and what to do about it, but all he hears from our elected officials is , people looking for someone to blame or point fingers at. 545 is the number of people that make the laws of the land for 600 million citizens, and so far, in the past 40 years, the lawmakers have added new laws, and rescinded some good laws, that have been so bad, that we are now in another depression, that some are calling a recession. Millions of people are out of work and they are working on the wrong problems. Everybody needs to take a refresher course. Everybody has been so busy going to college, serving in the military and making a life for our family and they trusted Congress and the Senate was doing their jobs, and they didn't and what is sad is, they still are not doing it.

Just to bring a little levity to the moment, here is something, they didn't teach in High School and they should have, if they had been in invented by then.

A LOT OF THINGS HAS BEEN INVENTED SINCE HIGH SCHOOL.

The only tools you need in life are: WD-40 OIL, and DUCT TAPE.
If it doesn't move and it should, then use WD-40 oil.
If it moves and it shouldn't, then use DUCT TAPE.

STUDENT HANDBOOK

In 1958, Elbert received the 1st edition of the Student handbook. Boy, does it cover everything. I want to read, to you a sentence, from the section on Home Room. In home room, at the beginning of each school day, the roll is checked, announcements for the day are read, and the morning Devotional is given. Elbert's most memorable, home room teacher was Mrs. Pauline Anderson.

And, in the section on the Cafeteria, The last sentence, says: A brief prayer period is set aside during each lunch period. Neither of these two prayer periods is available to Elbert's grand children today and you might say what can he do about it? Well, for starters do not re-elect any incumbents. Elect someone that will run for office and correct what is wrong, with America today. It is simple, stand up and say, enough is enough.

THE ANNUAL, 1959 TALON

Different classmates and some of the teachers and other friends wrote notes on the inside cover pages. In the front and in the back are treasures, these comments were lovingly left as cute reminders, you had friends and people, that would miss you in the years to come. Here are some quotes:

Elbert, you are about a crazy son of a gun, just the same, Lots of Luck always, Bobby Watkins.

Gopher, I sure will miss you next year. I have really had a blast with you in "Callaway's Room". You're the greatest in my book. Loads of Luck in the future, cause gophers can hardly get a job!!!!! Pat Cox. (Gopher was her pet name, for Elbert and Elbert was her pet)

Elbert (Gopher) you're a real great guy and I like "YA Loads. I hope you'll always be happy and have good luck. P.S. Don't be a paper boy.

With all of them people pulling for him, how could he have gone wrong? He is sure you have many of the same comments. He always felt he had a special group of people in his class. He knew there were some in classes below his that were real friends and that made it even better. He loved and misses every one of them.

In looking through his annual again and again something kept bothering him and he couldn't put his finger on it until recently in his annual, there is not one teacher, male or female, that has gray hair. There must have been one heck of a market for hair coloring or we must have been the nicest kids in the world to teach since sliced bread.

THE MINISTREL SHOW

This was a show put on at school and they even charged money to see it. Admission was fifty cents and it was on February 19 and 20th, about 1957. Elbert didn't remember who the teacher was, that put it together, but she was short and wore her blond hair pulled back into a bun. She was also the teacher that took them downtown to a Hotel, to eat a meal, to teach us about meals served in courses and which fork to use to eat what. She was also in charge of the Photography Club. Elbert remembered being in it. Elbert played a character that was a baby in a diaper, sitting in somebody's lap. They made a mistake of giving him a baby bottle of milk, and he squirted, whoever it was, on their black face and it started running in his eyes and the crowd went wild. Elbert and whoever it was, was a hit and a star. There is a picture in the annual, near the back, announcing the show with a bill board. I don't think you can have minstrel shows in school now days.

DANCE PARTY ON TELEVISION

Dance party, was on TV every week and the participants would be from schools all over Memphis.   Well, one day, here came a lady to the school, from the station to sign up those that wanted to appear on the show, with Wink Martindale. Well, going and being on the show seemed to go by so fast. It seemed like they just got there, when it was over. But I am getting ahead of myself. Elbert couldn't remember who he went with. But he just found out who it was and who it should have been. It should have been Gloria Warren, but her father, being a devout Baptist, didn't want his daughter, on that show, dancing on TV. So, to honor her father's wishes, she refused to go with him and Gloria is of the opinion, it was Emma Jane Oaks, unless she is mistaken, that went with him and danced to "A White Sport Coat and a Pink Carnation".

FIRST GIRL FRIEND/BOYFRIEND

One day, he heard through the grapevine, there was a girl that likes him. Not just likes him, but really likes him. You know what he means. He asked who it was and he learned her name. Then the private notes started coming and going back and forth. Then, the phone conversations began and they were told by their respective parents, to get off the phone, a million times then the invitations to go to her church sometime. Well, one Sunday Night he got to go to her church somehow. They sat on the back row, where all the other young people sit. This was so they could hold hands without you know who, frowning at them. After church, he walked her home and it gave them the privacy to talk and hold hands etc. This was the first time they kissed and he understood it went straight to her diary. They said their good bye and he started walking for home. It was quite a ways but that was alright. He was on cloud nine.

Now his mind is on girls and it's time to start thinking about, how in the world, was he going to date? He didn't have any money or a car. How was he going to take her to a movie with no money? How could he take her Roller Skating? How was he going to buy her a hamburger and a coke, much less fries?

Realization just set in. The real world just showed its ugly head. While at that age, he knew his mother didn't have the means to just fund his activities. She worked three jobs, trying to support herself and three boys. He needed to make some money. So, he started a whole series of jobs. He cut grass with a lawn mower, his Grandmother loaned him the money to buy it. He got a paper route. He pushed an Ice cream Cart, all over the neighborhood, for several summers. Every penny he made he gave to his mother, to help keep him and his brothers in a nice house and a car with nice clothes and food on the table. A Girlfriend was just something he could not afford.

They double dated with someone one night and they went skating, then straight home. He didn't remember who it was, they double dated with. They parked somewhere and the front seat got busy and they stared at each other and kissed. Then they informed the front seat that they needed to go home.

He slowly, called her less and less, as he had no right to prolong the inevitable. He couldn't afford a girlfriend. He didn't have any idea how to say it. He didn't have any idea what to say. He wondered, is this where you start lying, and making up excuses? He didn't want that.

FIRST JOB WITH A PAY CHECK

You have to be careful what you ask for, because you might get it. He had been praying for a job that would give him the money to date and do things. Well he got it. The only problem was, with this job, he now had money, but he worked the same hours you normally would date, or go to a basketball game etc. So, he was back where he started with his girlfriend status and dating.

He got a call from his Aunt Bertha. She worked at the Cross-town Theater. She was calling him to see, if he would be interested in going to work every afternoon when he got out of school.

Are you kidding? This is great, now his prayers were answered. Now, he would have a pay check every week. He was RICH! Well, don't go crazy Elbert. Not only are you not going to get rich, but, now you will be at work every night. There will be, no dating. You are going straight to work, after school. And when you get off work, you can ride the bus home and Oh by the way put your pay check on your Mother's dresser before you go to bed. Because, if you don't, she will wake you up and ask for it. Don't get the wrong idea, here. This was, just the way it had to be for them all, his Mother and brothers, to have what they had. And the most important thing here is that they had each other.

After a while, He learned his girlfriend was dating someone else. That was good, she deserved someone who could date her and do things together. Now, reality raised its ugly head again. As time went on and he got into a car, his money started going to any and everything but a courting relationship. This was cars, tires, gas, and drag racing. And even when he had a tender thought about and towards girls, he had to face another reality.

When he took inventory of himself, he found he had nothing to offer a girl. He had no idea what he wanted to do with his life. He had no idea, how he was going to ever amount to anything. And then one day, he woke up to reality. He found himself down and out. He knew it was time to join the Air Force. Why in the world the Air Force? He went into the service, so they would make a man out of him and give him the training he needed to one day, have a career at something. And they did both.

MARRIAGE

When he was probably ten years old, he realized not all marriages were made in heaven. He knew of happy marriages and he knew of bad marriages. His mother was married six times and she married his daddy twice. He remembered one day asking his mother, is there someone out there for him? Is she in Memphis or some other city? You know what she told him? There is someone out there for you and one day you will know it. When you are ready, and you know it is time, go for it with all that you have in you.

Make her number one, in your life; don't even let your mother come between you. Love her forever and ever be a man and make the best living you can. And make your marriage vows mean something when you say, forever and ever and until death do us part.

Elbert and Janice have been together for 50 wonderful years. They are not slim and trim as they once were, but they belong to each other. They had two wonderful daughters and have three wonderful grandchildren. They have a lot to be thankful for and a lot to be proud of. But most of all, they have each other.

Mont eagle, Tennessee

They were just getting out of school for the summer of 1956 in a few weeks, when Elbert and his brothers learned, they were going somewhere for the whole summer. Their mother had agreed to run a Lodge, on top of a Mountain, in Mont eagle, Tennessee, for the summer. The deal was they would take a black lady with them, one of the ladies that cooked in the cafeteria at Kingsbury, to be the cook. His Mother would hire a local person to help clean, etc.

So, one day, they loaded up with, his mother and the black lady in front, with Elbert, Wayne and Neal in the back seat, they left Memphis in a 1951 Chevy. They took highway 64, all the way there. Now, back in those days, there was no expressway, and it seem like it took all day, but we got there okay.

I remember the day we got there going to the top of the mountain, the road was so steep we passed a big tractor trailer and the driver was standing on the running board with his door open, while his truck was poking up the mountain.

The Lodge was really an old two story house with a wrap around front porch, built in the early 1900's. All the furniture was from the 1920's or 30's. This facility was called the Assemble Grounds was a compound that must have had, probably fifty of these old houses. Some were lived in year around, some were occupied only for the summer and some were lodges for people to visit and stay a day, week, month, or all summer. Our Lodge was called the Northgate Lodge.

Mother hired a young married girl, to help make beds, wash and clean. She was a mountain girl that had never been off the mountain and had just had a baby. One day, she didn't show up and we learned she had a death in the family. His mother inquired about the funeral and she went. He will never forget when his mother drove up, after coming from the funeral. She got out of the car crying,   he asked her, why was she crying and she said, the one that died, was that girls baby and they buried the baby in the front yard of their house. That was common in the mountains, they learned.

They had people that came and stayed a week, some longer. One older lady stayed a month. There was an outdoor, clay tennis court. Elbert got the summer job of dragging it every morning and putting down the white lines. He of course played with anybody that wanted to play. He also got the job of delivering the newspaper for the summer. He met a lot of folks that were there.

And there was a swimming pool too. The life guard was a girl, probably five years older than he was. She was beautiful and wore a black one piece bathing suit that was out of this world. His heart throbbed every time she spoke to him and he couldn't take his eyes off her. She of course probably didn't even notice him. Her name was Jane Law. Next to the pool was an indoor basketball court and that is where they had dances on the weekends and other activities during the week.

Out the back gate and to the left, down a dirt road about a hundred yards was a trash dump. One day Elbert and his brothers walked down there and they seen an old trunk. It was locked, so they got a screwdriver and a hammer and got it open. Inside, were German uniforms and some helmets? There were medals and campaign ribbons. Like any other boy, they took the helmets and pretty stuff and later at home, in Memphis, swapped it for other things, boys swap things for.

One day they decided to go to the drive in movie that night. So, they all piled in the car, even the black lady was with them. When they got to the ticket booth, the man said: "You can't bring her in here, black people are not allowed on the mountain after dark. You better take her back to the Assembly Grounds." That was the first time Elbert really ever seen that black people lived by different rules than white people. He was just old enough to be embarrassed and seen another side of reality.

Elbert learned to drive while there and he had his first fender bender, by running into a tree while trying to find the brake. This was truly one of the most memorable summers of his life. At night, he was invited to meet other boys and girls his age, and they danced and had parties.

Through the years, we have stopped and rode through the grounds and nothing has changed. It is identical to the day he was there as a young boy. This is the only place in the world that he knows of, that has not changed at all. The town has changed, but not the Assembly

Grounds, at Monteagle, Tennessee.
KINGSBURY CAFETERIA
Elbert's mother being the manager often cashiered the serving line. However from time to time, she hired students to take the money. Jean Hurt was one such girl to do that. Jean was very nice. He seen Jean at his 50th class reunion but he didn't recognize her until after the reunion. Then a year later, he learned she died. They made eye contact once but he got busy and never spoke to her. He hates that.

The head cook, in the kitchen, was a lady by the name of, Christine Townsend. One day when he arrived at school he went around to the back door of the cafeteria, to see his mother about something. Just as he opened the door, wouldn't you know it, a wasp stung him on the very end of his nose. Boy did it hurt, man did it hurt and did I tell you that it hurt? Well, Christine, the head cook seen what happened and she came running over to him and said: "Honey, stand still and I will make the pain go away. He thought yeah but thought go ahead. She took tobacco juice out of her mouth and dobbed it on the end of his nose and said:" There now go on in to school it will quit hurting in just a minute. "Well the first thing he noticed was, it didn't hurt anymore. The next thing was to look in the mirror, to see what everybody else seen. The third thing was to get his nose washed off before any of my buddies seen him and ask what is that on your nose? Being the appreciative nice kid that he was, he smiled at Mrs. Christine and thanked her, then ran as fast as I could, to wash his nose off.

Christine, had a son named, Ed Townsend. Ed Townsend had made a record and it became a hit record. He was an immediate famous person. His song was: "For Your Love, I Would Do Anything. " It was 50's music, that inspired the way we slow danced. This song was a belly rubbing song that comes out of the black Motown Era. To this day, Elbert's wife says he dance like a black person. Hey that's cool. Everybody likes to dance with me. Just ask Bobbie Kay Warren. If she doesn't acknowledge it, it probably is an early sign of senility.

PAPER ROUTE and the CAR WRECK
Well, as was mentioned earlier in Elbert's stories. He had a paper route for a while. Normally, he spotted my papers in stacks, then

started walking and as he walked, he was folding and then throwing them on the front porches as he went along. He got pretty good and could hit a small front porch from the side walk almost a hundred percent of the time.

Well, this one morning, his mother had gone out of town with some girl friends and she said he could drive her car, even though he didn't have a license, only to deliver my papers. So, he picked them up and spotted them in the neighborhood like he always had. Then he delivered them and when he got through, he was going back to the bakery to get hot donuts and chocolate milk, go home.

Well, coming down Macon road, when you get to Leadwood Baptist Church, you better be stopping. Because, you have to turn left or right, you can't go straight. If you do go straight you would knock down the guide wire holding the telephone pole up and jump a big bush and knock down two post holding up the car port, side swipe the car there, and wake up the little old lady that lives there that just got home from the hospital after having open heart surgery. That second pole holding the carport up came through the windshield and stopped inches six inches from the end of his nose. His first thought was to put it in reverse and get the devil out of there. But the back tires were spinning on the boards and blue smoke was rising, and he couldn't get back over that bush mentioned earlier. About that time, he got out and was staring into the eyes of a scared little old lady. He didn't realize it at the time, but he was walking around with his rubber boots on, that had captured a lot of the glass from the windshield, and it was cutting up his feet, without him even feeling or noticing it for hours.

The police came and a wrecker, his mother was on her trip to Hot Springs, Arkansas or Little Rock, he didn't remember. So he called his dad and he came to get him. Now all this was happening at 4:00 in the morning and now you're going to say, "What in the hell, was you doing out at 4:00 in the morning." He knew you would. He had a paper route remember? That little strip of stores had a bakery, and that is where we got our papers to go deliver and we always come back to eat a donut and drink chocolate milk, he just fell asleep at the wheel, just as he got there, because he remembered getting there, he just didn't stop, and

the next thing he heard was the crash.
JOHNNY CASH
Elbert went to school with Jan Cash. Jan's mother and Johnny Cash were brother and sister. One night, Jan had invited several of us over to her house to play some 45 records. We were having a good time when Johnny Cash came in the front door and walked straight into the kitchen to see Jan's mother. He wasn't in there but a minute or so, when Jan's mother said: we had to move our party somewhere else, Johnny had a head ache. We did, but he never liked him after that.

As you know, Elbert had a paper route and he delivered the Commercial Appeal to Johnny Cash. Johnny Cash had a little brick house on a cove, or cull de sac, with a one car carport. He had a white Imperial with a chrome rack on top to carry the band and their instruments. And he had a Pink and White Lincoln, for a personal car. He was married to his first wife at that time. Well, Elbert was out collecting for the paper, and it was Christmas time. He was getting a quarter and sometimes a half of dollar tip, since it was Christmas. But when he got to Johnny's house, he was coming down the driveway and looked at him like , what do you want, so he told him he was collecting for the newspaper, and he ask Elbert how much. He told him, and that is exactly what he gives him. No tip at all. Now, Elbert already didn't like him and now he really didn't like him. Elbert often wondered maybe if Johnny knew Elbert didn't like him, Johnny did buy a half page ad in our Annual at school, his senior year.

BUTCH McCarter
Butch McCarter, was many things, but most of all, he was Elbert's friend. So you can talk about him if want to, you just better watch what you say about Butch around Elbert. Butch has passed away, but he will be remembered in the hearts of all that knew him. He was a really unique character. Kingsbury High School would not have been the same, if Butch had gone to a different school. Elbert don't know of anyone in our class that could have replaced his personality. Butch was a cat of a different color. He was unique and he was a friend to each and every one he knew.

Butch had something wrong with his kidneys and was in the hospital once. Jerry Matthews and Elbert went to visit him, and on the way, they stopped and bought him a half pint of liquor. They had just handed it to him when a nurse came in so Butch stuffed it under the covers to hide it. We all thought she would just be there a minute but here come another nurse and announced they were going to change his linen. Oh hell, Jerry and Elbert said: "Well Butch, we'll see you, "and headed for the door.

Another time, Butch and Elbert fought in the hall between classes about something for two days then they made up and went out fooling around for the next two years.

Butch, Winston Williams and Elbert, one time moved into an apartment together. That was an experience.

Needless to say, he missed Butch at the 50th Class Reunion, Butch was one of the nineteen that wasn't there because they had passed away.

MY PARENTS DIDN'T PUT ME IN TIME OUT, THEY WHOOPED MY BUTT.

Yes, that was a part of growing up where everybody wanted to show him they loved him enough to beat his tail. We all remember it to some degree. Elbert can tell you every time he got a paddling at school he got another one, when he got home. He used to call it, double jeopardy but his mother called it, you better not ever do that again. This is another page that you can read comments other people have made through the years. You know what? He thought he was the only kid that ever got a spanking until he read where others got them too they just didn't come tell him about it.

I RODE THE ZIPPIN PIPPIN AND LOVED IT

For those that don't know what the Pippin was, it was a roller coaster that used to be at the Fairgrounds in Memphis. Yes, this was at the fairgrounds, I can still remember the smells and the excitement in the air and the rides. The cotton candy and candy coated apples, the rings you threw at bottles. The dimes you threw onto plates the people walking around with Teddy Bears that they had won. Millions rode the Pippin and many, rode it over and over again.

CASINO, at the Fairgrounds

Not many people know it, but the big round building at the front gate was called the Casino. The Casino, used to be a hot spot for dancing. His mother and daddy went there for years before they even got married. Many people in the 1930's and 40's danced the night away, to the Boogie Woogie at the Casino not gambling but dancing. Many love affairs were started and ended in that dance hall, enough about that, it was before Elbert was born. He was but a twinkle in his daddy's eye.

SILVER SLIPPER and the COTTON CLUB

Both of these night Clubs were favorite haunts of mother and daddy before Elbert came along. Both places were still in business when Elbert got old enough to go there, but they were not the magical places of his time. The Silver Slipper burnt down and the Cotton Club became a dump, in their last years.

GAISMAN PARK

It was just far enough away, that he only went there to play little league baseball two years for Pantaze Drug Stores. The only things there at that time, were a bare field and one baseball park. It later become a big park, that the City of Memphis supported with employees and the money to provide everything you would ever want for kids.

THE SUMMER AVENUE GANG

This was not a gang in any sense of your imagination. This is classmates before us and after us that went up and down Summer Avenue night after night laughing and looking to see who else you might know, is out riding around. There were car loads of girls looking for boys and car loads of boys looking for girls, and then when they found each other they wouldn't speak. It was more fun to look for them, than to catch them.

Some had been to parties, skating or movies. Some had six people in the car at the drive in hang out. But when that same car went through the gate at the drive in movie, there was only a driver and a date visible. When they got parked, the other four in the trunk would come crawling out. The boys and girls that hung out late, were the ones that just had to see their boy friend or girl friend, one more time before going home for the night and then getting on the phone under the covers to talk way into the night. Neither would be the last person to say good night, don't let the bed bugs bite.

It snowed on Summer Avenue one night while Elbert was cruising. The parking lot of the strip mall, next door to Zayers was vacant and covered in a few inches of snow. It must have been 1957, or 58. Jerry Mathews and Elbert noticed a car pulled off the road into the parking lot and since it sloped down towards the stores, he lost control and spun around and around. Elbert was driving, and told Jerry, that looks like fun, watch this. He got a running start and pulled into the parking lot and spun the steering wheel to the right and they spun around and around. Well, it worked just great, and it was fun, but they went on to the Krystal Drive- in.

Well, some other guys got the same idea they did, but one of them hit a light pole in the middle of the parking lot, broadside. One ended up in the ditch that separated the two parking lots there. And one guy's car, ended up in one of the stores. Boy, were they lucky!

GOLDEN GLOVES

There were three, prominent, Golden Glove Boxers, in his school. They were their versions, of Rock Balboa. Charles Shuttles worth was the Novice City Fly-Weight Champion in Memphis, and runner up in the Mid South. Paul Sylph, was the City Open Middleweight Champion and Jimmy Burette won the South Memphis Golden Bantam weight Championship but had to concede in the City Finals, without fighting, due to illness.

Butch McCarter and Elbert fought for two days in a row, in the halls of the school and the cafeteria and Mr. Crothers, the principle, paddled them. But Charles, Paul and Jimmy, got their picture in the 59 Talon Annual wearing bathing suits. Go Figure. Elbert don't remember what Butch and Elbert were fighting about, but they were friends for the rest of their lives.

NEW YEARS PARTIES AND CELEBRATIONS

As Elbert got older, he got more and more interested in being an adult, and doing adult things. He heard about the Hotels, downtown Memphis, as being one of the best places, to enjoy celebrating New Years Eve. So, he started going there with some other friends that were older than Elbert, and really enjoyed it. Getting dressed up and dancing to an Orchestra, playing Tommy Dorsey and Glenn Miller music, with a little Boogie Woogie and the Charleston was wonderful. Did you know, the Hotels, even had Saturday afternoon tea dances? This was, the one time, when older couples, middle aged and couples his age could get together and have fun and laugh. Everybody was in their teens in their minds and nobody related to being older than the other they were all at the same age, in our hearts. He has really missed that about Memphis. He has never found that venue again. He knows it exist, but not near where he lives.

Elbert and his wife were invited to a formal attire Ball recently at a Golf Club Banquet Room, in Sun City, Florida. When they went in and were seated, it brought back memories of those nights at the Hotels in Memphis. They danced to some of the same music as then. But now, "they" were the age of their parents then.

CROSSTOWN THEATER

Elbert worked for Malco Theaters for three years, and a lot of exciting things happened. He was at the Cross-town Theater for a year and a half, as a concessionaire and an usher. Then he went to the Memphian Theater as the assistant Manager to work under Jim Burch. He was there for a year and a half.

ELVIS PRESLEY

While at the Cross-town Theater, they got a call that Elvis Presley was coming to the theater and would be there shortly. Once the movie started, it was his job to clear the lobby and wait at a side door for Elvis knock. That door was an exit door, to an alleyway between the store next door and the theater. It wasn't long before Elvis knocked on the door and Elbert slipped him and his friends, inside and upstairs, into the balcony. Well, it wasn't but about 45 minutes, when the police come to the front door, asked if Elvis was in there. Elbert told them yes he was. They said to tell Elvis, to stay inside after the movie was over, until they come for him. Because people had found his car, he had parked across the street behind a super market and was stripping it to pieces. Elbert went upstairs and told Elvis and he didn't even act concerned. Elbert walked over behind the super market across the street to see his car and there sat the skeleton of a 1957 Purple Caddy Convertible. They had stripped it clean. It was jacked up and the wheels were even gone. The police later, came for Elvis and took Elvis somewhere. That was, the first time Elbert had ever seen Elvis.

AROUND THE WORLD IN EIGHTY DAYS

This movie ran for so long, Elbert could almost quote everybody's lines. He saw it, 47 times. The only other movie, that ever ran that long, was THE TEN COMMANDMENTS, and he seen it, forty something times.

They showed that movie, AROUND THE WORLD IN EIGHTY DAYS, for over a month, two shows a day. A Matinee at 1:00 and the evening show at 7:00. Well, that left them with nothing to do all afternoon but hang around. So, one day, they are sitting around talking and across the street at the supermarket. They had a huge display of gallon jugs of Apple Cider, in the window. There were three of them and one of the guys, went across the street and bought each of them a jug of Apple Cider. Now these jugs were the kind, you could lay in the crook of your arm and hold it, with your finger through the glass ring. They were pretending it was moon shine they were drinking, like in the movies. They were sitting in the floor leaning against the wall in the upstairs balcony lobby.

Well, one of the guys, named Luke, went downstairs for something. This other guy Ray was mad at Luke that went downstairs about something, and while Luke was gone, Ray took Luke's bottle of cider, into the bathroom and peed in Luke's jug. Then, Ray brought it back and set sit down, like nothing had happened. Well, Luke came back from down stairs and they all tilted their jugs up and drink away with big swallows. Then Ray, starts laughing and then they all are laughing at him. They are all rolling in the floor laughing until it dawns on Luke he don't know why they are laughing. So Luke says, "What are we laughing about? "Then Ray told him. Then Luke said, "No, you didn't do that. " But Luke did have that suspicious look about him, and said: "I don't believe you. "

About that time, they heard someone down stairs, so they went to check on it and found the Manager had just come in, and he ask, "What was up, what are ya'll laughing about so hard? " Luke told him and everybody started laughing again. The manager said: "Well, you can tell if he did it or not."

Luke said: "How?"

He said, "Shake all three bottles up and set them down on my desk. If Luke's bottle has more foam than the other two, then you know he did it." So, they all shook our jugs of cider and Luke's jug foamed way up into the neck. Ray took off running down the street, with Luke close behind and he had a big broom. Luke stopped and laid it across the curb and broke the broke the broom part off and continued on after him with that big broom handle. By the time they closed up the theater that night, Luke and Ray were friends again.

MISSED THE LAST BUS FOR THE NIGHT

One night, the movie had run long, and by the time Elbert closed up the Cross-town Theater. The last bus had already run for the night. There wasn't anything to do but walk up Watkins Street to Jackson Avenue and catch the bus there. He knew he had better hurry, so he started running at a pretty good pace and it also served to keep him warm, as the temperature had dropped quite a bit during the early hours of the night.

Well, wouldn't you know it, from about a block away, he seen the last bus going out to the National Cemetery, cross Watkins. That meant, he was in for quite a walk, all the way home. And it's now after midnight and freezing.

He slowed down and walked slower now, as there was no hurry to catch a bus, because the last one for the night had just gone by. He started to get cold and then a lot colder. He found some newspaper along the way and he had learned from the Boy Scouts that paper was a good insulator. So he slipped a section up his back and a section up his front and he rolled some and slipped it up his sleeves. He immediately felt warmer and he walked on home and didn't get home until after two o'clock in the morning.

His mother ask him the next day, was it after two in the morning when you got home? He explained about missing the bus and she made him promise to call her and she would come get him. What she didn't understand was there were no pay phones along the way that he knew of. The only bad part was going over the Jackson Avenue via a duct, and the smell from that plant under the bridge was terrible. Plus, the wind while on the bridge. There were street lights all along the way, so he could see where he was walking, it was just a long walk.

MEMPHIAN THEATER

Elbert was promoted and transferred to the Memphian Theater, and in the next year and a half, a lot went on there.

One night, a lady went to him and complained, there was a naked man on the very front row. Jeez, how can this be? He thought to himself lady, what in the devil are you doing on the front row? He had to check that out, and sure enough, there is this tall naked man, wearing a trench coat, but gaping wide open, stretched out, and spread out on the front row, watching the movie. Elbert hustled him out and he never come back to his knowledge, but Elbert was cautious about every man in a trench coat in the future.

Have you ever wondered how do they clean up all that pop corn, candy wrappers, and coke cups? It's easy one guy comes in the next morning with a blower and blows everything to the front in a pile.   He then, shovels it up   and wet mops the sticky stuff and he is through, now you know the rest of the story.

Elbert always like that song" KANSAS CITY, KANSAS CITY, HEAR I COME," so he took a 45 record of that up to the projection booth one day. They wouldn't be open for another couple of hours, and he was there taking inventory. He put it on and turned up the volume. Boy, wow, those six foot high speakers was spitting it out. You should have seen him dancing by himself.

You remember those big posters in the glass cases out front? Well, he used to change those and throw away the old ones. The other day, on the Antique Road Show, somebody had saved a lot of them and they sold at auction for enough to buy a Rolls Royce. That is $250,000, if he had only known.

One day, Elbert stood in the concession stand and eat buttered pop corn, almost all day, and half the night. The next day, he thought he would die. He had to go to a doctor, and the doctor gave his mother a prescription for a fleet enema. He didn't have a clue what that was, until as they are riding along on the way home and he was reading on the bottle what you did with it. And all of a sudden, He said: "Oh Noooooooo." Well, when the pain became worse, than the embarrassment. He took the enema and lived to tell this story. Now, let's go on to something else.

ELVIS and the MEMPHIAN THEATER

Several times, ELVIS would rent the whole theater. As did some big companies, to hold meetings, during the day when we weren't open. Elvis would rent the whole theater sometimes early in the morning and sometimes late at night. It would appear we were closed and not open for business, but there would be a parking lot full of cars. The outside lights would not be on, and paper over the windows in the front doors, but you could smell, the pop corn cooking, a dead giveaway.

GHOST AT THE MALCO

One day, we removed every other row of seats from the Memphian Theater and staggered the seating, so you would always look between the two people in front of you, to give you a better view of the screen.

We then loaded all the excess seats on a truck and hauled them downtown to the basement of the Mapco Theater. The Malco Theater building was built over a hundred and fifty years ago and has several basement levels. There are dressing rooms everywhere down stairs that still have the gas lighting of years ago, before electricity. Electrical lights were installed when they come out but provided very little light. This place is covered in dust and spider webs, smelling musky and very scary. The Malco in Memphis is comparable to the Fox Theater in Atlanta, Georgia.

The man in charge, at the Mapco, was a very tall man wearing a solid black suit and a white cowboy hat. He looked like an undertaker, wearing Hop a long Cassidy, big white hat. His skin was as white, as his shirt and hat, and he never smiled or made a comment. He might have been the nicest man in Memphis, but to Elbert, he was the scariest. He looked to be a hundred years old. Elbert was not kidding this man looked like a zombie with no blood in his veins

Elbert explored all through the place and if he had walked up on that man in the dark he would have made a mess. This place still had drapes from the 1800's and early 1900's.

ELVIS HOME COMING PARTY FROM THE ARMY

When Elvis got out of the Army, George Cline threw a party for Elvis at Elvis big house. George Kline was one of Elvis closest friends they went to school together at Humes High School. Jim King went to Treadwell High School and had a band that George managed. George invited Jim King. Jim King invited Francis Perry and Francis invited me. So, Francis and went and had a pretty good time.

The party had been going for a while before we got there. Elvis was up stairs most of the time and didn't come down until very late with a girl they thought to be Lana Wood. Lana Wood was a local TV personality and at the time, well, they were very close. Back then, the room on the left, coming in the front door, was the Teddy Bear Room, the walls and the ceiling, were covered with Teddy Bears. The room on the right was where the party was. On the back wall, was what appeared to be, the end of a Giant Wooden Beer Barrel with about six beer dispensers, with bartenders serving the beer.

Elvis walked around like the king of the castle and he was too. He wasn't very friendly, but he probably didn't know half the people there. He didn't appear to recognize me from the Cross-town or the Memphian Theater.

MY FIRST CAR

Elbert learned Mr. Lowe had a car he wanted to sell. Mr. Lowe was Richard and Nancy Lowe's dad. Also his neighbor three doors down the street. It was a 1936 Chevrolet Coupe, it ran good and even though the paint was faded and the tires were dry rotted, it was just right for his budget. The price was $60. And he could pay $10 a week for six weeks. And he did for five weeks. But one day his mother came in saying they were going on vacation. Well great, in all the excitement and while they were gone, he missed that last payment. When they got home, and were unlocking the door to the house, the phone was ringing and his mother answered it. She just learned, he was the proud owner of a 1936 Chevy and he had missed his last payment of $10. Well, she said,

"Where is it?"

He told her, "About a block away. "

She said, "Go get it."

He thought to himself hey great, she will like it and she will surely be happy. Wrong............

When she seen it, she said, "Get rid of it by dark, and she meant it by Dark?" How do you do that? Well, I'll tell you. On Jackson Avenue, under the via a duct, is a junk yard. He drove it to the Junk Yard and sold it for $20. He gave the man the key and walked to the bus stop and rode the bus to the National Cemetery and walked the rest of the way home. He stopped by Mr. Lowe's house and paid him the ten dollars he owed him, and arrived home, just before dark and gave his mother the last $10.   Well that took care of that.

MADE THE HEADLINES

It was January 1st, 1959 at mid night. A new law had just gone into effect that Elbert had no idea would have anything to do with him. The law was if you are not driving, but are a passenger in the car or standing on the side of the road waiting for the drag to conclude, you are just as guilty as the driver of said vehicles Drag Racing. Well, he was riding with Jerry Matthews and they had just beaten this guy twice, but he wanted to run one more time and Jerry said Okay. As they have now, beat him for the third time, and are just about to slow down, a State Patrol car pulled long ways across the road in front of them and they were almost, not able to stop, without hitting him broadside. But they did get stopped, only inches from the patrolman. The patrol man pulled up to Jerry's side and told Jerry to get in the car with him. The patrolman was in a hurry to go catch the driver of the other car that had tried to turn around and had got stuck on the side of the road. As Jerry got out of the car, Jerry had left the car out of gear and it started rolling. Elbert slid over behind the wheel to hit the brake and put the car in gear, so it wouldn't roll. But the Patrolman thought, he was going to drive off, and he shouted for Elbert to hand him the keys. He tried to explain, he was only trying to put the car in gear so it wouldn't roll, but he thought Elbert would run.

To some degree, it was funny, how many people read the

headlines, about Elbert Alberson and Jerry Matthews but, it wasn't funny, when his mother read about her son. He should have known she would read about it, as she always reads every word in the paper, every day. Jerry lost his license for a year and Elbert lost his for three months. When Elbert got his license back, Jerry's daddy made Elbert drive Jerry everywhere they went for the next nine months.

DRAG RACING-JAIL- BAIL

One night on Summer Avenue at Graham Street Elbert was sitting at a red light when a light green 1957 Ford custom pulled up beside him. As soon as Elbert looked over at him, Elbert recognized who this was. This was a young boy, driving his daddy's car that really was a fast car. It was what they called a sleeper. It looked slow, but it had a monster engine in it and it was a Hoss, if you know what I mean.

Elbert had heard about him and now he had just challenged him. Well, Elbert had a V8, it was a full house flat head with three two barrels, and he was anxious to try this guy on for size for a long time. So when the light turned green Elbert obliged him. Elbert beat him badly. The only thing wrong with his victory was, a Police car was sitting behind him and he never seen him when he left the light.

There was a buddy of his with him, and he was free to go, but Elbert got a free ride, in the back seat of a police car. Now this happened before that new law in Tennessee that said a passenger was as guilty as the driver so they let his buddy take Elbert's car.

Now they had just built this new Jail in Memphis out on his side of town. But initially they set him down on a bench while they made their report. So while he was sitting there, two more policemen come in and Elbert recognized them as the cops that come by the Memphian Theater and he had let them watch the movies free and give them pop corn free. Well he didn't know their names, but he recognized them and they recognized Elbert. So they came over smiling and asked, "What they had me for? " He told them drag racing, but he didn't know what else. One of the cops stayed with Elbert while the other one went to see what he was charged with. He came back smiling and he asked, "How much money do you have on you? " Elbert told him, "Thirty five dollars. " He said, "That isn't enough. You need twenty more dollars. " Elbert asked, "Could he call somebody, like in the movies?" The officer said, "Yeah and when they come they can bail you out. "So, Elbert called Jerry Matthews. Jerry left work and went to the Krystal Drive Inn, where they hung out and raised the money from other guys to come bail him out.

After the cops Elbert knew left, they put him in a cell. It was bare and didn't even have a mattress. It was brand new and had those electric sliding doors, clang. After about forty five minutes, Elbert heard some cars pull into the gravel parking lot and somebody burst through the doors and yelled, "Elbert, where are you? " He yelled back, "Here I am. "They opened the cell door and led me to the front desk. Between the money Elbert had and the money they brought, he was released. They had charged him with Speeding, Reckless driving, Drag racing, Loud pipes, no Inspection sticker, no City sticker, and the license plates were registered to a different car. In Tennessee, you have two tags. He put one on one of his cars and one on the other, to save money.

BOZO WARE

He never did know, Bozo's real name. Bozo was one of the guy's that he hung out with. Bozo worked nights like the rest of us, and hung out late like us. Bozo, run the Pippin Roller Coaster at the fairgrounds, well Bozo got off work and drank a little too much, no he drank way too much. So they, Elbert and Francis Perry decided to drive the three of them home. But first, they have to sober him up somehow. So, they decided to take him to the Holiday Inn Motel and throw him in the pool. When they did, and he immediately sobered up. But when he tried walking out, he would pass out again. After awhile, they decided to just take him home anyhow. So, when they got to his house, they held him up and rang the door bell. His mother let them in and asked, what is wrong with him? They said, "He was sick, but they would put him to bed, and he would be fine in the morning. When they took his wet clothes off him his mother took his wallet, she opened it and found his pay check, but it was unreadable because of the water. She flew mad and locked the front door and called the police.

She made them sit there in the living room until the police came.

One of the policemen took them out to the car, and one stayed talking to her. After a few minutes, the other cop come out to the police car and got in. Both cops are laughing and said: "Look boys, the next time you take one of your buddies home drunk. Don't ring the door bell and talk to parents. Just ring the bell and run like hell." Laughing about it they laughed too, seeing they weren't in trouble.

Then one of the cops asked, "Where do ya'll live?" They told them, then he asked, "How were you going to get home? " They told them they would walk. They said, "No, we will take you home, and if your parents have any questions, we will explain it to them. "They immediately said, "Noooooo, let us walk." But they wouldn't have it any other way. When they got to Elbert's house, it's now almost three in the morning, with blue lights flashing. You don't want to know what his mother said, he really don't remember either.

WILD PARTY, YEP, LIKE IN THE MOVIES

Francine Moore, a girl Elbert went to school with, married while they were still in school. She married Bob Collins. Bob went to Treadwell high School. Bob was raised and he lived with an Aunt. One day Elbert went to see him, while Bob was still single and when he let me in the front door, he said: "Don't sit on the couch, but to sit in a chair against the wall. " Elbert looked at him with raised eye brows and Bob explained. His Aunt had a man friend visit one day that week and he sat on the couch. Well, his aunt had a Siamese cat and the cat took off and run up the man's chest and the cat's rear feet clawed the man's lip, as the cat run up the curtains and the blood started shooting out of the man's lip. The man had to go and have it sewed up it was laid open by the cat's sharp claws.

One night Elbert pulled into the Krystal Drive Inn and Butch McCarter flagged him down. Elbert parked and joined him. Butch said, he was waiting on Francine and Bob, to show him the way to the party at Francine's sisters house, or it might have been Bob's sister, he didn't know, where ever, they were having a party. All of a sudden, Bob's yellow and white 1958 Ford Convertible came flying into the Krystal Drive In off Summer Avenue, on two wheels. It is Bob Collins. He yells to us, to follow him.

One or the others sister, was married to a man that owned all the Gould Beauty shops in Memphis. They had said it was okay to have a party at their house, while they were in Hawaii, on vacation. Well, to make a long story short, there must have been over a hundred people went through that house that night. Half the people there, they had never seen before. They cleaned out all the man's beer, liquor, wine. What wasn't consumed was hauled off.

Well, Elbert was dancing and having a good time, when Butch yells, Elbert, come on, not wanting to be left behind, he took off and they all jumped into Bob's convertible. Butch, Bob, Elbert and somebody else, left with the top up but, Bob is driving and he is snockered, but he didn't go too far down this dirt road and stopped. They all piled out to make water (Pee)……. And they are all lined up doing their business, when Bob, got back in first and decided to lower the top. As the top was going down into the hole where it went we heard glass breaking and the smell of liquor was strong. Somebody had stuffed fifths of liquor down in the hole where the top went, and when it was lowered, it broke them all and liquor went everywhere. Bobs takes off, and the tires are spinning but the car is not going anywhere thank goodness, it give Elbert that few seconds he needed to dive onto the trunk and grab the top and hold on. Here they went, Bob is flying and fish tailing and Butch see's Elbert is about to lose his grip and yells STOPPPP. Well, Bob slams on the brakes and here Elbert came flying through the air, across the front seat and into the floor, of the front seat at the feet of Butch.

This is the party of the century, Bob and Francine was in big trouble when the vacationers got home from Hawaii. This was just like "Animal House "in the movies. They eventually, got back to the Krystal on summer and they went inside to eat. After that, Bob got into the yellow and white 1958 Ford Convertible, and was headed home. As he left the Krystal, he shot out into Summer Avenue, jumped the curb across the street, made a hard left turn between an iron telephone pole and the building, going down the sidewalk, and back out into the street and the car went dead. He passed out at the same time. Well, wouldn't you know it, but the police are sitting in a grocery parking lot and see the whole thing. Yep, car 36, 28, or 77, one of them, pulled up and arrested

Bob. Yep, Bob went to jail. Nope, none of us could hardly stand up or talk, so we were not going to go talk to the police about bailing him out.
H

SKINNY DIPPING ---- MCKELLER LAKE

Elbert had been to McKellar Lake water skiing, several times with different people, and at the time, it was open into the Mississippi river. Well, they closed it off from the Mississippi and made it a real lake. Well, the dam had a paved road on it that may have dead ended, because you had to turn around and leave the same way you came, to the lake.

Well, somebody came through the Krystal Drive In one night yelling from their car to: "Follow us " we are going "skinny dipping." Well, about four car loads of guys and girls followed these maniacs, out of the Krystal Drive In and headed up Summer Avenue. One of the cars was Elbert, Jerry and Brad.

It was a pretty good ride to McKellar Lake, and one or two of the cars with us, peeled off and went back. When they finally got there, as they pulled up and their headlights shown out into the water's edge, people were already running out into the water to hide the fact, some were naked. Some were yelling for them to turn out their head lights. And the same amount was saying, No don't turn out the lights. There seemed to be, about as many girls as there were boys. Some were in their under wear and some were naked. There were as many that never got out of their car as did. Elbert, Brad and Jerry were ones, to stay in the car.

A group of people pulled up beside them and got out. They stripped off their clothes leaving them everywhere on the ground and run hand in hand into the lights of the cars, with people in them, bare butt naked and into the water, laughing and having the best time. Who knows where they went to school, or hung out?

When suddenly a car coming across the dam, turned on its flashing blue lights Elbert first looked at the blue lights and when he looked back at the swimmers, they were running as fast as they could to their cars. They cranked up and started towards the blue lights. The Law didn't appear to be in any hurry. Elbert drove normal and as they passed them, he noticed they were probably, just out to break up this kind of fun, before it got out of hand. Or somebody got hurt.

This same thing happened again months later, and several car loads of them drove to a lake somewhere down in Mississippi. That place had a big beach and groups that knew each other went skinny dipping. Nobody, in their group did, they went all the way down there, for nothing.

NEW ORLEANS WEEK END

There were four of them that planned a trip to New Orleans for a week end. There was Brad Guthrie, two other guys Elbert barely knew and himself. One of the guys had a 1955 Chevy two door and that is what they went in. They left on a Friday, and took off down highway 51 South, into Mississippi.

They drove and drove, and drove some more. Then it got dark. Back then, there were no expressways just two lane black top narrow lane highways. As the time got later and later into the night, they went through some small towns that closed up for the night and nothing was open, not even a gas station. The closer they got to New Orleans, they seen nothing but swamp and water on both sides of the highway.

Somewhere in the middle of nowhere, the generator light came on. Which meant, the generator wasn't putting out electricity and they were running on the battery? Since, it was night time, they had the headlights on and they draw a lot of juice. They started looking for a town, hoping to find one soon. They knew eventually the car would just stop, when the battery was used up and it did. The car slowed down and got slower and slower, until it died.

There was nothing to do but get out and push. Luckily, we were on the outskirts of a town, somewhere in Mississippi. Then, shortly, they saw the headlights of a car coming towards them. It was just poking along and it eventually got to them. It is a policeman. He was very nice and when they explained what was wrong, he turned around and pushed them, with the police car on into town to the house of a black man that worked on cars. The policeman told us to just wait and he would go wake this guy up. He walked up on the man's front porch and banged on the front door with his flashlight until they heard, the man answer, okay, okay, I'm coming.

The policeman, told the black man to get up and fix these boys generator. He said, okay for us to push the car into his garage next to his house. This garage building was leaning, and Elbert wondered if it might fall down any minute, but they pushed the car inside like he told them to, and the policeman waited with them. The man, worked on it for a while, and finally gave up, he couldn't fix it, they needed a new one. The black man said: "Push it on down to the truck stop and that mechanic there could fix it. So, they pushed it out into the road, and the policeman pushed them on down to this truck stop.

The policeman told this guy there what their problem was and the man said, "The mechanic wasn't there. "About that time, the policeman got a call, on his radio, so he told this guy to push us, on down the road to the next place that might fix it. So, he came out and got in a 1950 ford and pushed them on down the road, to the next truck stop.

Another man now came out and they tell him, their problem and he says he can fix it, and goes to work. Meanwhile, the guy that pushed us down there is sitting in his car, waiting for something. Brad and Elbert walked over to the passenger side of his car and thanked him for pushing us to this place.

The man replied he didn't want any thanks he wanted $20 for pushing them down here. It hit Elbert wrong, and he told him, all he was getting was a thank you, the policeman is the one that told you to push them and it wasn't, but a couple of hundred yards. If you want $20, take it up with the policeman. No sooner, had Elbert got all that out, the man reached over to the passenger seat and picked up an army colt 45 pistol and pointed it at Elbert. The hole in the end of that barrel looked huge. Brad was standing beside Elbert and Elbert told Brad, he only had $10, for god sakes, pay him whatever he wanted.

Brad paid him and the guy went back to the other truck stop. They pooled their money and bought a used generator and the man charged their battery, and then they took off again, for New Orleans.

As they pulled into the outskirts of New Orleans, they seen a Motel that they might be able to afford. This Motel was a series of little one room houses, with a shelter on the side to park your car. It didn't cost much. It looked like the Motel, Humphrey Bogart stayed in and they had a sub machine gun battle in the movies.

They all got cleaned up, and were ready to hit Bourbon Street. They decided to ride the bus into town and back, to avoid driving with maybe a little too much to drink. The bus driver told them, the last bus for the night stopped running at eleven o'clock , so don't miss it, or they would have to walk. They had walked enough so far on this trip, so they went into new Orleans seen what they came for and caught that last bus back to the Motel They got a good night sleep and headed back to Memphis, the next morning. Their trip home was uneventful.

When they got home, somebody asked if they went to some place? Elbert remembered that they did, and ask why do you ask? He said: "Everybody in there, is a man dressed as a woman, did you notice that? " "What? You have got to be kidding. That can't be true. If that was true, they sure fooled them." That's how dumb they were, they never knew it. Needless to say, there are things out there in this world that is better left alone. But for four young adventurers, they were in awe of everything.

This was a trip they had no business on but that is the way it is in growing up. It would probably be wise, to remember, "Curiosity, Killed the Cat."

CHARLES TILLER

Elbert met Charles Tiller late one night after he had got off work and locked up the Memphian Theater. He had just pulled into the Crystal Drive in on Summer Avenue, when someone yelled, Elbert come on jump in, we're going to a fight.

He didn't remember who it was, but it had to be one of his friends. He hurried and jumped in the back seat and there sat a guy that handed him a beer. Everybody was talking at the same time and they all seem to know where they were going and who was going to fight who. Elbert was just, along for the ride. This time they went to the Treadwell High School, play ground . Now, it is about one o'clock in the morning and when they got there, Charles, who was sitting beside Elbert, was the guy to do the fighting. He climbed out and pulled off his shirt and he looks like Charles Atlas, in the magazines.

Most of these fights were simply, one side of town, fighting their side of town for bragging rights. Sometimes, it was Charles fighting somebody or George, Charles cousin, or sometime Mike Tiller.   About the time a circle was formed and they were just about ready to fight, somebody yelled, "Here comes the Law"

Everybody, run for their car, to get out of there before the law got there or you get a ride to jail and pay a $51 dollar fine. Well, Elbert dove into the back seat and Charles come jumping in and they took off. They all headed to the Krystal Drive in, to see if they wanted to try another place, but nothing materialized, that night.

Well, from that night on, whenever Charles seen Elbert, he would holler at him to come ride around with him and his buddies. Now, what do you say? No? Remember, this is the guy that defends our side of town and Elbert is a 90 pound weakling compared to him. He always had cold beer in the car and they would drink well into the morning. And no body, ever messed with Elbert, mainly because of whom, his friends were.

Charles, come to his house to pick him up one day and he met Elbert's mother. Now, Charles had a vocabulary and manners, Elbert was worried his mother wouldn't like him, but they liked each other. Of course, she had no idea, how rough he was, late at night, routinely taking on guys twice his size and more times than not, knocking them out.

Well, they had a lot of good times, riding around at night and going to different fights around Memphis. They later went their separate ways. Elbert was in the Air Force, in Japan about five years later, when he got a letter from his mother and a newspaper clipping, where Charles "Dago" Tiller was tried and convicted of murder and sentenced to life in prison. He still has that clipping. That was in 1962, or 63.

Some might not understand, but to Elbert, Charles Tiller was a good guy. Elbert didn't learn whatever happened after that until the year 2009. A friend of his told Elbert, he could look Charles Tiller up on the internet and he found a story about him. He had been in a fight in prison and a prisoner hit him in the head with a ball bat. He didn't die right away, it was years later, but he died from those injuries.

Elbert learned, Charles graduated from Christian Brothers High School and had three years of college and an offer to play pro baseball. He hit the coach, one day, and got thrown off the team. He was going to medical School, until something happened that ruined that. He could have really been somebody, but drinking and fighting ruined his life. The Charles Tiller he knew was a lot of fun to be around and a super nice guy. Elbert once asked him, was there anybody he wouldn't fight? Charles laughed and said, "Yes, his cousin, Mike. " Elbert asked, "Why is that?." And he said, "Because, he is crazy if you fight him, you would have to kill him."

Everybody in Memphis heard of the Tiller boys. Any policeman could tell you. They hated to get a call if a Tiller boy was involved. You didn't go by yourself, you waited for back up.

Elbert recently went to a fifty year class reunion and found several, of the guys he went to school with, were retired policemen. One of them said to Elbert, "I always thought you were the quite, super nice guy and after hearing your stories, and exploits late at night. You were really, a James Dean, or Marlon Brando type.

Thank God, Elbert went into the Air Force when I did. He went into a whole different kind of world which led him into a different life.

HOT RODS

Elbert, being in the group that hung out together that liked old cars. Would sit and talk, swap parts and hang out at a body shop on Summer Avenue, across from Matthews Market when they were not sitting at the Krystal Drive Inn. There was a guy there that did pin striping and Elbert learned from him. Elbert made some pretty good money pin striping dashes, hoods, trunks, and door handles. He used to paint tear drops running, they had arms and legs and big round eyes, and turtles as a trademark.

Brad Guthrie, had a1951 Mercury two, lowered all around, painted with dark gray primer. This was one cool, lead sled, hot rod. When it rained, it shined like it was painted.

But one of the more memorable autos Brad drove, was one, his Mother had just bought Brand new. She bought this 1957 Chevy Blair, solid white four doors. Beautiful car and it had a V8 with a four barrel

Power Pac motor. This was one strong motor with a Duntov cam and dual exhaust with a straight stick tranny. Well, one night they took it to a guys shop and a guy let them, put two four barrel carbs on it and then they went out on Summer Avenue, to try it out. Well it started raining, the streets were wet, and so every time Brad would cram second gear, the car would fishtail. They were afraid of messing something up and it was getting late, so they decided to just go home and change the carbs back later.

Well, the next morning, his mother, a school teacher, mind you, got up and went down town shopping, leaving him asleep. She was on Poplar Avenue and as she approached Cooper Street, where the Memphian Theater is. She changed lanes and eased it into second gear and gives it the gas and all hell broke loose. She hit that dip in the road and the tires broke loose, it scared her so bad, she spun out, now keep this in mind, this is early morning traffic and people trying to go to work. Hearing this now you can imagine her with big eyes and her mouth wide open trying to scream and nothing coming out, going round and round in the middle of a three lane street, full of cars. She didn't wake Brad when she left, but she did when she got home. Elbert was at home, and he thinks he heard her screaming because something woke him up. They put everything back like it was suppose to be, and didn't have but one more problem later. One night, Brad, driving her car was drag racing with somebody, and when he crammed second gear, the shift lever broke off in his hand and he had to drive it home in second gear. Brad is a big guy and didn't know his own strength. Brad owns a couple of Barbeque Restaurants in Memphis, Tennessee as of today.

Ollie Bailey, had a 1940 Ford Coupe, lowered all around. Most of it was dark gray primer, but he was having one fender fixed at a time and painted with about ten coats of solid Black Lacquer paint. It had 1957 Corvette tail lights in the rear fenders, and the last time Elbert seen it, the whole front cap was finished beautiful. Like all of their cars, that were lowered, they all had to come into the Krystal Driveway at an angle, because their cars were so low.

Elbert had a 1954 Chevy Blair Convertible. It was white with a white top, lowered all around, shaved hood, door handles, and trunk.

The doors were electric. It had a 265 Chevy V8 with two four barrels, under the hood, with 184 louvers punched in it and a floor shift. One night at the Krystal Drive In, on Summer Larry young who was J.D.Young's brother, pulled into the Krystal in this car. He and his dad had built it, and it was for sale. Elbert bought it and don't remember the amount, but drove it for quite a while and went to Halls, Tennessee on the weekends, drag racing it under D Gas Class.   Sometimes, he won and sometimes he didn't.

One night, Elbert was just out cruising around. It was late and he was wide awake and didn't want to go home. He decided to drive down Main Street and had stopped at the red light in front of the Malco Theater. This 1954 Chevy pulled up beside him and the driver lowered his window and indicated he wanted to run him when the light changed. It had tinted glass and it was a six cylinder. The driver thought, since Elbert's car was a 1954 Chevy Convertible, it had a six cylinder motor also. What the driver didn't know was, Elbert had a V8 with two four barrels. When the light changed, Elbert smoked him. At the next light, the driver of the other car rolled the window down and waved. It was then Elbert recognized him. Elvis sometimes rode around in a 1954 Chevy four door, with his buddies, so nobody would recognize him. Elbert had just drag raced with Elvis, and beat him. You can imagine what Elbert was thinking probably that, this was his 15 minutes of fame.

On one of these Drag racing trips to Halls, Tennessee, Elbert was on his way back to Memphis, when he raced a 1956 Power Pac Chevy and blew a head gasket. He ended up trading this car for a 1950 Ford Coupe with a full house flat head v8 with three two's. Then, one night Drag racing, he blew that motor all to pieces. He then bought a 1949 Lincoln two door.

Raymond Sweet had a 1957 Ford Purple Convertible with a white top. It was so low to the ground he had a washing machine roller under the back bumper to keep it from dragging when he came in the Krystal Drive In.

Jerry Mathews had a black 1958 Chevy convertible for a while, but traded it for a 1958 white hard top, that was one bad machine. Then he sold it and bought a 1955 Chevy hard top, beige and red.   Later in my stories, you will read more about these cars.

TEXARKANA, TEXAS

Jerry Matthews called Elbert one day, wanting him to ride with him to take his grandmother back to Texas. She had been visiting for awhile and was ready to go home. Elbert said: "Fine, let's go," so off they went across the Memphis and Arkansas Bridge. They had an uneventful trip and we dropped her off and headed back to Memphis. They were riding along when a vibration started up, Elbert looked over at Jerry, to ask, "What is that? " Suddenly, Bammmmmmm Elbert looked at the floor shifter and it had a big white ball on the end and it was bouncing up and down and Jerry said: "Grab the shifter, so Elbert grabbed it and was trying to hold the transmission up off the highway, but it was too heavy and all he was doing was, helping to hold it, when it bounced up and off the pavement. When Jerry finally got the car stopped and onto the shoulder of the road they got out and looked under the car. The ears of the transmission were still bolted up and the transmission was just sitting on the highway. There was no drive shaft. So, they started walking back where they came from, looking for the drive shaft. But, they didn't find it. When they walked up beside the car, they noticed something in the back seat and there was the drive shaft, it had bent double and come through the floor just behind the front seat.   Boy was that a wild ride. They hitched a ride to a telephone and called his dad and his dad sent a wrecker to pull them in to Memphis. This was his 1955 Cream and Red, Chevy Belair Hardtop.

TEXARKANA, TEXAS AGAIN

Jerry and Elbert was sent to Texarkana to get his Grandmother this time, so they lit out for Texas in his 1958 white Chevy Impala. When they got there, they visited with his relatives a while. His uncle, had a grocery store, just like Jerry's dad. He told them they could stay at his cabin on the Red River that separated Texas from Arkansas. He knew, Jerry, liked to go frog gigging. As they got out of the car at the cabin Jerry said: "Let me go in first." Elbert said: "Fine with me, but is there some reason?" Jerry smiled and looked at Elbert and said: "One time, his uncle opened the door to go in, and there was a rattlesnake coiled up behind the door." Sure enough, there was the sign on the floor, where they had shot the snake, with a shot gun. They set their things down and Jerry walked to the bed and started peeling the covers off the bed, one piece at a time. Elbert asked: "What are you doing now? " Again, he smiled and said: "They had also found snakes between the covers. Elbert said, "I'll tell you what, how about we sleep in the car.

Jerry laughed and said, "Come on, let's go gig some frogs. " Elbert had never done that before and was anxious to see this. They got two big long poles with three sharp prongs on the end and climbed in a boat with a big light. These were the biggest frogs, Elbert had ever seen and they were quick too. You would just about touch the frog, then you just jabbed him. But not ever having done this. Elbert would almost touch the frog, then drawback to jab him and the frog would jump in the water. He learned not to draw back just jab him and they got about fifteen that night. One would paddle the boat and hold the light, while the other, gigged the frogs. They finally quit, and took the frogs to his uncle, then they went to find a drive in and local hang out.

While sitting there, everybody coming through noticed the white 58 Chevy that had not been there before and the Tennessee tags. It wasn't long before a 1959 Chevrolet Impala pulled in and these guys walked over and wanted to know, did they want to run that thing? They said fine, let's go. So we followed them, a little ways out of town and run him three times. Jerry beat them every time. Then, they went back to the local drive in. One of these guys took a likening to Elbert and Jerry and climbed in the back seat and started telling them about the town. He told them the state line ran down the middle of Main Street and one side was Texas and the other side was Arkansas. On the Texas side of town, there were legalized Brothels. Now, they are looking at this guy as though he is lying and he senses that. He then offers to show them.

So, they crank up and go to see what he is talking about. Well, he is right, Elbert and Jerry were too chicken to go in, but there were these three old houses two story just like you see in any town and the house numbers were 7, 9, and 11 on 4th street. The yards were the parking lots and they were surrounded by a high wooden fence so you couldn't see the cars. This guy said: "At the front door, there was a living room with a juke box, and couches, and a hall way, with doors on each side.

And, at the back door, another living room with couches and a juke box. Jerry, and Elbert had made the headlines before and they didn't need that again, so they dropped off their new found friend and headed back to the cabin on the river. They had breakfast with his family, got grandma and headed on back to Memphis, with a grin on their face. The biggest problem they have had was, they didn't tell this for years, because they didn't think anybody would believe them. It didn't turn out that they weren't believed. Nobody believed that they didn't go in. It was just like in the movies.

MOTHERS WILD RIDE

Elbert almost had him a beautiful new car that probably would have got him killed, or at least, into a lot of trouble. Pat Bechem had a 1959 black Chevy two door hard top Impala with red interior, three two's and a four speed transmission, and it was for sale. This was almost a new car. He asked his mother, to co sign for him and she said she would, but to let her see the car first.

So he got Pat to go with him, to show it to her. She then, wanted to ride in it, so she got in the back seat and Elbert drove. Elbert went about a block away, and turned around, to come back. When he got to the intersection, he had pulled too far out into the intersection and a car was coming that Elbert didn't see, at first.

For some reason, Elbert pulled it into low gear and stepped on the gas and the car went air born, laying rubber with smoke coming from the tires. Elbert looked in the rear view mirror at his mother and she had her mouth wide open and her eyes were as big as saucers. He knew right then, he had messed up.

Something, Elbert didn't tell her was, this car was the Super Stock Champion at the Halls, Tennessee, Drag Strip for 1959. When they got home, she got out and didn't say a word. Yep, she had lost her breath. As a rule, his mother was never at a loss for words, but she was that day.

CONFESSION TIME

At his recent 50th Class Reunion, Elbert and his wife, sat with Ray Weaver and his wife in a booth. They visited for some time and laughed the whole night away. As they were getting up to leave, Elbert bumped into the person sitting in the booth behind them. It was Gilbert Phillips, it was so good to see him, they were shaking hands and smiling and all of a sudden, he ask Elbert a question that brought back memories of one night in his life, when Elbert was 15 years old and had took my mother's car for a joy ride. You guessed it, he wrecked it down at the end of Graham Street. The same street, his High School was on.

Elbert was flabbergasted, that Gilbert even knew about it, much less remembered it. Elbert is still amazed, and Gilbert never did say, how he knew about that or even remembered it, or if he knew the rest of the story. Elbert now wonder's, how many other people know about that.

Well, let's get this out in the open. It was one of those moments in time when it wasn't funny and Elbert wasn't proud of it, he really was ashamed, but I will go ahead and tell it for him, as he has talked all around it and maybe Gilbert will tell him one day, how he knew about this.

Well, his mother had gone out on a date and he knew where the key to her car was. So, he got his brothers in bed and he slipped out and took his mother's car for a joy ride. Well, he seen Richard Lowe and Francis Perry and they were just sitting, in Richards 1947 Plymouth, talking. They decided to ride around the block and go by his school. Elbert was leading the way and he was almost to Graham when he came up behind a slow moving car. So he passed him and about the time he was back in his lane, he seen he was in trouble. Back then, when you got to Graham, you had to turn right. You could not go straight, or turn left, so he hung a hard right and the tires are squealing and wham, he hit the curb and the wheel folds up under the car. Elbert jumped out and was looking at it, when Richard and Francis drove up. Elbert run over to Richard's car and jumped into the back seat and said: "Quick, take me home. " On the way, he told them if they were asked they haven't seen him. They dropped him off at home, and when Elbert went into the house, his brothers asked, "What is going on?" He told them, to get back in bed.

Well, it wasn't long before the phone rings and the police ask for his mother. Elbert said: "Oh, she has gone out with a friend, and wasn't there. They asked if she driving her car? Elbert said no, it's in the driveway. He asked are you sure, and said to go look and make sure. Elbert said ok, then counted to 15, like Mickey Rooney would have done, in the movies, then, told him with enthusiasm, Somebody, has stole our car, it is gone.

A little while later, his mother came home and the first thing she asked was where her car is? Elbert said: Mamma somebody stole our car and the police called and they found it, and it is wrecked. She called the police and they told her where the car was, so her and Marvin, whom she later married. Went to see how bad the damage was.

Well, the next day, Elbert is in class when his mother, came to the door and ask the teacher could she see Elbert and called him out into the hall. They started walking back to the cafeteria and her office. She hasn't said a word yet and he is wondering, what this is about? So, he asked her, where are we going? She never looked his way and never missed a step as she said: "You're going to jail.

"What, do you mean?

"You took my car and you wrecked it, didn't you? "

"No Mama. " Lying like a dog.

As they walked into her office, there was a Detective waiting in her office. He was a big fat man with a Fedora hat on and eating a piece of pie. He started talking, still eating the pie, with food in his mouth. He says, "Well son, we know the whole story, so you might as well tell us the truth. We have already talked to Richard Lowe and Francis Perry, at Treadwell School, and they told us the whole story."

Now Elbert is thinking, the jig is up and the cat is out of the bag, what would Mickey Rooney do? So, he confessed. Boy, the truth hurt. The detective told his mother they would stay out of it and leave it up to her to punish him and he left. Thank god it was without him. Meanwhile, Elbert was thinking, wait until he gets his hands on Richard sand Francis.

Later, when he got to Richard and Francis, he learned, they didn't know what he was talking about, it became clear, the detective and his mother had tricked him into confessing. So, now you know the rest of the story, about the young idiot that he was. Confession is good for the soul. And he never did that again.

Chapter 4   1959 to 1962

LITTLE ROCK ARKANSAS

After graduating from High School, Elbert's mother, his brothers, Wayne and Neal, was moving to Coronado, California, to be with her new husband, Marvin "Blackie" Blackburn, who was still in the Navy. Elbert had decided not to go with them. It was time for him to leave the nest, and go out on his own. So, shortly after graduation, they packed up and left Memphis, crossing the Mississippi River headed west. When they got to Little Rock, Arkansas they dropped Elbert off at Jerry Mathews Aunt's house, and they continued on to California

Jerry and Elbert stayed with his Aunt and found them jobs. Elbert started looking for a Draftsman job, and passed over a job painting bill boards at a $100 a week. He found a job as a draftsman, and really enjoyed it as he loved doing that kind of work. His major in school was Industrial Art and minored in Math. The work was clean, in an air conditioned office, and he thought he had it made. They held back two weeks pay, and when he finally got a pay check, he was floored. After taxes, etc., he   took home less than thirty dollars a week. That just didn't sit right with him. He was so proud to get the job he failed to ask just how much it paid. So, now, it was time to ask, and he did. He was told $45 dollars a week.

He explained he had turned down a job that paid $100 dollars a week that required no training. And he took a job that required training for less. But he couldn't do this and he quit. He went back and took the $100 dollars a week, working in the cold in the winter and hot in the summer job, only because it paid more. Somehow, he felt like a fool , this just wasn't what he thought it was going to be like, after getting out of school and on his own.

Things just didn't work out like he had hoped it would and he decided to go back to Memphis. He told Jerry of his plans and Jerry asked, "When do you want to go? " He told him tomorrow. Well, tomorrow was in the middle of the week. Jerry asked, "Why don't you wait until the week end and he would take him back to Memphis? Elbert told him, "He didn't have but one bag, he would just hitchhike if he would just take him to the Highway." This was late in the afternoon and since Jerry had to be at work the next day Jerry said he would take him right then. Elbert said "Great, let's go." Elbert told Jerry's aunt good bye and thanked her for all she had done. Jerry, tried to get him to wait until the week end, but he dropped him off and they agreed to see each other in a few weeks. As it was, Jerry moved back also, several weeks later.

HITCH HIKE

Well, Elbert is standing on the side of the road in the hot summer sun. As he looked up the road, he could see the heat waves coming off the concrete highway. He also noticed, you can see grass growing in the cracks of the concrete. When you're in a car going down the road, you can't see those little details. The tar in between the slabs of concrete literally bubbled and burst leaving a sticky residue on tires as they passed. All along the side of the road, you see things people threw out the car windows, cigarette butts, baby pacifiers, parts that had came off of cars.

Looking behind him, he seen another guy hitching and darn it, he will be picked up before him. After a while, Elbert stopped walking and sat on his suit case, and that other guy did the same. Elbert knew he needed space between him and that other guy, as people would stop for one person, but not for two, as a rule. After a few minutes, he see this 1955 Chevy stop and that guy walked over to the car and they was talking for a minute, then the car drove off, leaving the hitcher still there. Elbert was wondering what that was about, then the car came on down to where he was standing and stopped. He had the window down and asked, "Do you want a ride? " Elbert said: "Sure "and hopped in. They rode along for a while making small talk. About, where he was going and where he had come from etc. The sun was starting to go down but not anything close to dark yet. And out of the corner, of his eye, he seen this guys right hand move close to him. Then he made a comment that readily identified him, as gay. Oh Crap..... What in the Devil??????.....

Elbert still laughs to himself when he thinks about what he said, when he said, "If you don't mind, I will get out right here. Can you imagine, if you don't mind? "Hell, he wanted out and right now." He pulled over and stopped and Elbert was out like a bullet, with this guy making all kinds of reasons, why he should stay in the car. Finally, Elbert told him to get out of there and he drove off. But he didn't go far and turned around and started back towards Elbert at a high rate of speed and on his side of the road. He thought what the heck? Is he going to try to run over him? There was a corn field right there and there he went, running up the rows of corn, where he couldn't see him. He stopped, but never got out of the car, and slowly drove on off, back towards little Rock. So, after a few minutes, Elbert walked back to the side of the road and started hitch hiking again.

After a little while, it was now getting dark, but not really dark yet. Some cars had their lights on and some didn't. It had started to cool down and he had tied the sleeves of his jacket around his waist and was just walking along, when he heard a car coming and it started slowing down. Elbert stopped and turned around, to see this black 1951 Chevy Fleet line, torpedo looking thing, come to a stop, beside him. The guy, in the passenger's seat, said: "You need a lift?"

Well, ah yeah Elbert muttered for a second, and said: "Yeah, he sure did." Now, you need to understand, this was a car in the middle of nowhere, and it's getting dark and there are four black men. What in the world do you think he was going to say? No? That he was just standing there for the heck of it? So, he said: "yeah, I sure would appreciate it."

The back door opened and out comes the biggest, tallest, black man, Elbert had ever seen and he turned back to the inside and brought out a spare tire. He looked down at me and said: "climb in the middle. Yep, he did. About the time Elbert got nested, he handed Elbert, the spare attire, and he put it, in front of him and the man climbed back in. Now, you have to imagine this, here is this skinny white boy, sitting in the back seat of a 1951 Chevy on the highway, holding a spare tire between his legs, in between two black men , with two more black men, in the front seat. And off they went.

After a few minutes, they began to talk, and Elbert just listened, and you know what? They talked about the same stuff everybody does. They ask me, where he was going and where he had been. And ask Elbert, where in Memphis, he wanted them to drop him off. Elbert didn't remember what they talked about after that, but he will tell you, as they crossed the Memphis and Arkansas bridge, Elbert had got comfortable, but he was glad to be back in Memphis. Going down Crump Blvd., he seen a bus, and told them, he would like to catch that bus. They sped up and got in front of that bus, He was talking about, and let him out. Elbert thanked them for the ride and run to catch that bus, as it would go right to his grandmother's house, "Big Mamma ".

I know what you're going to say, you think he was crazy. Believe me, back then, hitching a ride was as common as the sun coming up and going down. Millions of Military people hitched rides, to go home, to see their girl friend, if for only a few hours, and then hitched a ride back to the base. Back in the 40's and 50's not everybody had a car and the buses didn't go everywhere. So people often hitched a ride, sometimes only a mile or so and sometimes hundreds of miles. But I don't know how many got picked up by a gay guy, or a car load of black men, in one day?

BACK IN MEMPHIS FROM LITTLE ROCK, ARKANSAS

Elbert spent the night with Big mamma his grandmother, his Daddy was living with her at the time. He let him use his car that night and he went to the Crystal Drive In to see all my friends. That was when he found out about, Larry young wanted to sell his car.

He also learned of a job at Osborne and Abston Auto parts warehouse located on Crump Blvd., pretty close to his grandmother's house. He went to work there in the warehouse putting up parts. He worked there for a year and a half. During that time he was promoted to, Rush Order Filler, the Parts Counter in the main store, Jobber Inventory Control Auditor. His mentor there was Mr. Smith the warehouse Manager. Elbert dated his daughter for a while and he liked him even though, his daughter liked somebody else.

Anyway this is how he bought hi 1954 Chevy Convertible through the credit union. Mr. Nor fleet, the General Manager, also liked him, and he is the one, that promoted him into inventorying the jobber stores, all over the southeastern part of the United States. They had 60 stores at the time and they were bigger than NAPA Auto Parts in Memphis. Of course, years later, that changed. Mr. Abston was a little man in statue, an older man that spent most of his time traveling to Africa, on Safari's, shooting big game. Mr. Osborne had passed away some time, before Elbert went to work there. They were great people to work with and for. His last job there, consisted of on Monday Morning weekly, he drove to an Auto Parts Store with a big book ten inches thick, and then counted every item in the store, writing down, how many, of each item, was there. It took a week of doing that, all day long, to finish an inventory. Then Friday night, he turned in that book, full of information, and got another to use the following Monday.

He will never forget, going to an Auto Parts Store in Grenada, Mississippi. Around lunch time, the store owner, called out to him, to come and go to lunch with them. He said: He appreciated it, but he was really busy at the moment and he would go later. The owner walked back to where Elbert was and said: "You don't understand, you have to go with us, if you don't, no restaurant in town will let you in. You have to be a member of each restaurant and have a membership card to get in. It was a black man issue. So, he went with them and sure enough, when they got to the restaurant, he had to put a card in a slot, to open the door. That was the most extreme thing he ever noticed. He knew all over Memphis, as he was growing up there was White water fountains and Black water fountains, White Rest rooms and Black rest rooms. Elbert quit his job there, when he went into the Air Force.

    He was hired again four years later, after returning married, after four years in the Air Force. He will get back to his job there, when we get to that period of time in his life, later.

    WHY THE AIR FORCE AND WHY NOW?

    Since he was in the mood to bare his soul, he has a story to tell about why he decided to join the Air Force. Butch McCarter, Winston Williams and Elbert, got an apartment together and they were doing okay, but it was really too expensive for them, so they parted and went their separate ways. Elbert got a room in an old house, off Jackson Avenue, and the rent was $10 a week, for a room, up stairs.

    Well, one day, he got up to go to work, and he was running late, and wouldn't you know it, one of the two cars, he had, wouldn't start. Well, he went to the other one and it, wouldn't start. So, he walked to, the corner bus stop, to ride the bus to work. While he was standing there, the light turned red and cars stopped for the light. He looked down into the back seat of the car nearest him, and he recognized one of the girls he went to school with. He was staring at her, trying to remember her name when the light changed and the car started to move forward. About that time for a fleeting second, their eyes met and it seemed she was looking at him trying to place him.

    It bothered him so much he went back to his room, to look in the mirror to see what he looked like. Why didn't she recognize him? What he seen in the mirror was, a 17 year old boy in a dirty shirt, wrinkled clothes, and somebody that hadn't shaved in a week that had been out parting every night, for weeks. Someone that had blood shot eyes and hadn't had any breakfast. It hit him so hard, that he wasn't doing well and this had to change. Especially if he ever expected to make something out of his life so he called Benny Utley.

Benny Utley and Elbert had been talking about going in the service and Elbert ask him if he was ready to do it. The idea was to let the service make a man out of him and to give him a career field, so that when he got out of service, he could get a good paying job, doing something.

So, Elbert went and picked him up and off they went to sign up. Now, it was funny if you could have heard them talking about which branch of the service they were going to join and why. They decided against the Army, they walked everywhere and a sniper might get them. They decided against the Navy, because they didn't like that little white hat and bell bottom pants, with no pockets. And if their ship sunk it was a long swim. They decided on the Air Force mainly because they wanted to be trained on Jet Engines so that when they got out they could get jobs at the air port and be able to drive a Cadillac like a friend of Elbert's cousin, Charlie "Sonny Boy" Lockett. Sonny Boy, had a friend that drove a Burgundy and Cream, two door hard top, Cadillac Coupe De Ville and he was a jet engine mechanic for one of the air lines at the air port.

Besides, the Air Force wore a hat, with a bill on it. So, they started laying out our requirements like they had to stay together for the next four years. The recruiter says oh yeah no sweat no problem. So they looked at each other and signed up. Boy, this is great all you have to do is stand your ground, and tell them what you want, and they agree. Well, they stayed together through Basic Training. Then, they got separated and Elbert never seen Benny Utley again after that. It's been fifty eight years now. He sure would like to see him again, so we could laugh at how stupid they were, when they thought they were so smart. The next thing was to go to the Veterans Hospital for a physical so off they went.

Well, there were others there when they got there and they got in line to get their physicals along with others. After several test, Elbert was called over to the side and told, there was something wrong with his urine. He thought, oh no Diabetes. It had run rampant through his daddy's side of the family.   They said not to worry, he was being sent to a private doctor for his evaluation. Elbert told them, just give me the Doctor's address and he would drive there now. They gave him the address and ask if another guy could ride with him. He said: "Sure, let's go." The doctor checked them out and told him he was okay, and he could forget it. However, the other guy had something wrong with him that was going to prevent him from going in service. They went back and everybody was getting ready to board a bus and Elbert thought he was going to be left behind, but they said for him to go ahead and board the bus.

There was a phone on a table there in the room so Elbert picked it up and called his Daddy. He needed to tell him what he was doing and he needed him to come get his car. Everybody around him could hear what he was saying, and he said the Lincoln is in the parking lot and the keys are under the seat. He looked up and several of the guys had gone to the window to see this Lincoln in the parking lot. What they seen was a ten year old Lincoln, that he had give $50 for.

They did get training that led to a career, at least Elbert did. And they made a man out of them.   Elbert didn't get the Jet Engine training he wanted but he ended up being a crew chief. He knew a lot about every system on an air plane, but he wasn't a specialist on any one part of it. He was the boss of a crew that took care of an air plane. He ended up working on copier machines after leaving the service, and after a short time, he became a manager for twenty seven years.
BASIC TRAINING

So it's off to Lackland Air Force Base, in San Antonio, Texas. A few things come up during the training that he laughs about now, but he didn't at the time. The training went fine and he had no problems at all. It got exciting one day at mail call. All of a sudden this voice comes over the speaker in the barracks and this voice says, for Airman Alberson, to come to the Commanders Office your mother is here to see you. Boy that was the last thing he wanted all the guys to hear and they teased him forever it seemed. It seemed his mother had got a letter from the

Chaplin that her son had just joined the Air Force. Elbert seemed to have forgotten to write and tell her. Well she was in California and he was in Memphis, it wasn't like he could run it by her yesterday.

So, he hurried over to the office and sure enough there is mother and she starts crying at the sight of her son in a baggy military uniform weighing a skinny 129 pounds. She and his brothers had decided they didn't like California and they stopped to see him on their way back to Memphis.

One day, they were told, to prepare, for a sand storm. He had no idea what to do but one of the guys did and they taped all the cracks around the windows and doors to keep the silt out. It came at night and they didn't see the effects outside until the next morning. A thin film of dust was all over everything in the barracks how it got in, they don't know. They had grass yesterday now nothing but sand everywhere. A car parked outside had sand piled up on one side over the top of the car. When he removed the sand, he found the sand storm had sand blasted his car on one side. There was no paint on the driver's side just shiny metal, no paint. He had paint on the rest of the car.

Then, there was a little excitement just a few days before we were to leave to go to their next assignment, which was a school somewhere. They had one last thing to do before passing their basic training and that was to qualify on the firing range with an M1 Rifle. It was a two day affair. The first day they went to learn the positions and to go through the motions of firing the weapon, but with no bullets, it was called dry fire. Well, there was this guy, from New Jersey, that marched next to Elbert on his right, everywhere they went. He didn't like Elbert, and Elbert didn't like him. He would intentionally bang his knuckles against Elbert's while marching and Elbert would do it right back. Well, they got to dry fire and the Sergeant asked if anyone was a NRA Shooter? Elbert didn't have any idea what he was talking about. Well this guy says, yeah, he was. So the sergeant told him to come forward and show everybody the three shooting positions. Well, he didn't know them either and was told to get back in ranks.

The next day, they marched back to the firing range for live fire and to qualify, with our rifle. They said: "When your name is called, come forward and take a shooting position, if you have a malfunction, do not attempt to clear the weapon, raise your hand and someone will assist you. If you attempt to clear your weapon, you will be disqualified. After you have finished firing your weapon, return to ranks and wait for instruction."

Well, everything went smoothly for Elbert and he went back to stand in ranks. All of a sudden Elbert seen this Yankee from New Jersey, working on his rifle then the Sergeant seen him and disqualified him. Then, here he came, walking towards Elbert and Elbert is smiling. As he approached Elbert he said something, to Elbert and Elbert ask him, "What happened to you, NRA shooter? " Well, that did it, he took a swing at Elbert and he hit him right between the eyes. Then, here came the sergeant and broke it up. Well, Elbert slept on the far end of the barracks, down stairs, on a top bunk. He slept on his back, with his arms folded across his chest. And sometime during the night, he felt a blanket cover him and he received several punches from several guys. None hurt, because the blanket woke Elbert up, and he immediately sat up, and yelled for a buddy of his at the other end of the barracks, to stop them and don't let them get by. But it was too late, they had already, run past him, and up stairs, where all the Yankee's were. So, Elbert and a guy from South Carolina started up the stairs, when a hail of boots come flying through the air. Elbert ask the barracks guard, who was it that came to give him a blanket party? He played dumb and wouldn't tell him. They went back to bed, but Elbert kept hearing somebody whispering. So he got up and found the barracks guard, telling another guy, all about it. Elbert tapped him on the shoulder and when he turned around, he told him. "I don't know who hit me, but you will know who hit you, and he laid him out. The next day, they shipped out to the schools they were assigned to. Elbert never seen that guy again after that and he has never been fond of people, of the northern persuasion, since then.

TATTOO

After nine weeks of basic training, they finally allowed them to go into San Antonio. There was this buddy of his, that wanted to go get one of those big tattoo's, of a black panther, with red claw marks. But he didn't want to go, by himself. So Elbert agreed to go with him. He didn't know what it cost, but it took a long time. While Elbert was waiting, he was walking around looking at the pictures of all the types of tattoo's this guy does. Well, after they finished, he looked at Elbert and asked which one do you want?

Elbert quickly answered, he didn't want one. He asked why not? Elbert told him he didn't have any money for one thing, but maybe later sometime. He asks, do you have a dollar? Elbert said Yeah. He said look, I will write your name and put it in a ribbon and add some color, for a dollar.

So, Elbert thought, what the heck. He would be flying for the next four years, and it would help to identify his body, if it was ever necessary, so he said okay.

Well, he didn't write his name, he printed it. He didn't put it in a ribbon, he put a curly queue under his name, and the color he mentioned, wasn't what he expected either, it was two red dots, that later, disappeared.

And no, unlike 99% of everybody that got them back then, he was not drunk. Sometimes, he wished he had of been, and then he would have had some kind of an excuse.

AIRCRAFT MAINTENANCE SCHOOL

It was back to school again, but this time, it was on something exciting and adventurous. He loved every day of it. The most exciting was he would have to say was running the engines. There is a really great feeling, to start them up, and hear them roaring, feeling the vibrations and the power, of these big engines. This type aircraft, was a KC-97, it was really, a flying gas station. This aircraft refueled B-52 Bombers and B-47 Bombers. KB-50's, were used primarily, for refueling fighters and helicopters.

He learned a little, about every system, on this type aircraft. They refueled Bombers in flight, so they could keep going, wherever they were going, without landing to refuel. About the time, he got out of the air force, the KC-97, was replaced by jet aircraft, mainly the KC-135. That plane was more ideal, as a tanker.

When they refueled a B-52, they had to climb as high as they could go, and start a slow descent to keep up with him. And the B-52, had to fly as slow as he could, without falling out of the sky, to stay with us long enough to refuel him. B-47's wasn't a problem. He still remembers the engines they had they were R-4359-B Pratt and Whitney Engines.

He graduated with flying colors and was assigned to, Hunter Air Force Base in Savannah, Georgia. He went back to Memphis on leave after school and before going to Savannah, Georgia. He tried to look up all his friends, but they were at work or off in College. Reality set in that now, mature life had just started. Memphis had become a town in another time zone.

He went to the Krystal Drive In that first night home and there was a different generation parked there yelling at girls and talking about other guy's cars. No one was there that he knew. The party was over it was like everybody went somewhere and left him. He was in the real world now with no one, to drag race with and no one to party with.

A friend of his wanted him, to meet her for lunch down town, and he got there way too early. She worked at the Fire department, right across the street from the Main Library. So he walked to the Library. While there, he met a lady in the Genealogy Section and she started showing him how to look up his ancestors. He found it fascinating and the next day, he went back and spent a couple of weeks, working on his family tree. That was in March of 1962. Through the years since, he has traced his family back seven generations.

Well, after his leave was up, he left Memphis again and headed for Savannah, Georgia, his new assignment. His dad gave him a 1951 Chevrolet Coupe, this car at one time was owned by his uncle Clyde. Clyde had passed away and his dad became the new owner. It was a nice car, and he packed everything he owned and headed to Savannah, Georgia. Back then, there was no expressways, it was two lane black top highways, all the way. Elbert left Memphis, headed for Tupelo, Mississippi then to Birmingham, Alabama, then, Atlanta, Georgia and on to Savannah. This trip took 25 hours. Gas back then, was .22 cents a gallon.

The front gate to Hunter Field, as we called it, was quiet and the guards on the gate, looked bored at two am in the morning. But he slowly approached and one of them, walked over to his car with that question on his face, as to say, what do you want? He told him, He had just got to Savannah and he wanted to check in. The guard explained, the offices were closed and he couldn't come on base until 8am, in the morning. Ok, he was exhausted, as he had been driving for ever, it seemed. So, he turned around, and went looking for a place, he could park and get some sleep. He parked under a gigantic Natural Gas Tank that was called the Globe, because it was painted just like a globe.

The next morning they let him on the base with no problem and he got checked in. He was assigned to a very nice new barracks. It was a new building and appeared to be, just like you see in college dorms. He found his room and found out, he had a roommate. He was a tall lanky guy from Needles, California. And come to find out, he was a jet engine mechanic. Wouldn't you know it, that is what he wanted to be, but they trained this cowboy, from California. His name was Duane Carr.

This was the beginning, of the rest, of his life. He made some friends while in Savannah, that are with him, to this day. This is where He met his wife and they have been married for 50 years. He started a 30 year career, with the Xerox Corporation while in Savannah, and their first born girl child, Janet Lynn was born in Savannah.

Elbert has often said: " He always wished he could go back to his childhood days, but now that he has lived so long, he would love to also, go back to his Air Force days, in Savannah, too. He has lived a wonderful life and can honestly say he has enjoyed every day of it. Well, most of it, anyway.

Saint Patrick's Day in Savannah is the day you want to be in Savannah. The parade is out of this world, and the partying goes on for a whole week and it is compared to the Mardi Gras in New Orleans.   It is the party time of the year, in Savannah down town on River Street.

Military pay is and never has been much, so you eat off base when and if you can afford it. But, when you are broke, you go to the chow hall. There you get this great stuff called SOS, often referred to as (s--- on a shingle), but is cream beef gravy. You usually poured it over biscuits and on a cold day and it really stuck with you, when you need it. Of course, everything is on a buffet and the guys would lead you to believe, it was terrible, but if you can learn to like it, it is pretty good. Now and then, when he got paid , he headed for the taverns , that were having a oyster roast, or the one down the street that is having a fish fry. You can get fat eating the food that is free, to get you to buy beer.

Savannah has a street that, reminds him, of Parkway in Memphis. It is called Victory Drive. Years ago, the people of Savannah, planted Palm Trees, down both sides of the median, in memory of those, that died in World War II. There were so many, that they are planted them, real close together and real close to the road. Elbert was there from 1960 to 1962, and he noticed, almost every tree had marks on it where someone had hit them since they were so close to the road. And today, there are a lot of them that are missing due to cars hitting them.

Duane Carr would one day become his best man, when he got married. They have remained friends, for fifty something years.

Duane had a girlfriend that called him, her war hero. Surely she was joking. She was from a small town in South Georgia. No, a little bitty town, in South Georgia, called Nicholls Georgia.

Well, when the weekend came around, Duane told Elbert, he was invited to go to his girlfriend's family farm, for the weekend. He thought, boy, this is great, but he didn't want to intrude, and Duane said no, he was more than welcome and Etta, probably, would have him a date lined up. Etta's mother and father's name was, Leroy and Lucy Grantham. This was the start of a great friendship that is still going, even though Leroy and Lucy have passed.

Leroy had a big farm, a dairy farm, where he had a herd of about 300 cows and he milked at least 150 of them twice daily. He grew all the components of his cow feed and made his own feed. They ground, cow feed every weekend for the rest of the week. He also had a chicken house with thousands of little chicks running everywhere with automatic feeders and waters. They stayed there until eggs started appearing then trucks would come and take them to hatcheries, someplace.

Leroy also grew tobacco, and Elbert got an education visiting them almost every weekend. He was raised in the city, with limited knowledge of farm life. He looked at everything as exciting and fun.

However, the boys that grew up on the farm, considered it hard work and they wanted to go to the city.   Elbert lives in the country today, and love it where he lives. Elbert doesn't think he could ever live in a big city again.

The first morning in Nicholls, Georgia, at the Grantham Farm, he was awakened at 3 am in the morning to go milk cows. You have to be there, to get the best of it all, but they opened the gate and let 30 cows come into the milking parlor, at a time. The cows walk right in and go to their individual stalls and start eating. They know the routine and just stand still while he washed their udders and stuck a suction cup on each tit. Boy, was that a big bag, full of milk. If you just get it anywhere close to the tit, it jumped on it. It was like a day old baby starving to death. The vacuum machine immediately started sucking the milk through the glass tubes that went into another room and emptied into a large stainless steel tank. Then, later that day, a big tanker truck would come and get the milk and take it to the dairy. When all the milk had been retrieved, they removed the vacuum tubes and the cow would just walk out and another would take his place.

When they finished, they went back to the house to eat breakfast. Lucy would have the table set for them all. Now this is as the biggest breakfast he had ever seen. There was ham, bacon, sausage, eggs scrambled, some fried, and grits and biscuits. There was orange juice, coffee, and ice water. The biscuits were called "Cat Head biscuits," because they were so big.

 Some mornings, they had pancakes, and or waffles. But the thing that caught his eye was: Lucy had sliced in half, biscuits, from last night's supper. She then, dipped them in egg batter and deep fried them. Then, they poured syrup over them and eat them with a fork. Well, Elbert thought that was the cat's meow. They tease him today, because, they said he got quiet and wasn't saying anything, because he was eating so fast. They said: that first time he ate that, he ate almost the whole platter full. Boy that was good.

It wasn't, all work and no play. Sometimes, we fished or hunted or went water skiing. But, at 3pm every afternoon, we had to milk the cows again.

Now, cows making whoopee in the pasture, was not the best way to increase your milking herd.   So, they artificially inseminated the cows that were ready to have a calf. This, you have to see. Duane, put on this long glove that went all the way up to his arm pit. Then he had this long metal thing that holds the semen and he sticks his arm in the rear of this cow and feels around for the uterus and leaves the semen there. Then the stork, fly's over the farm later and brings a cow. No, no, just kidding.

Now, if you want a pretty cow, you used one type of semen, if you wanted a lot of milk and a lot of those bit tits, you used another semen. You have got to laugh along with Elbert about this. If Mrs. McGinnis, his high school English teacher, had put more humor in her English class, he might have remembered more of the things she taught them.

Yi was a black man that lived and worked on the farm. Yi was his name. Elbert never knew his full name. Yi was quiet and you never heard him say anything. He lived, in a tenant house, there on the farm. He lived alone and he wanted it that way.

Every meal they ate in the big house, Lucy would fix Yl a plate, piled high of the same food they eat. Yi would take kit and go off and eat by himself. Again, that's the way Yi wanted it. So, one day, Elbert ask, about him and learned, his name was Ira something. He was born on this farm and had never lived anywhere else. Never married, but he did have family in town and on other farms, in the community, that come to see him. Yi died a few years back. He was family, but he never started a conversation. Elbert ask what they paid him. Now listen to this carefully. It was $ 5.00 every Saturday night. Elbert ask what? Why? Well, they bought all his clothes, pay all his bills and give him a place to stay, and pay his utilities, and provided all the food he ate. They took him to the doctor when needed, and paid for his health care. He didn't need or want anything else. Elbert said, well, what about going to town, to ah get ah, you know what, and maybe a beer?

Oh, he does. He has a girl friend he see's, but he never brings her home. And he buys him some liquor. And the $5.00 is plenty. Are you sure? Oh yes, every Sunday morning, Leroy has to go to the sheriff's office and get Yi, out of jail and pay his fine, for walking home in the middle of the highway drunk. He walks the center line. And his fine is, fine is $26, 00 every Sunday morning. Yi would take his five dollars and spend half on bonded whiskey and the other half on moonshine, and then owe the sheriff $26.00. Simple, now do you understand? Well, enough of that, now it's off to the chicken house to make sure the automatic waters are giving 50,000 chicks enough water and the feeders are feeding the chickens and to pick up two or three dead chickens that were too dumb to eat or drink.

Now, on Sunday, after the cows are milked, we go to church, then eat a big lunch, and then it's time to go water skiing, until it's time to head back to the base for another week of playing War Hero's until next weekend

BLUE LIGHTS OF THE RUNWAY

Upstairs, in the barracks, there was a guy that worked in the Tower, he was an air traffic controller, and would always brag, he could bring a plane down onto the runway in a storm with zero visibility.

Well, usually the blue lights Elbert is talking about, are down each side of the runway, landing or taking off at night. One night, we are coming in to Savannah, Georgia, from Newfoundland, but this night, a dense fog had settled in the area and visibility was zero and we were trying to land. The tower was bringing us in and we couldn't see a thing. Elbert was sitting on the navigators table behind the pilot, looking over his shoulder. When all of a sudden, he seen the blue lights and the nose wheel was clipping them out. That meant they were running over the blue lights on the right side of the runway. That meant, the right landing gear, was in the grass and only the left one was on the runway.

The pilot jammed the throttles forward and pulled back on the yoke and they were air born again instantly. They had just performed what is called a touch and go landing. They made a go around and finally landed okay. Later that night, in the barracks, Elbert was in a small skirmish in the hallway of the barracks. When he told that idiot in the tower, how much he was impressed that he almost, got them killed. They never spoke again, after that.

HILTON HEAD ISLAND

Elbert and his buddies would occasionally go to Hilton Head Island, in South Carolina, on the week end. Elbert's car had a problem with the transmission and he didn't have, low or reverse gears. As they, would leave Savannah, Georgia. At the foot of the Tallmadge Bridge, was a toll booth. They had to come to a complete stop and pay a toll, then immediately start up a very steep tall bridge. Now with four of them in the car and taking off in second gear, it took all he had to get up that bridge.

 Once they were on Hilton Head Island, they could drive right onto the beach and go for miles. There would hardly, be anybody on the beach and they could camp out overnight if we wanted to.   This was 1960-61. On one of their trips there, they all fell asleep on the beach and got so badly sunburned, they couldn't hardly, wear their clothes the next day at work. That is when they were informed that if they couldn't come to work, they could be court martial, for damaging government property. The government property was them.

Because of over development on the Island, those days are gone now. It is amazing to see what a difference of 50 years makes. Today there are six lanes of traffic red light after red light, and you can't drive on the beach.

NEWFOUNDERLAND

When, they flew to Newfoundland, there were always three planes, in their flight. One right after another, usually fifteen minutes apart. They were, always going to relieve three other planes that were sitting on alert, fully fueled and ready to go, on a moment's notice.

In the event of war, a horn would sound and they would run to their planes, start the engines and immediately taxi to the runway and get airborne. Elbert normally, spent three weeks in Savannah, and two weeks in Newfoundland. It was their job to refuel B-52's and B-47's coming from the United States, on their way to targets unknown, possibly Russia, but who knows.

Sometimes, and sometimes more than once, they would sound the horn, and they would run to the planes and start the engines and just before we taxied, they would cancel the alert. This was a test, just to keep us on our toes.

One day, the horn went off and it was my job to stand the head set, out in front of the plane facing the aircraft, after removing the engine panels installed, to keep birds, and snow out of the engines. He would indicate to the flight engineer, ready to crank, engine number two. They always started with engine number two because, the hydraulic pumps were on that engine and that way, all hydraulic systems could be checked, and they would have brakes. Then engine number one, three and four. Then, he would remove the head set and extension cord, and then pull the chocks, from the wheels. Then stand where the pilot could see him and salute the flight Crew leaving, if he did.

Behind their plane, there was more planes, lined up almost put of sight, wing tip to wing tip, and nose to tail. It was a sight to behold, when all the planes had their engines running and you didn't know if this is it or not. After a few minutes, they would all shut down their engines, and we would secure the plane again, until they called another alert, or the real thing.

It happened on one of these alerts that Elbert thought someone on the ground had walked into a turning propeller. He was standing head set one day and they had their engines running, when all of a sudden, somewhere behind our plane, Elbert seen bits and pieces of a parka flying in the air. It looked, just like, pieces of green nylon and fur. He was trying to figure out, what happened, when it dawned on him, He was wearing a parka of green nylon and a fur lined hood. He thought, oh no, somebody, just walked into a spinning propeller. It was always a possibility and he thought please no. There wouldn't be much left if you walked into a prop spinning. Well, everybody shut down their engines and they went looking to see what had happened. One of the Combat Defense Troops, had took off his parka, and left it lying on a fence post. When they cranked those engines, the wind picked it up, and blew it into the planes behind it, and it got chopped up into a million pieces. Thank goodness, nobody was wearing it, at the time.

They had another, incident like that, months later. Somebody left several cases of hydraulic fluid stacked near the alert pad. Snow had covered it, and here came a snow plow one day, when he hit that hydraulic fluid, the fluid is blood red, by the way. The pretty white snow being thrown up into the air suddenly became blood red. Elbert didn't see it, but the ones he talk to, said everybody just knew including the driver, that he had run over somebody and chewed them up in the snow plow.

INFLIGHT EMERGENCY

One day, late in the afternoon, they are the last of three planes heading to Newfoundland. Well, they were about thirty minutes out of Savannah and over water, when they heard a Mayday call. It is the plane that took off just before them, and he is in trouble. He has shut down, two engines and has a fuel leak on another engine. Eighth Air Force called their plane and told them to go find him and escort him to the nearest airport. As a rule, Elbert normally sit on the navigators table behind the pilot, and they are flying along trying to find this plane almost in the dark of night. When all of a sudden, there he was and they are rapidly approaching his rear. Elbert's plane was closing at 350 knots and this plane ahead of them is way to close and slow. The pilot called out, gear down, flaps down and power off. Elbert looked at the throttles and he had pulled them almost all the way back and they literally fell out of the sky and slid directly under that plane, ahead of them. He just knew their vertical stabilizer would hit them as they passed under them but they didn't, thank god.

They slowed down and flew with him, on his wing tip, until he could land at Cherry Point, North Carolina. This was a runway built for marine Fighters, not a big four engine Tanker. We circled and watched him land. From what we could see, he landed alright, but we learned later it was almost a controlled crash. He had cracked all three landing gears and blew all the tires, and done structural damage to the air frame. Sounds like a crash to me.

It was months later, after flying landing gears and engines, into Cherry Point, did they fly it home . Then it sits, for another year, pickled like they do them at, the bone yard, in Arizona

We flew on into, Dover Air Force base in Dover, Delaware. We refueled and started to leave and wouldn't you know it, but engine number three wouldn't start. We took off the old starter and found the dog or splined part of the shaft had sheared off and fell into the engine.

That meant we had to have another engine. They had another engine, there on the base, but it would take about ten hours to change it, run it, and check it out.

So the flight crew decided to catch a cab and go to a baseball game in Baltimore, Maryland. Elbert said, fine he would stay with the plane. Well, the engine people were faster than everybody thought, and they got through in about five hours. Now, here Elbert was, standing around waiting on a flight crew to return from Baltimore and a ball game.

About that time, the Flight line Maintenance Officer drove up and wanted the pilot. He explained, there was a message for him and Elbert had better go with him, to receive it. So Elbert hopped on his metro truck and off they went. At base ops, they hand him a phone and there is a voice on the other end yelling at him, wanting to know, "When will you be in the air? "

Elbert told him, "Anytime now, just as soon as the flight crew gets back.

The person on the other end, said: "Back? Back from where?"

Elbert said: "A ball game. "

"A ball game? What ball game? "

Elbert answered, "Oh, one of the World Series games in Baltimore."

All of a sudden, this voice yells at Elbert. "Get that flight crew back to that airplane and have the pilot call me, ASAP. This is General so and so, at Eighth Air Force now, and I mean now.

Elbert said: Yes sir, just as soon as possible.

When Elbert got back to the plane, the pilot and the crew drove up, about the same time. He met them at the car and they went to base ops to call the general. All Elbert could think of was, Thank God, he stayed with the plane.

They weren't gone long and they immediately got their butts in the air and on to Newfoundland.

MARION, INDIANA

Elbert's mother had been after him for some time, to take some leave and come home. He had just bought a 1953 Ford four door sedan and it was a plain Jane car. The paint was dull and in many ways this car was ugly. But it run great and his 1951 Chevy had finally give up the ghost, and died. So, he headed home to go with the family to Indiana. His mother wanted to visit her brother, his uncle Floyd, Aunt Betty, Saundra and Linda and she wanted him, Wayne and Neal, his brothers, to go with her, so they did. When Elbert got to Memphis, his mother, had just bought a new car, it was a 1962 white Chevy Impala, two door hardtop, with red interior.

So they loaded up and took off for Indiana. Well, sometime later just as it was getting dark and somewhere north of Tennessee. Traffic comes to a halt. They are sitting there behind a line of cars trying to figure out what the holdup is when Elbert noticed water is on both sides of the highway. And way off to their left is a white house. They sit there about another 30 minutes and Elbert noticed that house is half again closer to them than it was earlier. He opened the door and look down and he can see the pavement is under water about two inches. That meant the road was about four to six feet higher than the lay of the land and it was flooding. And that house he mentioned earlier was getting closer and closer. It kept coming until it was about twenty feet from them and it finally stopped.

About that time the traffic started moving again slowly thank goodness. The water got up to the bumper and then we pulled up out of the water onto dry pavement. It took a little ways for the water to drain out of our brakes, and then the motor started missing. It wasn't bad and they made it on to Uncle Floyd's house. The next morning Uncle Floyd took it to the Chevrolet place and they replaced a spark plug, that had cracked, due to it being hot, and exposed to cold water.

Later the next day, the cousins, Saundra and Linda, wanted to take their cousins out to meet their friends. They went to their local hang out and they watched them wave at their friends and call them over to hear their cousins talk funny. Elbert and Wayne were a hit. Neal stayed at the house because he was too young. Elbert told them, "we don't talk funny, they did." Later, they decided to get something to eat and the local hang out didn't have hamburgers, they had veal burgers instead. Elbert and Wayne had never eat veal before and didn't even know what it was When they told Elbert, that it was a baby calf, he knew he didn't want any of that.

Elbert couldn't wait to get back to Memphis and go to the Crystal Drive in, or to get a Barbecue sandwich and especially where the people didn't talk funny.

While he was in Memphis, he took his car to Earl Sheieb's Paint shop to get a $29 paint job. He could choose from a funny looking green, or two other weird colors, he chose the green. He dropped it off one morning and picked it up about three that afternoon. Boy it looked a 100% better.

When he got back to Savannah, Georgia, it was time to renew his driver's license. So he went to renew his license. He parked and when he got out of the car, he noticed a big hole in front of the left front wheel. He thought to himself, when he comes back, he needed to watch that hole and not hit it. He went inside, and some problem arose. He stormed out the door, and the door slammed accidentally. But he just knew, they thought he did it intentionally. But no one said anything. When he got to his car he jumped in and forgot about that big hole and he hit it, BANG!! He jumped out and seen the bent bumper and bent fender and he slammed the car door and heard the glass break. Now he is really mad. He took off leaving a dust cloud behind him and while riding along, the ring around the left head light fell off and bounced on the road. He stopped and picked that up and went to the service station he worked at part time and told the guy working, to fill it up. Back then, they raised the hood and checked the oil etc. Elbert is standing inside talking to the owner and watching the guy checking his battery and Elbert noticed something running down the fender. That idiot had set the battery holder that held a squeeze bulb of acid on the fender and acid is running down the fender. Now, in a matter of less than an hour, he has tore up his freshly painted car. This was a bad day from hell.

PISTOL TOTER'S LICENSE

While in the Air Force in Savannah, Georgia, at Hunter Field. He worked for a Tech Sergeant that was a member of the Air Force Rifle and Pistol Team. Sergeant Hinkle and Elbert would go to the rifle and pistol range, and shoot, every now and then, and one night, he invited Elbert to eat supper with him and his wife. Afterwards, they were talking about pistols and Elbert mentioned he wanted to get him one to have, as he was on the road a lot, going back and forth to Memphis on leave, and he traveled by himself mostly. He went and got one from another room and said he would sell Elbert that one, for twenty dollars. It was an H and R, chrome plated, 22 caliber target pistol, with a nine inch barrel. It was one of a matching pair that he bought at a gun show, but had no idea where the other matching pistol was. It was great. It was the most accurate pistol Elbert ever had.

So, Elbert went to the Police Station to get a license and had no problem. But he noticed something funny. In bold letters, it read Pistol Totter's license. He thought they ought to be a little more serious minded about something such as that, but who was he to question it.

Sometime later, Elbert was home on leave and the subject of a pistol come up, and he told his father, he had a pistol that I kept in the car. First thing he asks was, do you have a license to carry it and He told him yes. He didn't believe him, so he pulled it out of his wallet and showed it to him. He handed it to him and didn't think anything about it and his father said: "Son that will get you in trouble. Elbert ask what he meant. His father started smiling and asked, "Where did you get that, out of a Corn Flake box?" The license said: "Georgia Pistol Toters License"

Georgia changed the name of it later, through the years. Now it says Georgia Firearms License.

The only time he has ever needed it, and he did pull it on somebody was, he was on leave and was on the way to Memphis and he was in Mississippi somewhere. The highway was about six feet higher than the lay of the land and he was starving to death. He was in the middle of nowhere and it had just got dark outside. He was just rolling along, when he noticed way up ahead, he seen a light and the glow is that of what appeared to be a hamburger joint. So, he was thinking, when he get's there he will pull in and get him something to eat.

As he got there, he pulled off the highway and drove down into their parking lot and rolled right up to the building under the lights. He had no sooner turned off the motor and the lights, when it dawned on him this was a hangout for black guys. Not a white person was in sight. Oh shit....

So, he started the motor put it in reverse and threw his arm over the passenger seat, so he could see behind him to back up and leave. But, a car pulled up directly behind him blocking his way. He turned around in the seat and looked out the windshield, and somebody come to each door and started beating on the top of his car. The doors were locked and his pistol was lying in the passenger seat. He reached over and got it, and looked at his driver's door glass, all he can see is a big belly and belly button. So he leaned towards the passenger seat and pointed the gun at that belly. He was thinking, should he shoot through the glass or should he roll down the glass a little? No, he'll just wait, but if they break a window, to get in there to him, he was going to shoot this belly button and everybody in sight.

About that time, the guys standing in front of his car seen the pistol through the windshield and they yell to the others, he has a gun. The belly button moved and two big eyeballs are staring at the end, of the barrel, of his pistol. Within seconds he is running, everybody is running and the car behind him moved out of the way. He slowly backed up and got the heck out of there and hauled buggy. He just knew they would chase him, but they didn't. To this day, he has never needed a gun, ever again. But, the one time he needed it, and had it, he was glad and lucky. But somebody would have died, if they had broke one of his windows out. And it could, have been him too.

RUNAWAY PROPELLER

In the winter, in Newfoundland, the snow was piled up so high between the taxi way and the runway, that when a plane was landing or taking off, you could hear it, but you couldn't see it until it started to rise out of the snow, on the horizon.

Anyway, it was time to go home to Savannah they had been there for two weeks. But, there was a blinding snow storm and the visibility wasn't good enough for them to take off. They had completed their preflight inspection, and were waiting on a clearance from the tower. There were three planes ready to go and they were just sitting there waiting to take off, when the tower closed the runway. They really, wanted to go home so the flight crews of the three planes went to the Base Operations, to discuss the situation.

Elbert's pilot, Major Hedgewald, had a green card. Which meant, he was authorized to take off with less than minimum visibility? They weren't gone long and when they drove up and parked at the wing tip. They got out and yelled, let's go, get this thing in the air and they did.

They took off down the runway with Elbert sitting on the navigators table looking over the pilots shoulder when he pulled back on the yoke and they lifted off. Now for a few minutes, you couldn't see anything, until finally they rose through the snow storm and was above it, in clear sky with the shining sun. That was the first time they had seen the sun in two weeks.

Yeah, they said. Alright, they are in the clear now, but wait. They have another problem. The propeller on number two engine is not responding and the engine rpm is climbing in RPM. In fact it is running away. So, they try to feather the prop, feathering it means, to turn the blades where it bites more air and would slow down the engine, but that didn't work, and its getting faster and faster. Take off rpm was 2850 and once at our cruise altitude, it was reduced to about 2350. But right now, that engine was turning 2900 rpm's. The pilot asks Elbert to go look at the prop hub and let him know what color it was. Normally, it is silver in color, but as it gets faster and faster, it turns red, and can come off. It was cherry red. That's bad. Elbert reported back, it was red, so he laid the plane over on its right side and we flew in circles continuing to try to feather that propeller. By flying on our side, if the propeller sheared off, it would fly over the fuselage and not into the fuselage. It's bad enough to lose a prop, but you don't want it to come off and cut the plane in half. The RPM rose to 3000 rpm, then 3100 and they finally got it feathered. Which meant, they had that engine shut down? We returned, to normal level flight and headed back to the base on three engines. Now flying with three engines was okay, but since we were over water, and if we lost another engine for some reason and went down. We, wouldn't last, but about, 20 minutes in the cold water below.

Elbert was sitting in the cockpit when it was decided to go back and change the prop and without thinking, Elbert said: "Oh no hell no don't go back into that show storm, trying to land on a runway we couldn't even see. " Then it dawned on him he was speaking out of turn. This wasn't his decision to make.   He looked around and everybody was smiling, so he said: "Oh, I am sorry, excuse me" and laughed with them.

The weather had cleared, but the only way you could tell where the runway was, it was higher than the rest of the land, because it was covered with snow and ice. The tires on our plane had wire sticking out. It would cut your hand but it sure was good on ice.

We landed okay and they towed the plane into a hanger to change the propeller. When the prop people were finished, they pushed the plane outside, between two hangers, to run up the engines, and check out the prop. Elbert hooked up the head set and cord and walked out in front of the plane, and instructed them to crank each engine in order and when they were ready to take the prop up to max power he closed the hood on his parka to keep the wind and snow out. When they brought the engine back to idle rpm, he opened his hood and there stood the nose gear of the plane, just inches in front of him.

What that meant was, the plane had slid forward, when they took the prop up to max power and it almost run over him. He should have kept his eyes open and he never shut his eyes again after that close call. Jeez, another close calls.

CRASHED   KC-97

One day, Elbert and another guy on his crew had to take something to a trash pile. Somebody told them where to take it and when they got there. There were the remnants, of a plane that had crashed. Looking closely at it, they realized it was a plane just like theirs. So, when they got back, Elbert ask about it. What he learned was, about a year, before he got to Savannah. That plane was taking off and as he went down the runway, the engines were back firing and missing. They had already passed the point of no return, so he lifted it into the air but within minutes, the engines quit and the plane crashed killing eleven men.

What had happened was, when it was refueled. The fuel man had put jet fuel in the plane. It was the wrong fuel. The jet fuel melted the pistons, and it crashed. Elbert remembered that, the rest of the time, he was flying. He made sure they got the right fuel. A jet can burn any kind of fuel. But a propeller type plane has to have, what they call, AV gas.

STOCK CAR RACING

Elbert got to be good friends with the crew on the plane parked next to them, and learned the Tech Sergeant used to drive stock cars. This other Staff Sergeant, he knew, used to build engines for stock cars. Elbert had always wanted to get into stock car racing, and this seemed like a good time to do it.   So the three of them got together and bought a 1937 Ford two door sedan. Elbert bought a Buick V8 nail head engine and they bought a six two barrel log manifold and built this beautiful race car number 97.

Elbert had previously gone down to Jacksonville, Florida. He bought a 1930 Ford coupe with a Chevy engine, but they wouldn't let them race it, because it didn't originally have a steel roof, when it was manufactured. It didn't matter that it had a metal roof on it now, welded on. So they built the 37 Ford. They would take it to the track on Tuesdays and they would let them practice and tune up the car for the Friday and Saturday night races. Elbert had a ball running around the track of course he was out there all by himself. They wouldn't let him drive in races, because he wasn't 18 at the time. He later found out, he was supposed to lie about his age, as that was what the other guys did. He wasn't raised to lie he had done forgot how.

Well, the night of the first race for their new car, it caught fire and almost burnt up. All because of the log manifold. So, they changed the intake manifold and carburetors for the fast heat and they tried again. It happened on the sixth lap, of the race, when an Oldsmobile, ran up underneath their car and caused it to turn over. Every time the driver's side comes up, that car would hit it again and again, until everybody stopped.

The ambulance come and hauled away the tech sergeant and he was unconscious for 41 days. Elbert worked part time at a shell station, at 37th and Bull Street and there was a mechanic there that wanted to buy everything they had. Elbert wanted nothing else to do with racing.

He was through.

He bought a 1958 Chevy Impala, hardtop with an automatic. He drove that car like an old man. He decided right then, no more spinning tires, or driving faster than the speed limit. He washed that car every day, mainly because of the residue that fell out of the air from the paper mills and because it was a black car and showed everything that got on it.

Well, things got serious back at the base one night, and word was out over the radio for all military people to report back to their unit ASAP. So, he headed straight to his plane, at the base. They were told to get enough clothes to be gone for 90 days and get back to the plane, they were leaving, ASAP

MORGAN'S BRIDGE

One day, somebody told Elbert, of a good place to go swimming. It was a few miles from the base, so off they went. There was, Elbert, Duane and Kenneth and a guy named Bobby. Elbert had a four door car at the time and they all piled in and headed for the Ogeechee River on Highway 280. Just as you get there, you turn off, onto this old dirt road that goes to the old wooden bridge. So, they were rolling down this dirt road, slowing down, because they could see the bridge ahead of them and about that time. A big long black snake started across the road ahead of us. Elbert hit the brakes because Kenneth Vickers, is yelling Stopppppp, stopppppp and they came to a sliding stop in the dirt road. Kenneth, jumps out first, then they all got out, watching Kenneth, catch this snake, before it gets away.

Kenneth caught the snake and pulled it out into the road and starts to sling the snake around and around in the air. Elbert knew, what was going to happen, so he started for his car, ahead of the other guys. Kenneth slung that snake through the air, and it wrapped around the neck, of a boy with us, named Bobby. Bobby started screaming and clawing at that snake, until it fell into the road and crawled off in the bushes.

The next thing Elbert seen is, Kenneth running with Bobby chasing him towards the bridge. I think Bobby wanted to discuss the situation and maybe in a violent manner too. Kenneth climbed up on the railing, turned his back to the water and did a back flip off the bridge into the water. Elbert thought to himself, I hope that water down there, is deep because if it is a foot deep, he is dead or paralyzed one or the other. Luckily, the water was ten feet deep.

CUBAN CRISIS

Elbert threw his things in a duffle bag and headed to the flight line. When he got to the plane, they took a full load of fuel and did a preflight inspection, before the flight crew even got there. After everyone was aboard, they taxied to the runway and went airborne.

They were told that, they would learn of our destination, only when airborne. And that is when they learned, they were headed to the Azores, in Portugal.

What had happened was, President Kenned, had just given instructions to Russia, for a ship loaded with a long range nuclear missile on it, to turn around and head away from Cuba. We didn't learn until we landed, that the ship had not turned around as yet. It later, did return to Russia. However, we were on alert in the Azores for twenty six days.

We played pool, eat and played cards for twenty six days, waiting for something to happen. We had a poker game that ran for the entire twenty six days. When we couldn't stay awake any longer, we would sell our seat in the game, for $10. And go take a nap. Then, when we would come back and buy back into the game, somebody else wanted to sleep for awhile.

There was a door that separated the poker game, from the liquor store in the NCO Club. Every now and then, somebody would take $5 out of the pot and go next door and get us a bottle of Jack Daniels, usually a fifth. Those that drink would pass it around the table about twice and it would be empty.   So, a few minutes later, somebody would get us another one, with money out of the pot.

 Elbert remembered one game where it came down to him and another guy to declare their hand.   Elbert laid his hand down, but called it wrong. Which meant the other guy had won? But, this guy just threw his cards down and stormed out of the room. Elbert looked at everybody at the table, as to say, what do I do? Everybody smiled and said, rake it in, the pot is yours, and he left the table. So, Elbert just won

$360. He quit and took a nap after that.

They had been told that they would not have any practice alerts. So, if the horn went off, that meant get to your plane, they were at war. Well, one day this plane landed, that had come from Newfoundland, and they ask why was he flying? Why wasn't he on alert, like us? He said, there were so many planes at the base there that they were parked even on the fuel depot. Then, there was a fire, at the fuel depot, and the only way to move the planes fast enough, was to blow the horn. He said there were flight crews throwing up and running to their plane at the same time. He said they got airborne and was told to come there. They stayed with them for the remainder of the time they were there.

On the way home from the Azores, after it was all over, they flew down to Cuba to see what was going on there. They had heard, there were American war ships, one mile apart, all the way around Cuba. Well, that part was true. They approached an aircraft carrier, and as they got close, you could see people waving at them, as though they thought they might try to land. They had no intention of that, but the Navy complained to 8th Air Force, and the flight crew got into trouble, for flying so low around an aircraft carrier.

BOOM OPERATOR ON THE JOB TRAINING

On the way home from the Azores during the Cuban Crisis, They got a call to meet a B-47 as he had a fuel leak and needed fuel badly. They informed him they didn't have any jet fuel, but they had AV gas that would work, if he wanted it. The pilot said fine, he needed 7000 pounds of fuel.

Well, the Boom Operator they had on board, had talked Elbert into transferring from maintenance to being a Boom Operator, just as soon, as they got home. So, he told Elbert to go ahead and make the hook up and it would give him some experience. So Elbert lay in the bed and released the boom and was just flying it getting the feel of it. He moved it right and left and up and down, and extended it and retracted it. Then he saw the B-47 coming up behind them, getting closer and closer. He got so close Elbert could read his name on his helmet.

All of a sudden, a door opened and Elbert could see the receptacle that he had to put the nozzle into. All he had to do was get it close, within inches, and it would slip in magnetically. Flip a switch and he would get 600 pounds of fuel a minute.

Well, just as Elbert was about to punch him, they hit an air pocket and he moved the boom to his left and it went out of sight. It happened so fast, he didn't realize how much to the left and out of sight it was and to find the boom again, he moved it to the right. Well, here it came, and it hit the little door on the B-47 and knocked it off and the B-47 backed off and the plane shook. Elbert's pilot asked over the intercom, "What in the hell is going on back there?" The sergeant quickly said: "Oh nothing, no problem, just a little on the job training." Elbert apologized to the bomber pilot and he came back. They give him 7000 pounds of fuel and he left happy, and without a fuel door.

When Elbert got back, he had changed my mind about being a boom operator. And was glad he did. If he hadn't changed his mind, he never would have went to the Far East and been on the assignment he was on there.

NICHOLLS, GEORGIA

Well, it's Friday afternoon, Elbert, Duane and Kenneth Vickers, another boy from Nicholls, are headed for Nicholls, Georgia for the week end. They are in Kenneth's car. He had a black and white with red interior 1957 Chevy. Elbert always drove and all three rode in front. Well, they took a short cut through an Army installation, and they come around a curve, and there stood, ten deer, in the middle of the road. Elbert jerked the wheel and they started spinning and finally come to a stop, broadside in the road. They missed every deer, and the deer were still standing there, looking at them. That was the weirdest thing. The car had gone dead, but it started up and they went on down the road, and they never seen a deer again. Duane and Kenneth both said: It was a good thing all three were in the front seat, because it kept Elbert from being slung out from under the steering wheel. He told them it wasn't luck. It had to be a guardian angel, or the lord himself that kept them from getting hurt.

Later on down the road, near Glenville, Georgia, they were riding along and they were hungry and they passed an old country Baptist Church called Watermelon Creek Baptist Church and wouldn't you know it, they were cooking something on an outside grill. There were a lot of people there and they each had a plate of something and big glasses of Ice Tea. Boy, it sure looked good and the smell was terrific. Elbert told Duane and Kenneth you know they might not notice it if three more people got in line and fixed a plate and we could slip off to the car and eat in the car, and nobody would be wiser.

What he didn't know, because he was raised in a big city, where you didn't know the neighbors two houses down the street was, these people had grown up in that community and went to school and church for generations with each other. Heck most of these people were kin to each other, one way or another. And if we had pulled up and got out, everybody would have known they were strangers. They probably would have all stared at them, wondering, what they wanted.

But, in all reality, they probably, would have come over and invited them to come and eat with them. Now, don't get excited, they didn't stop. They went on down to Baxley, Georgia and eat at the Dairy Queen.

When they finally got to Leroy and Lucy's, Kenneth dropped them off and Leroy met them. Leroy said, "Hurry and change clothes, we are going to move irrigation pipe in the tobacco field." So they did. Every two hours, they turned the pump off and stretched out across the field and picked up the sections of pipe full of water, and carry it twenty rows over and sit it back down. Then they cranked up the pump and let the water flow for another two hours. This is what they did all night long. Well, about 7:00 pm somebody brought them some fish, a fish cooker and all the things to make hush puppies and they deep fried fish and drink sweet tea until, they were full.

Then, about 10:00 pm, somebody broke out a fifth of Four Roses Liquor, and they drink that. Now that is a sight to behold. There were ten of them, with mud all over them, and now they have a fifth of liquor in them and they are carrying that pipe, 22 rows some time and 18 rows another, and after a while, it got to be daylight. So, they head to the big house, for breakfast. Then, they milked a 150 dairy cows, then, they headed to a neighbors tobacco field, to start helping him, irrigate his field. Because, he had helped them irrigate Leroy's. They eat lunch in the field and supper that night in the field and at 10:00 pm, guess what else, was broke out yep, the Four Roses, again. Well, they got through and now they have been in the field for two days and two nights. They went to the big house and cleaned up and changed back into their uniforms. Kenneth come and picked us up and we headed back to the base in Savannah, Georgia, after another great, outdoor experience on the farm.

MINOT, NORTH DAKOTA

Well, today we are flying to Minot, North Dakota, to take some Generals furniture, he is being reassigned to Minot and they have no idea what he did wrong, to get that assignment. It is in the middle of nowhere. They flew for what seems like all day and land there that afternoon. As they approached Minot, Elbert looked out the hatches, (windows) to you, on each side of the plane and all you could see was a checker board on the ground. Everything is laid out in squares and the roads were long and way off in the distance. They run together like the rails on a railroad track, long and straight as an arrow.

Once they had landed, he got out and looked around and not a tree in sight. He could see for 300 miles in any direction, except for that one lone tree off in the distance looking east. He noticed fences lying on the ground and asked about that. They said in the winter time, they raised those fences, to form snow drifts to help keep the runway and taxiway open and easy to clean with snow plows.

They refueled, unloaded the Generals things and back into the air they went. They were there less than an hour. So it was time to take a nap. He got used to the fact military planes are uncomfortable, no plush seats, and only fold down cots hanging off the wall of the plane. He even got use to the noise, as there is no insulation either. But they did have a urinal, a latrine, a coffee pot and GI rations. It was a lot like dog food, packaged in 1944 and it was now 1962.

RIDE IN A SINGLE ENGINE TWO PASSENGER PLANE

One day, Duane, Kenneth and Elbert were on their way to Nicholls, for another weekend of farm life. They seen this hitchhiker and Elbert recognized him as one of the flight engineers that flew his plane once in a while. So, they stopped, and picked him up, and ask where he was going? He was going to Waycross, Georgia, where he kept a small plane that he flew on the weekends. None of them had been up in a small plane before. He said: If they took him all the way to his plane, he would take them up, one at a time. They said sure. They did and it was great fun. He went by himself at first, to check out everything, he then came down and took us up, one at a time. And he let us fly it for a minute or so. Well Elbert is leading up to another story, so here goes.

FLYING A FOUR ENGINE PLANE

One day, weeks after riding in the small plane. They were on their way to Newfoundland and as usual, Elbert is sitting on the navigators table behind the pilot, just enjoying the flight and watching the pilot and wondering what it would be like, to sit in the seat and actually fly the plane.

About that time, the pilot got up and starts by Elbert and as he is going by him, Elbert smiled and said: "No sweat, I'll take it while you're gone, and the pilot said: "go ahead, and sit there, he wanted to use the latrine and stretch his legs." Elbert thought, hey great and he climbed into the seat. Now the plane is on autopilot and flying itself, Elbert is just sitting there and he sees the yoke moving little by little and the pedals are moving, ever so slightly.

About that time, Elbert put my hands on the yoke, to get the feel of it moving, and out of the corner of his eye, he seen the copilot look up briefly and when he did Elbert said, "Okay, I got it and without looking at Elbert, the co-pilot reached up and released the autopilot. Now, Elbert is thinking, did he do what I think he did? Then the thought came to him, if he turns the yoke a little to the right he will see if anything happens. Un knowing to Elbert, the flight controls of a 270,000 pound, four engine, air plane, carrying 174,000 gallons of fuel, is real sensitive, you know?

Well, the airplane immediately turned right, and the right wing went down, and Elbert is saying in an excited but firm breath, for the copilot to take it, take it!!!!!!! About that time the door came open and the pilot came out of the latrine, zipping up his flight suit and he had just peed all over the latrine. The copilot, put it back on auto pilot, and Elbert got out of the way. The pilot smiled as he went by Elbert and they all had a good laugh and no harm done. He never tried flying that again.

ORDERS ASSIGNED TO JAPAN

Well, they went to work one morning, to learn, the base was closing. It would no longer be an Air Force Base, so they were all being reassigned to other bases. Hunter Air Force base was part of the 8th Air Force, Strategic Air Command (SAC). It would soon become Hunter Army Airfield.

Elbert had two choices. He could go to Dover, Delaware or Japan. He pondered which way to go until he got a picture of a friend of his from Delaware. He was sweeping six feet of snow, off the wing of an airplane. That did it for him. He hated cold weather. So he went to Japan. Now, you have to understand, he would probably jump out of a perfectly good airplane, at 10,000 feet, before he would go to Delaware, because, he was cold natured to the extreme.

SAYING GOOD BY

Well now to say good bye was tough, real tough. He had made some beautiful friendships there, and it ripped his heart out to think, he may never see these people ever again. He hugged them and did not see them for almost three years, but they stayed in touch through the mail. There were two very sweet ladies he got to know. He had dated one of them for awhile and there was another, that he had only recently met, and had really, had only one date with. The one he dated for awhile sent him one or two letters in two years. But the one he had only recently met wrote him a letter every day for the time he was overseas.

If he didn't get a letter from Janice one day, he would get two, the next day. This courtship became so real, that when he came home from overseas, he didn't go straight home, he went to get Janice in Savannah, Georgia. Then he went home, to see his family in Memphis and to show them, who he was marrying in two weeks, in Cob town, Georgia. They were married on June 21, 1964. They moved to Memphis, Tennessee for only six months and then to Birmingham, Alabama. Today, they have been married 50 wonderful years.

Then there were his friends in Nicholls, Georgia on the farm. They became like a second family to him. They treated him like one of their family.

Elbert loaded up everything he owned in his car, a 1958 Chevy Impala, and headed home to Memphis, for 30 days leave and 11 days travel time to Japan. He had an extra Chevy V8, disassembled motor, in the trunk of his car. He mentions this now, because of what happened to him on his trip home.

TORNADO

Back then, there was no expressways and they occasionally paved a dirt road that became a short cut and as he was leaving Birmingham, Alabama. It was raining cats and dogs, and the wind was blowing, but he was determined, to keep going. He wanted to get to Memphis before daylight. It was probably one or two in the morning and he had the radio on real loud to keep him awake. This road was the new Jasper, Alabama road, and they had just sprayed tar and gray rock gravel on it and a steam roller had mashed the rock into the road, giving him a good grip on the road. Well, he is riding along listening to the radio, when he heard an announcement, there was a tornado sited and it was moving towards this little town somewhere. Then he heard it again say, the tornado is one mile west of this little town and it is headed directly to it. He didn't remember the name of the town now. But, about that time, he saw a sign that said: That town, one mile to his right.

Then all hell broke loose, all of a sudden, he couldn't see anything, mud was flying everywhere, and the noise of the tires on the gravel suddenly got quiet, no tire noise, then all of a sudden the car swerved and the windshield cleared and the tire noise came back. He kept going, until he came into the outskirts of Memphis, and he needed gas.

He pulled into this gas station that had a little white wooden office, it had stopped raining. He walked to the front of his car and he couldn't tell, what color his car was, for all the mud. The wind from that tornado, had put him off the road, into a fresh muddy ditch, and then back up on the highway, again. Thank god, he had the weight of that extra engine in the trunk. There was so much mud on his car he couldn't find the windshield wipers.

His Mother had bought a new house out in Raleigh and had a beautiful concrete drive way where he parked and went in. Later, Wayne and Neal helped him wash his car. They then moved it into the street and parked it at the curb, while they got a wheel barrow and a shovel, to haul away the mud, off his car. That tornado, had put him in a ditch, and brought him back out onto the road, and he didn't even know it, until he got to Memphis. Some may think he was really lucky. But he thinks that was more than Luck. He really thinks the Lord was in that car with him.

What makes him think the Lord walks with him?
 He was run over by an armored truck. He has been mauled by a big dog. He got my arm caught in a washing machine wringer. He broke his arm, an ankle and teeth out. He dug a cave that caved in on him.   He has been in speeding cars with a drunk driver. He has wrecked two motorcycles, and several cars. He has drag raced with near miss collisions. He has climbed mountains. He has been in airplanes on fire, with engines shut down, lightening struck, run off of runways, been in controlled crashes, crashed into a hanger one time. Slept in the jungle, with Cobra's, Python's, and wild Elephants he has been in Tornado's, drove stock cars, and flew airplanes, been shot at on the ground and in the air. He has had emergency's scuba diving. He has hauled moon shine, Snow skied, Water skied, Drove Bull dozers, Excavators, tractors, big Trucks.   YES, HE IS STILL HERE, only because THE LORD LIVES and HE HAS SOMETHING ELSE FOR HIM TO DO.

FAMILY   TREE, GENEALOGY

While home on leave, before going overseas. He spent many hours and many days, at the Main Library, down town Memphis, tracing his family tree. The lady, in charge of the Genealogy Section of the Library, really helped me a lot. She started him out with Census. The first Census taken in the United States was in 1790. There has been a Census every ten years since.

He learned very quickly, there is a lot to this. Years ago, people used cursive, or long hand when logging census information, and some of their penmanship is quite frankly, terrible and in some cases unreadable. The information is still good, however by association with a previous census. In later years people with more education and more legible penmanship made the data more valid.

Another source of information can be found, in the City Directory, this was very useful and informative. It contained information such as addresses, employer, and telephone numbers that was fun reading. One day, he told his father the address, he had ever lived at, since first coming to Memphis. It blew his mind, that he had found, that information.

He has traced, his mother's family tree, back seven generations. Taylor was her maiden name. He has traced his father's name Alberson back seven generations. And, he has traced his wife's Mother's maiden name Sikes, back seven generations. He traced her father's name, Nail, back, four generations.

He says Generations, because he can document in detail, these he has mentioned. Cemeteries tell him a lot also. Especially, if he visited them, and can read what is on the head stones? And he can see who is buried with them in the same area. This helps, to tie people into a family.

This is a great job, for someone retired and has an interest in this. Some people will pay dearly, to have some of this information. Some people have the need to trace family, because of medical histories and to settle estates. A lot of librarians can tell you of people that do this for a living, and those that do it for a hobby, and those that are better than others, i.e. more detailed or with factual, back up documentation.

GRAND PA AND HIS CADILLIA

By tracing his mother's maiden name, he found out that at one time, his grandfather, Albert Larimore Taylor, was one of the richest men in Macon, Tennessee. He went to town one day, with his sons and bought a 1930 Cadillac. One of the sons, drove the car home, and it sit in the yard for weeks, and months, on end. Albert had a horse he rode and it was one of the fastest horses in the county, it actually was a race horse.

Albert rode that horse, everywhere he went. One day, Floyd his uncle, drove the car to town without asking, Grandpa. Well, Grandpa Albert, came home and he noticed the car was gone, and ask, where it was?

Lizzie, his wife, said: "Floyd was in it, the last she seen. " Well, Grandpa sat in his rocking chair, smoking his pipe and waited for Floyd to come home. He smoked Prince Albert Tobacco, in a can.   Well, about dark, Floyd comes walking up the dirt road, to the house.

Grandpa Albert, ask Floyd. "Where is my car? "

Floyd told him, "It was about a mile back down the road, it had run out of gasoline.

Grandpa said: "Gasoline, what happen to what we had?"

Floyd tried to explain, "You have to buy, more gasoline."

Albert said: "You mean I have to buy something else to make it go?"

Floyd, told him, "Yes pa."

Albert said: "I am not spending any more on that car. It can just sit in the yard, for all he cared."   And it did too. They went on horses and pulled it home and it sit for almost a year.

HANGING THE RAPIST

Tracing your family tree, you will eventually, find out things, you didn't expect. Albert, his Grand pa, and his horse went with some other men and hanged the rapist of a white woman, under a railroad trestle. Sometime afterward, the word got out who was involved. The sheriff sent word he was going to have to arrest them. So the family, loaded up the Cadillac, and went to somewhere, in Arkansas, he never learned where. In essence, he abandoned his farm and he was gone long enough, that he lost the place and everything he owned, including his horse.

Years later, Albert got word from the sheriff, there would not be any charges and he could come back if he wanted to and he did. He never amounted to much after that, it all took something out of him. His wife died and he lived alone for years.

When he walked, he walked funny to Elbert, as a kid. He picked each foot up deliberately and then put it down firmly, almost like a Tennessee walking horse. When he asked his mother, why he walked that way, she said: " It comes from years of walking in loose soft dirt, behind a mule drawing plow.   You would have to see a man walking in soft dirt, behind a mule, to understand, I guess. Believe me, it was different

My Uncles, mothers brothers, were wild boys, growing up on the farm back in the 1900's and 20's. They entertained themselves on the farm. They fought real fights and took real dares. One of my uncles had some fingers missing. Elbert ask mother what happened to his fingers and learned. One of her brothers, dared him to put his fingers on top of a post, and he would chop them off. He did and he did, and from that point on, he didn't have, all of his fingers. Oh, that hurts, just to tell it. Two other brothers were arguing one day about something. One picked up a double bit axe and threw it at the other one, running away, and it landed in the calf of his leg.

They grew peanuts, just to eat year round. When they were ready, they would have a peanut pulling. They would pull up a wagon full and then, they would sit around telling stories and pull the peanuts off the vine. Then they boiled them and roast some. Well Elbert's other, had a three year old brother that eat some raw peanuts and got colitis and died.

To this day, he will eat boiled and roasted peanuts, but not very many at a time.

TIME TO GO TO JAPAN

Well, it's been fun, but it's time to go. Elbert went to see one of his best buddies, Jerry Matthews. He asked him if he knew anybody that might be interested in buying his Chevy. He said yes, he wanted it. So Elbert sold it to him, for $800 and he paid Elbert in $20 bills. Well, it's late in the afternoon and the banks are all closed, so he can't get a money order and he has to be at the airport in an hour or so. So, here he has eight hundred bucks on him in cash. He has money stuffed in every pocket. There was another buddy of his that was going with him and they were traveling together. He was from Dyersburg originally. Well, his mother, Wayne and Neal took him and this guy, to the airport. They said their good buys and wave to them as they walked to their gate. When they got to the gate, they learned that flight has been cancelled for some reason.

Elbert looked at the ticket lady, with the firmness of someone with

$800 dollars in my pocket. He told her he had already said good bye to his momma and he wasn't going through that again. To put them on the next plane going west, he didn't care where, but he wanted out of Memphis tonight. She laughed, and put them on a plane to Dallas, with an overnight stay in a downtown hotel. Now, he has watched the cowboys and Indians for a life time, on TV and in the Movies, and everybody knows the Indians are naked, so, it must be hot anywhere west of Memphis, Tennessee. So neither Elbert nor his buddy had a coat. Luckily, Elbert did have a crew neck sweater that he bought, to outdo Larry Rhodes in High School and a sports Coat. His buddy had nothing, but a long sleeve shirt.

So, when they landed in Dallas, Elbert thought they would freeze to death. It was colder in Dallas, than it was in Memphis. So, Elbert broke out his sweater and the sports coat. They spent the night in Dallas with Elbert wearing the sweater and his buddy wearing the sports coat. The next day they flew on to San Francisco. When they got there, it was colder than in Dallas. He couldn't believe it. So, they swapped and Elbert wore the sweater and he wore the sports coat. Their flights were different from there to Japan. He was going to a different part of Japan than Elbert was. So Elbert said so long to him and he never seen him again since. The song, " San Francisco " was popular in march of 1962, and he heard it until he was sick of it.

His flight, from San Francisco was on a C-118. That is a plane, like Eisenhower flew during WWII. This is not a jet. It was loud and shaky too. He rode that thing to Hawaii, and hung around the air port for a couple of hours and got back on that thing and went to Guam. They landed and more people got on and some got off, then he sat next to a crying baby with a stinky diaper for a while. Then, they landed at Wake Island. That place is four miles long and a mile wide. While they refueled, they went to the water's edge in a small hut and got a beer and sat under a palm tree looking at the clearest water he had ever seen. Then they got back on it and flew on to Tokyo, Japan.

CHAPTER 5   1962 THROUGH 1964

TOKYO, JAPAN YOKOTA AIR FORCE BASE

Half asleep, Elbert was awakened by an announcement they will be landing in Tokyo, Japan very soon. The lights came on and the stewardess is asking for everybody to bring your seat in to the upright position. It's about nine o'clock pm, Tokyo time. He looked out the window and was amazed, at the lights below. Tokyo is as big a city as New York City, and the lights go for ever.

As soon as the plane, had stopped, he gathered his bag and quickly moved to the door, to be one of the first, getting off. He found his way to baggage and found his duffle bag. He had no sooner turned around, to look for the exit, when he seen two air force guys holding a sign with his name on it. As he approached them, they smiled and introduced themselves and said, they were there to pick him up.   That was a relief, and he gladly followed them outside to a jeep, double parked outside. It wasn't cold there at all, and he gladly threw his bags in the back and climbed in with them.

Yokota Air base was about fifty miles away, and even though it was night time, he immediately, started noticing the differences in our country and Japan. There was no sidewalks and people walked very close to the road and the further we got out of the city, he noticed the people were wearing more traditional clothing.

They got to the base, and these guys took him to the transit barracks, got Elbert settled in for the night and they left. The next morning, Elbert found the Admin Offices and went to check in. When he told them who he was, it was like, they were anxiously waiting on him, the admin clerk, immediately stood and said to follow him. He took him to the First Sergeant's office and he came around his desk and shook my hand. Now this is not, how it had gone so far, while he had been in the air force. Usually, you can expect no more than, the usual treatment offered any other GI.

The sergeant said to sit down. Elbert handed him his papers, and he reached over and picked up a file and come to find out, it was his service records. He already knew more about him than most people before he even got there. His first comment was, I see here you have been an assistant crew chief on a KC-97. Elbert said yes. He then asked him what the differences were between a C-97 and a KC-97. Elbert told him in detail, but mainly the only differences was a C-97 didn't have extra fuel tanks inside the fuselage, nor a boom to deliver fuel, and the hydraulic pumps were on the out board engines, and are opposite on a KC-97. He said for Elbert to go find something to do, until thirteen hundred hours and they would discuss his assignment when he got back. Then the sergeant got up and left him sitting there. Elbert thought that strange, but he got up and left, to find the chow hall and PX.

At one o'clock, (thirteen hundred hours), he was back sitting outside the sergeant's door, when he emerged from what looked to be conference room , with double mahogany doors. He motioned for Elbert to join him and inside, was a big conference table with three Air Force Generals, and the officers of two flight crews. They ask Elbert multiple technical questions, and inquired if there would be any problem with Elbert getting a top secret security clearance? Elbert answered, as he didn't think there would be any trouble. They then explained, they had a C-97 and needed a replacement crew chief immediately, as theirs, had an emergency and had already left, to go back to the States. Could he crew this plane. Elbert said yes. They explained, this was a special project, and he would not be assigned to a squadron, he would be flying strictly for (Blank) Air Force. Nobody was to know who they were, where they were going, or where they came from, was he comfortable with that? Elbert said yes. The flight crew commander, spoke up and said, he would take him to the plane and make sure the combat defense troops will give him access. They needed to have the plane refueled, and a pre flight inspection, as they fly at sixteen hundred hours, go get your belongings and bring them to this office, we'll wait on you.

Outside was a jeep was waiting and Elbert returned shortly. The Captain took Elbert to the plane and handed him a new security badge. He was introduced to the maintenance crew. They now worked for Elbert and nobody else. They went everywhere this plane went and was part of the project. Now, the only funny feeling Elbert had, about this whole thing was, he was an E-4. And he had a Master Sgt and a Staff Sgt, that technically, out ranked him, but yet he was the boss. But, Elbert never had a moment's trouble.

One of the first things he noticed as he approached the airplane was the tail number. He immediately recognized the plane, as one that was parked beside his plane, for two years, back in Savannah, Georgia. The story they had been told, when it was flown off one day, was it was going to Dallas Texas to be burned by the Fire Department on the air Base, to give them the practice and he knew the crew, that flew it to Dallas , and left it there.

The other thing was, there were four combat defense troops guarding this air plane. No one touched this plane, but his crew. They did not eat in the chow halls or stay in barracks on the bases, they went to. A bus would pick them up and take them off base, to a hotel. They wore civilian clothes off base, and on the plane, they carried 38 pistols, and no personal identification. Only a Geneva Convention card and a security badge.

SAIGON, VIETNAM

About twenty minutes before flight time the flight crew arrived and they were in the air twenty minutes later. They flew 15 hours and landed in Saigon, Vietnam. A blue bus arrived and picked them up, and took them into Saigon, to the Continental Hotel. The rooms they were assigned to had storm shutters on it like in the tropics. When Elbert opened his, he was told to keep them shut because the Viet Cong, would throw a hand grenade in the opening if they knew U.S. service person was in that room and the shutters were open. This hotel was on the corner of a big intersection. And just a couple of months before they got there, a Monk had burnt himself to death in the center of that intersection. You could still see the burn marks on the street. They stayed together and went to a bar and had a few drinks, then went back to the hotel, to eat. They were never to get in a cab alone, they were told to stay in groups of at least, two or three or you could end up dead in an alley, by the Viet Cong. The police in Saigon wore white uniforms with black belts across their shoulder and around their waist, and they carried machine guns.

The next morning, they had breakfast on the veranda and while they were waiting on the bus to take them back to their plane, a Vietnamese boy came and started shining Elbert's boots. Just as he got started, Elbert caught movement out of the corner of his eye, and someone kicked this boy in the chest, lifting him into the air and he landed on the sidewalk. It was a waiter. Elbert jumped up and almost hit him, when he explained the boy knew better than to come up on the veranda. In the past, a shoe shine boy had pulled a hand grenade out and blew up several people. The even ride a bicycle up and leave it against a wall and walk off with a bomb on the bicycle. So, Elbert learned quickly to be suspicious of things like that in Saigon.

The bus drove up and they left Saigon, and flew for another fifteen hours, landing somewhere else. And it was like this, for the next two years. They didn't get mail until they got back to Japan or the Philippines, sometime for weeks at a time.

SINGAPORE, INDONESIA

They flew over Malaysia, and the road to Mandalay, that was

Burma. That was a popular movie back in the states, with Bob Hope, when he was younger. Today, it is a suspected supply route, for the Viet Cong. They flew into Singapore and this was an experience, he will always remember. As they approached the British Air base they were headed for. Elbert was sitting on the navigators table, right behind the pilot. The co-pilot, said: "Keep an eye out for a surprise, because they were sending us a welcoming party," they being English, or British Fighters.

    It wasn't long before they noticed four black dots on the horizon, in front of them, and they were rapidly getting bigger and bigger when all of a sudden they went by overhead, and that was close   maybe a 100 yards from us and that is close. They weren't fighters, they were fighter bombers, the British call them Javelins.

    When on the ground they were led to be parked beside one of their Javelins. The Javelins also had their own private guards. The Bombers only had one guard and they had four guards. That looked a little silly as here was this big bad fighter bomber, probably armed, with one guard. And from all appearances our plane was a cargo plane, with no armament, and it had four guards.   Now what does that tell you. There is something special, about that plane and no one, is to get close to it, for any reason. Any idiot could figure that out.

    The flight crew went on into town, and Elbert stayed to refuel and fix something. So they could take off early in the morning. Elbert is sitting in the shade of the plane on the steps waiting on a fuel truck, when this rattle trap of a vehicle drove up and the guy driving is naked except for short khaki pants, sandals and no hat. His skin was dark from what appeared to be a lifelong tan. His hair was   blond from being bleached by the blazing sun. He did have on sun glasses. He stopped right at the door of the plane, and waved to the guards. They waved back and Elbert assumed, they knew him and he knew them. He shut the motor off and said with that British accent, Good morning. He got down and walked over to Elbert and was super friendly. They were soon laughing and talking about any and everything. Of course the heat was unbearable, and Elbert commented about the heat waves, you could see coming up off the concrete around them. He said, a beer sure would be good about now, wouldn't it. Elbert smiled at him and asked if he would like one? He said sure. They just so happened to carry beer with them where ever they went. They bought it for 15 cents a bottle in the Philippines, because in Japan, it was a dollar a bottle. So, they carried a large cooler with beer iced down. Elbert went and got them two beers and they sat talking.

Elbert kept staring at the Javelin, parked next to them and said, "That sure is a dangerous looking plane, I would love to see inside the cockpit. "

"Go ahead, it's okay."

"No way, that guard might shoot me if I go over there."

"He laughed and said, "No it's okay." He stood up and yelled to the guard, to let Elbert look inside the plane. The guard put down his gun and waved for Elbert to come on. As they walked over there, the guard showed Elbert where to put his feet to climb up and look in the cockpit. He even climbed up there and opened up the canopy.

Afterwards, they walked back and Elbert ask about this thing he was driving. He said they use it to tow airplanes and move them around. It was handy and he just drove off with it, when he decided to come to our plane. Elbert got him another beer, and Elbert ask him, what do you do here? He said he was the Flight Line Operations Officer. Elbert's eyes got big and he just knew, he was in big trouble. He laughed, and said he was a Major, but they don't get crazy like us Americans over uniforms and such. He laughed and Elbert laughed with him. The fuel truck drove up and once that was done, he dropped Elbert off at the main gate, and he got a taxi into Singapore to the hotel. They run into him every few months when they went back Singapore. He sure fooled Elbert.

Elbert noticed the taxis over there were Mercedes sedans and not an old one either. He asked how they could afford that and learned, a Mercedes is an expensive car in the U. S. But, in a lot of other countries it is a cheap car. And that is why they use them as taxis. He also learned the place to go, was the British Enlisted Men's Club. They called it the Britannica Club. It was a two story building that had everything you could imagine. Fine dining, to a sandwich shop, Barber Shop to a

Night club, even a health club with weights and such, massages, sauna, and a swimming pool. If you were military, you were welcome. Civilians were allowed as guest of military people, Officers and enlisted men and women alike.

He noticed a crowd of people out on a balcony looking down at something, and he walked over there. When he seen what they were looking at, he laughed. It seemed one of our guys, named was one of two guys that had decided to jump off the balcony into a pool below. The military police was down there trying to get them out of the pool, and they kept swimming to the other side from them. It was just like in the movies and everybody was laughing. Now, our man was a little guy that probably weighted a hundred pounds, if that. The other guy was a giant of a man with a full beard. It looked like, Mutt and Jeff, being chased, by the keystone cops. After awhile, somebody yelled for me to join them, as they were going into town, so Elbert left.

    They went into Singapore, Singapore, is in Indonesia and they are really bad about dishing out punishment by caning. That is rough. You don't want to experience that, believe me. Well, it was election time in Singapore and they had just built a large grand stand and the people running of office, were giving speeches. Well, some drunk jumped up on the stage and was patting one of the speakers on the back, saying vote for this man, then here came two policemen with machine guns and everybody is running. Elbert got down on his knees and crawled through the crowd into a record store. He then stood up with records in both hands and nobody bothered him. He soon found his buddies and they left the area. They didn't stay long and went back to the Hotel.

    The next morning, they met up at the plane. Everybody was there but the oxygen and Pressurization man. Oh no, please don't tell me he is in jail, surely not. They didn't think anything about him being in that pool. At best they thought they might throw them out of the place but surely not arrest him. The pilot and Elbert went to check and sure enough they had him on base in the Brig not in town, thank goodness. When they ask for him, they said they could have him. But when they brought out this giant of a man, with a full beard, they knew this wasn't our man. Somehow, they had got the names mixed up and give them some British sailor. Elbert said, "This is not our guy, we want the little guy that was with him. "then they brought our man out. The pilot read him the riot act and they hurried back to the plane and got airborne. Every day was different, sometimes they flew all day and sometimes they flew all night. They never knew where they were, where they were going, until they were airborne.

After about a year, Elbert became a flight crew member as a Scanner. They got a new crew chief from the states and now, he didn't work on the plane anymore he rode it and looked out a window watching for visitors, even at night time. One of the first night flights as a scanner he was sitting there looking out into the darkness of night, with an occasional period of time when they would be above clouds and have moon light. Most of the time, they are at 20 to 30,000 feet, and it is pitch black dark. Sometimes, it appears, someone on the ground is shooting flares up at them. The first time he saw that, he said over the microphone, "Somebody is shooting flares at us." The co-pilot said: "That isn't flares that is 50 caliber tracers. " Well, there had to be a first. After a while, he got to where he could spot tracers in the daylight. They glow red even in the daylight.

They only got hit once and they felt it when it happened. When they landed, they went looking over every inch of the plane and found a 50 caliber bullet welded into the right wing spar. The air frame people come and magna fluxed it and said, it had welded itself in and was no problem. So they cut it off and ground it down smooth, and they painted it red, and called it their badge of honor.

They got a little cocky about now and would occasionally joke around and say things like "You might hit us, but you can't knock us down" and they had a guy on the crew that was superstitious and every time he heard that, he would cringe and say don't say that. Then, they said it even more, just to aggravate him.

The price of things in the Far East was great in many ways. So when they had some down time, they would go sightseeing and shopping. Diamonds over there was a dime on the dollar, at the time. They bought things for their mom's and stereo stuff for themselves, and would ship it home. They had suits made, tuxedos, shoes, custom fitted and tailor made. You just couldn't afford some of these things back home. Dishes were another thing they bought hand painted things that were three to five times more costly back home. Elbert bought dishes and wedding rings in Japan, to save money for getting married when he came home.

STUDEBAKER CAR

While Elbert was in Japan, one of the guys he met was getting ready to go back to the states and he had a car. It was a 1950 Studebaker torpedo looking thing. Ugly wasn't the word for this car. But it ran good. The deal was, he bought it for a hundred dollars, with the understanding, when he went home, he was to sell it to another GI, for a hundred dollars. That way a GI would always own it and have a way to travel in Japan. Well, he got one of his buddies and they went to buy gasoline. Well, on base, he pulled up to the gas station and said to fill it up. He handed the guy a $10 bill and the guy gave him $9 and a dime back, change. Elbert asked, "What is this?" And he said, "It was only 90 cents." Gasoline, was only ten cents a gallon on base. Off the base, it was $3.00 a gallon. He knew right then he was going to like driving this car.

MOVIE CLEOPATRA IN TOKYO

One weekend, they were down for a few days, and he wanted to see the movie, Cleopatra with Elizabeth Taylor, and Richard Burton. Well, it was showing in Tokyo and he had never been to Tokyo, so he got a buddy and they went to Tokyo.

They were told how to get there and they are riding along on this road. It seemed like they should have already been there and was beginning to think they were lost. It was a bright sunny day and hot as the devil. The air seemed to be thick and smelled terrible, as they passed through some rice patties. They could see people out there planting sprigs of rice all neat in a row. They were almost but not quite knee deep in water and mud. They came to find out later, they used manure for fertilizer, and yes even human manure. The odor was terrific and would gag a maggot. However they just went faster to get past those fields.

After awhile, he decided to stop and ask if they were headed in the right direction. He found a Japanese man on the side of the road, and he pointed straight ahead and asked if Tokyo was straight ahead. The man smiled and bowed and said, "Hi, Hi "which meant yes. So feeling better they lit out and rode some more. Then it dawned on Elbert Japanese people are the most obliging people in the world. He might not have understood anything Elbert said, and just meant to please him. He decided to turn left and try again. When the man said, "Hi, Hi" again and it was a total different direction, Elbert said: Oh shit, he doesn't have a clue what he was asking, so he turned around and got back on the main road again. Luckily, after about thirty minutes, they started seeing the high rise building's on the horizon, and knew, they were on the right road.

When he was sure they were pretty close to downtown. He found a parking garage. He wanted to leave the car in a garage and he wanted a ticket, so that when they got out of the movie, he would be able to say, take him to the place printed on that ticket. He parked the car and got a ticket. Then they got in a taxi and showed him the clipping out of the newspaper and said, take us there. It worked like a charm. Riding along, Elbert began to smile and almost laughed. His buddy asked, "what is so funny?" Elbert said, "I just remembered, something somebody had said earlier, if you ride in a taxi, don't say, Hi yoc ko dozo. It means to hurry please. Well about that time, Elbert didn't think about it, but the taxi driver heard him and jumped the curb and crossed into oncoming traffic to turn left and take a short cut. He dropped them off at the movie theater. They were just on time, but first they went to get pop corn and a coke. Well, they didn't have coke, they only had orange juice. So, they got pop corn and orange juice.

They found good seats and the movie started. Well, guess what? Elizabeth Taylor and Richard Burton spoke Japanese. They didn't have a clue what they were saying. Then, they noticed at the bottom of the screen, they had English printed. So, while it was difficult, they were able to figure out   what was going on. But that was a chore, for a three hour long movie.

The movie experience is now over and they are outside trying to explain to a taxi driver, to take them to the address on their parking ticket. But after awhile they began to worry. Then a policeman came up, that understood English. He explained it to the taxi driver and they got back to the parking garage. Taylor walked up to the window and handed the ticket to the girl and she looked at him as though she didn't have a clue as to what he wanted. Damn! Now what? Then it dawned on him back in the states if you buy something in the department store they stamp your parking ticket for free parking. So they went inside and headed for a counter that sold something inexpensive. Elbert bought a scarf and as usual, not knowing how much money they wanted he held out a hand full. She took what she wanted and smiled at them. Elbert, then handed her the ticket, but she handed it back to him. Now what? Then he figured they were going to have to find somebody that spoke English. After asking several employees, the boss man came to them and he spoke English. Elbert explained they were trying to get their car out of the parking garage. He laughed and said he would go with them outside. He explained to the girl what they wanted and added there would be no charge. Elbert then thanked him, bowing, just like he did. Elbert never did learn how to get his car from a parking garage, but he doesn't think he will ever need to know that anyhow.

MAILMAN ON A MOTORCYCLE

Now, another time Elbert decided to go to Johnson Army base, to go to a movie about 20 miles from Yokota Air Base. It started raining cats and dogs and wouldn't you know it, his windshield wipers quit working. Well, he was sitting at this intersection and, the rubber fell off the wiper and it is scratching the glass, back and forth. He can't see anything but these dark objects coming and going. He saw a gap between two of these objects, so he decided to take off, between them. Oh no, Wham, this Japanese mailman, on a motorcycle, hits his front fender on the left, breaking the headlight and hurting his hand.

NOW, LISTEN CAREFULLY

Yesterday, Elbert had just been in a class about driving in Japan. They have a law there that says if you maim a Japanese citizen, then you have to support him and his family for the rest of their life. Surely they were joking, but he wasn't sure. They said, it would be better to back up and run over them again if they were not dead, to keep from having to support them forever. Now, all that, is going through his head, and he thought about it and decided surely they had to be kidding. God forbid they were serious, but he wasn't going to back up and run over him again. Today at this writing, Elbert would be saying to himself what a dumb ass he was. Anyway, here came the Japanese police, and they give him a ticket. He took it to the Air Police office and they scared him to death. They said he had to go to the Japanese Police Station and pay a fine, and a lawyer had to go with him. The guy there laughed and ask him, why didn't you just back up and run over him again. Now don't be laughing at him. That is what he said. So, on a certain date, Elbert and an air force lawyer went to this police station. Wouldn't you know it, they didn't speak English. They had to find somebody that could speak English. They pulled out about ten pieces of paper that Elbert couldn't read. They then stamped each of them with about ten different, rubber stamps. And announced, he owed this guy, 27,000 yen, at 360 yen to a dollar, it was $75 dollars. Elbert thought WHEW! He was tickled to death it wasn't more than that. He paid the fine and apologized to the man, bending and bowing with the biggest smile, he could come up with.

All he could think about was Thank God he didn't have to support him and his family for the rest of his life.

JAPANESE HOTELS

The Japanese Hotel described here, is mostly used by the Japanese people not foreigners. Mostly, because you would have to know where they are, as they seldom have a sign outside, in English. And they are usually on a side street out of sight. Foreigners stay in the more modern hotels, typical to their countries. One of the guys took Elbert to this hotel, probably for the shock value. But, maybe just to give him the experience of a lifetime, I don't know. Elbert could never have found this place, as it was off a side street and it was night time and no sign of any kind. It cost, 2000 yen a night that came to five dollars and a half, American.

Anyway, they paid the lady at the counter and she told Elbert to wait there and she took his buddy off down the hall, to a room somewhere. Taylor looked around and it was a wooden structure with sliding walls, made of light wood frames, with paper panels. It was hard to find the door, as it slid into the wall and looked just like the wall. They took off our shoes at the door when they entered the place and left them by the front entrance. The next morning, their shoes were by their bed, cleaned and shined. It wasn't long, before she returned and motioned for Elbert to follow her, so he did. She took him to a room that had a bed, which surprised him, as they usually sleep on Futon type bedding. She showed him a house coat and slippers and a cabinet for him to hang up his clothes. She motioned for him to undress and put on the hose coat and slippers, and left. While he was doing that she left and returned with a tray with a cup of hot green tea and a coffee cake of some kind. He was instructed to eat and she would return. He nodded and said okay, but she was gone before he could ask her why she was going to return. The cake and green tea was very good and hit the spot as they had not eaten hardly anything all day.

    After a few minutes she returned and motioned for him to follow her and he did. They went across the hall and down a ways to a room that had a sunken tub full of very hot steaming water. He could tell it was hot as steam was rising from it. There were faucets very low to the floor on the wall and a wash pan, soap, a wash rag and towel. About that time she removed his house coat and she seen he had on his briefs. She pointed at his shorts and it was very clear by her motions, he was to remove his shorts and this was going to be embarrassing. He said, okay, okay, and he did. She then made him sit on a little stool, while she poured warm water all over him and proceeded to wash him down. Now, he hasn't had this experience since he was a little boy.

    She then rinsed him off with fresh warm water poured all over him and she then motioned for him to get into that hot sunken tub. He eased down into it and he had to hold onto his privates, to keep from getting scalded. After a few minutes, he got used to it and was enjoying soaking, she then motioned for him to come out and she poured cold water all over him. Now he is shivering as she dried him off with a towel and hands him his house coat and slippers. She then motioned for him to follow her back to his room.

She then said goodnight, he thinks, and slid the door closed and was gone. The bed was a feather mattress, and he slept great. The next morning, he met his buddy outside and they took off looking for something to eat and get back to the plane.

OKINAWA, JAPAN

To be a Scanner on this flight crew Elbert had to attend flight training at Kadena Air Base in Okinawa, Japan. He arrived and all went well until the last day. Since his last name is Alberson and starts with an A, the A's are usually first to do everything. Like to get shots, or what have you, never to eat though. If it is a good thing, they start with the Z. So they are taking their final exam and they make an announcement that the only experience not completed as yet, was riding the Ejection Seat. They knew they would end up doing it, they had been wondering when it would be. And now, here it is.

The plan was to start with Alberson, and while he is riding the ejection seat, the rest of the class would be taking the exam. When he came back, they would tap someone on the shoulder and that person should quietly get up and go ride the seat.

So they took Elbert into a part of the building that had a real high ceiling. They have this old fuselage that has an ejection seat in it and the seat is on rails. So when it goes up, there is a loud bang and the seat in milliseconds goes to the top of the rails and slowly slides back down. You go through a sequence of events to give it some semblance of reality.

So, Elbert is instructed to climb in and strap on the seat belts and shoulder harness. Straight ahead outside the building is a man with a head set on, talking to Elbert, and he said, you have a fire in the engine and you must eject. Arm the ejection seat and blow the canopy. Now, eject at will. Elbert pulled the handle and there was a loud bang and something is bouncing around behind the seat and it hits him in the head and his hair is singed and no one is telling him anything, just staring at him. Elbert is trying to decide, is this part of the exercise, or what? He is thinking, get out. But, what if he is half way out, and this thing shoots up into the air. One more second and he decided to hit the quick release on the seat and climbed out.

This instructor says. "There was a malfunction, go back inside and don't say anything to anybody."   So, he did. Now, everybody is looking at Elbert, because they aren't taking somebody else like they said they would and Elbert smells like burnt hair and it was.

They came for Elbert again, and this guy asked, "Do you want us to sand bag the seat and show you it is okay now?" He said yes and they did and it worked fine. Then this guy asked, "Do you want to see me ride it, to show you it is okay now?" He said yes, again. And he took off his watch and handed it to one of the other guys. Elbert asked him, "Why didn't you tell me to take off my watch, "Elbert had just bought a $200 dollar Hamilton Electric watch, and was wearing it. He laughed and the seat worked fine.

So, Elbert then rode it and everything went fine. Elbert returned to Yokota Air Base and went on the flight crew as a Scanner. His seat, was near the tail on the right side of the plane and the window hatch at his seat, was really a bubble. He could stick his head out and see all the way to the cockpit. And all the way behind us and straight down.

JOHNSON ARMY BASE

One day, Elbert learned there was a movie playing that he wanted to see at the army base several miles away from Johnson Army base. So he climbed into his 1950 Studebaker and headed for Johnson. As you left the confines of the city and the base, you had to drive through the farming community of rice patties on both sides of the highway. He rolled up the windows and closed the vents because the smell was terrible coming from the fields. He tried to hold his breath, and he drove as fast as he could get away with, to hurry and reach the next town and the Army base. The smell was from the fertilizer. They used human waste, and it would gag a maggot.

Well, after the movie was over, he started back to Yokota Air base. Just as he was approaching the first field of rice and the odor he noticed there was a very nice Japanese car sitting on the side of the road. As he approached it, he seen it was a big car for a Japanese car. It wasn't a limo, but something close to it, obviously. The man had just got out and was looking at a flat tire. He appeared to be an older man and he was dressed in a suit, an overcoat and a hat. So Elbert pulled over and ask him, if he could help him. The man spoke broken English and indicated he would appreciate some help, so Elbert changed his tire for him. When Elbert was through, the man offered him some money. Elbert didn't know how much, as Elbert held up his hand, and told him no, no thank you, he was glad to help him and as Elbert turned to go, the man insisted he take his business card. He and Elbert both were bowing and smiling and telling each other thank you. They are the politest people you will ever meet.

Later, when Elbert thought about it, he asked the lady in the barracks, what it said on the card, as he couldn't read it. It was in Japanese. She looked at it and put her hand over her mouth and called the Japanese house boy that shined our boots, for him to look at it. They told Elbert, this man owned a well to do, highly regarded Geisha house. He had even written something on the back, in Japanese, but Elbert didn't remember what it said. Now, a Geisha house is not a house of ill repute. It is a house of highly trained ladies in the art of communication and conversation regarding finance, local and news from all around the world. They can carry on a conversation on probably more levels, than Elbert could. The impression Elbert got was he should have visited the address on that card, just to see what it was all about. But he never did. Shortly after that, they left Japan and moved to Clark Field, in the Philippines.

THE ROAD TO MANDALAY

Flying over Burma, Vietnam, Laos, and Cambodian jungles, you can only barely make out, a narrow winding road from the air. From the ground, they look like a big fat plane flying so slow, they can't be anything important. When they are noticed, it is assumed, they are a cargo plane of some kind and not worth the ammunition to shoot them down. The trees are so tall and the tops of the trees are so densely thick. The people on the ground some time hear them, but they can't see them. And because of that, they think Elbert can't see them. Wrong!!!

Not, only can they see them, they can tell how many are walking, how many are in two man jeeps, and how many are in the back of the deuce and a half trucks. They can even see where they slept, last night, and can tell how long they have been gone. Just knowing which direction they are headed, tells them, where they are going. And the size of their transportation, tells who they are. How long, they have been moving equipment and ammunition, tells what they are planning.

War is hell. When 200 trucks go to a certain point and turn around and go back empty. It's safe to assume there is a pile of supplies and ammunition in that spot. Knowing that then, it is safe to assume, that, if you bomb that area, there is a good chance of blowing up a supply depot delaying a push to advance any further.

Mine is not to understand or reason why but, to just do or die. Elbert has heard that saying all his life. And at different times, it may have multiple meanings. But, when you are flying for hours on end and there is nothing to do, but think, you figure out what is going on and where you fit in the picture. You soon realize you are but a pawn in a chess game. You volunteered for the ride and maybe you didn't fully realize you were writing a blank check for your life. Somebody needed information and somebody had to go get it.

THAT WAS RED BULL

Everybody has a job and everybody trust you are doing your job. Trust is more important, than anything else. Any one of them on that plane that fails to do his job could very well be responsible for them all to fail. And Failing, is not an option. The belief exist that, I like you, but I expect you to do your job. And if you don't do it, and do it right, you don't fly with me

SPRAY ON THE GENERAL

Every now and then, there would be visitors that would accompany them on flights, for whatever reasons. And they knew better, than to be curious about whom they were or what they did. They would at times, go into the different compartments that were off limits and talk among themselves. Occasionally, there would be a general with his little group that went everywhere the group went to fly with them. Well, one night, they had been in the air for hours and they had a crowd of people with them and it was night time. People are lying everywhere around Elbert, dozing or sleeping. Some are sitting up in the darkness, smoking a cigarette, or just asleep, with their eyes open. Well, in the rear of the plane was some small, stainless steel urinals, mounted on the wall of the plane. Elbert needed to get to one of them and do his business. He made it to the nearest one, without stepping on anybody. And with a sigh of relief, he peed in one of them. Well he didn't realize it, but he was straddling the head of somebody and the spray of his urine went all over the face of the guy lying below him. Elbert quickly, in the dark moved away, watching to see who it was, that now sit up. Elbert never seen his face, but he seen stars on his lapel and knew it was one of the Generals on board. Oh shit.

Elbert watched out of the corner of his eye as the General awoke, got up and started moving around. He seemed to have not remembered it or forgot it, until he started talking to someone and all Elbert could think of was, he is telling that guy what happened and he is telling him, as soon as he figures out whom it was, he will throw him out of the plane, without a parachute. Or, have him shot, when we land. Oh well, Elbert had other things to do, more important, than to worry about him so he forgot about it and hopefully, the General did too.

THE BRIEFING

As Elbert was thinking about, that little story, he remembered a briefing he went to in Japan, at Yokota Air Base. As they got to the door there was police stationed outside of the room, and again inside. They all had to show all their credentials and security badges etc, to get in. Elbert had never been in this room before and he was in awe, once inside. The room was dark and both the walls and the ceiling were black. On one wall, there was a big Plexiglas map of Far East Asia. What he seen was, every plane and ship in the Far East, not just ours either. Yes, we know where everybody is. That meant a great deal to him in knowing, if they went down, they would know exactly where we were.

His mind immediately went back to the Cuban Crisis. Often he had heard people say, and he thought it also. How come we didn't know more about what was going on down there in Cuba than it looked like we did? Well, the answer just come to him, when he looked at that board and seen what was there. Let me tell you now, there is nothing that we don't know and just about the minute that it happens, or materializes. With the advent, of the things we have put into orbit in space, believe me there is very little that we don't know about anything, including if your car is still parked in front of your house. Including what room you are in and quite frankly, what you are doing, washing dishes, or taking a bath and if the dog is asleep on your bed or in the den. On your way out today, look up and wave.

CLARK FIELD, IN THE PHILIPPINES

Well, Elbert has been in Japan for a year or more and he just learned, they are moving their operation to the Philippines. They have been in and out of there many times, so it wasn't any big deal to them. Off in the distance, you could see Mount Pinatubo. This mountain was a time bomb and we didn't know it. Years later, after being back in the States for years, this mountain erupted and was a lot worse than Mount Saint Helen in Washington State, ever was. They flew out of Clark Field for the remainder of his enlistment. They continued their routines of never knowing where they were going and half the time, where they had been. Japan, was neat and clean as compared to the Philippines. Now this is some poor people. And people, that lived a hard life in ways never known in the U.S. The town outside the base is called Angeles.

Angeles is a nasty, dusty, dirty, smelly town just outside of the U.S. Air base of Clark Field. The money exchange was in Pesos. Elbert forgot the exchange rate, but he remembers ten dollars, was enough money to be King for a Day, maybe even two days. The married guys that lived off base, had gardeners, live in cooks, housekeepers and babysitters. Just outside the main gate to the base, they could catch a Jitney (taxi) ride into town. Most of the bars, and there were many. Were owned and operated by locals. The Blue note Café is where they hung out when in town. It was owned by a colorful guy that was in the merchant marine during WWII. He married a Filipino and had several daughters. They are both educated and living in the U.S. somewhere. If you behaved yourself, he was a good man to know. If you got on his bad side, you better never come back in to the Blue Note.

He had bar girls, just like every other bar, but his head bar girl was the head of the bar girl association. She was responsible for seeing the girls didn't take advantage of the GI's and she ran for office just like other political people. She was educated, in more than book sense. She had been there, and done that. The bartender knew a lot about American drinks. And one night, out of sheer boredom, Elbert told him to mix him one. Then another different one and another different one until he said stop. Well, he doesn't remember when the lights went out, but you guessed it. He woke up the next morning with them telling him to drink a beer and he would sober up. They referred to it, as the hair of the dog, that bit you.

Let's go back to the Jitneys. They were everywhere, and the most colorful decorated jeeps you have ever seen. After WWII, the U.S. left millions of jeeps over there. It would cost too much to load them up and bring them home. The Philippine people had no cars to speak of. These jeeps became a gift to the Philippine people, as transportation. Other people salvaged damaged jeeps and they became Jitneys also, or a Taxi.

There was a Bus Line that traveled all over the Philippines. It was called the Blue Line. And yes, they were painted Blue. These buses, had a front and a back and a top and a bottom, but they did not have sides. So when you got on the bus, it was from either side. There was no center aisle. So to get on, you paid the driver and just climbed on one of the many seats that ran from one side to the other.

One day, Elbert and his buddies decided to go to blue beach. Blue beach, is where General Mac Arthur, landed the second time, and liberated the Philippines from the Japanese. So, they caught a jitney to the Bus Station, got on and sit in the very first seat about three fourth of the way from the front. The Dust rolled up and almost choked you, but it was cooler on the outside seat, than being stuck in the middle of the bus. It stopped at each village they came to and there was usually someone selling something, covered up, on a big tray, they balanced on their head. She would walk up to each arriving bus calling out, "BALLOUTES, BALLOUTES." A lady sitting in front of Elbert bought one and it appeared to be an egg. He thought, hey great, boiled eggs. He even started to buy one until the lady cracked it open and he seen and smelled what was inside. It was a dead chick. And she sat there and ate the whole thing. Elbert thought he would throw up. Once they got going and she finished it, the smell faded. He later learned it is an egg that has an Embryo in it and it is buried in the dirt for so many days, then they eat it like a snack. No thank you. After awhile they arrived and walked to the Beach.

    Looking around they seen several Philippine boys swimming and running around. They seen Bamboo huts along the sand dunes. They learned they could rent a hut and spend the night and they decided to do just that. There was a little store there, where they bought something to eat and snack on. They changed into swim trunks and were having a great time. All of a sudden, they noticed a boy coming from their hut. Well, you guessed it. He had a handful, of their wallets, watches and cash.

    Well, thank goodness, the Air Force seen to it they were not fat and slow. It turned into a foot race. They took off and ran the dude down. They got their stuff back. It may be hard to believe, but they got used to the humidity and the hot temperatures. At least you accept it and go on, without putting a lot of thought in to it. They slept pretty good in the Bamboo Huts, they were about three feet above the sand . During the night, wild dogs and hogs chased each other, even under their hut.

    They wish they could say it was a pretty and lush jungle, but it wasn't. They had a good time, but never went back. The water was pretty nice. There was a monument to remember Mac Arthur landing there, but even it, had run down, the words barely readable, and weeds growing all around. It was kind of disappointing to see that. As the bus passed through the villages, they could see, there were really poor people living everywhere. They had a hole in the wall of their house for a window. The floor was dirt with pigs going in and out. There might be a rag hanging over a door way, in the opening and   chickens everywhere.

    Back in Angeles, a lot of the local people worked for married GI's and their families. A married GI, living off base, was considered rich, compared to the Filipino's and often took advantage of it. They could go to the base, to a movie or the Airman's Club to dance, dine and drink while the live in maid, looked after the kids, while they had a night out.

There were older married people that didn't want to be transferred anywhere else they were living like kings and queens.

That part was good, but it was still dirty and dusty, and you were in the middle of nowhere. It was a long way to manila, the largest city. When Elbert was there in 1963 and 1964, the prime minister was a man named Diem. His wife became famous later for having so many pairs of shoes. When she and her husband, were run out of the country, the revolting people found, he took millions with him when he left, to live in other countries. This period of time, was referred to as, the Madam Nu, Regime. They were Catholic and as such, made it against the law to dance close enough for the fronts to touch. You had to dance at arm length. Elbert met several people and he has pictures of them, but he has long since forgotten their names or where they were from. He regrets that he didn't write, their names and addresses down, but didn't.

Elbert remembers this one fellow. He was an American Indian. He was from the Black Feet Tribe. He showed him a picture of his home and it was a very pretty white clapboard house with a white picket fence. He told Elbert he lived on a reservation and when he and their family went on vacation, they had to sign out with permission of the Indian agent. Elbert said:"That was pathetic and he was sorry it was that way. The Indians were here before any of us." He went home on leave while Elbert was there. He told Elbert, the reason he went was, he had too. Every ten years, the U.S. Government pays to the Black Feet nation, a cash sum, for the gold that was taken from the Black Hills of North Dakota. And as an adult descendent he got a share of the money. He never told Elbert the amount, but that was a part of History that Elbert didn't know about. He was a great guy and Elbert wished to this day, he could see him again.

TAKHLI, THAILAND

The sky is clear and they are descending, as they approach their destination. Elbert is looking over the shoulder of the pilot. The pilot is 40ish, quiet, and he doesn't say much. He is staring ahead and they are all looking for a visible sign of an airfield. They have to be almost on top of it or they should be. The co-pilot says over the intercom, "There it is, dead ahead. " Elbert didn't say anything at first, as they were still pretty high up. But the spot the co-pilot was talking about, looked like a postage stamp. They are getting closer and closer and Elbert mumbled to himself, you have got to be kidding.

Elbert is sitting on the navigators table looking over the pilot's shoulder and what he was looking at is the shortest runway he had ever landed on. It was so short they had extended it with that interlocking steel temporary runway. They flared out and the tires touched with the sounds of screeching rubber in a chirping sound. Then all hell broke loose with the rattle of the steel interlocking panels they were rolling on. They were rapidly running out of runway and the pilot was standing on the brakes. They were sliding and the green grass was all he could see. About that time, they seemed to gently roll off the steel, onto grass and they could feel the drag on the plane as they came to a stop.

They didn't crash they had just run off the end of the runway. They left a trail where the landing gears had plowed trenches and they are now mired down in about three feet of the muddy grass field. When Elbert unlatched the forward door and let it drop down it landed on the ground. It didn't go down far enough, for them to walk down steps, they had to climb out. There were Thailand Air Force mechanics standing there, as if this was an everyday occurrence. They surveyed the damage and found none. They were just stuck in the dirt but there was no damage. This Thailand officer said, "We will have you back on the runway before daylight. Elbert asked him, "How will you get it back on the runway? " He smiled and pointed to the edge of the jungle, there were elephants with men on their back slowly approaching. There were the elephants and it seemed like 20 or thirty men. They had this to happen before and they knew just what to do. Since Elbert was on the flight crew, he had no duties until they were air borne again. This U.S. Army guy drove up and said he was to carry me to some barracks. And here came several more to carry the rest of the flight crew into Bangkok, so he climbed in and off they went.

They drove off on a narrow road leading away from the air field into the jungle. And as they entered the jungle, the road narrowed to the width of the jeep. Now normally when riding in the front passenger seat of a jeep, your right knee would hang out but this jeep had a plywood door and it was   higher than your elbow, so you didn't drape your arm up on the top of the door. It was really quite uncomfortable and Elbert ask him, why was the door so high? He looked at Elbert and said, "This is the land of the King Cobra. And they are everywhere. If that door wasn't there and as high as it is, a snake along the edge of the road would stand up on their tail and strike at your knee as we go by. If you get bitten, more than likely you would die before we got you to a hospital. "Elbert hushed and rode on in an uncomfortable position but a safe one, from a Cobra.

They pulled into a clearing and immediately, see this long two story building stand on poles. It is screened in upstairs, but no windows. It was a barracks, built by the Japanese, during WWII. All the wood was mahogany or teak. It wouldn't rot, like so many woods in America. Underneath, on one end, was a chow hall, where a buffet was set up at meal time and tables for people to eat on, in the middle section. And on the other end, was a bar, with some tables and chairs, if you didn't want to sit at the bar.

Elbert's driver had told him earlier as they left the plane that he could stay in these barracks, or he would take him into Bangkok. Whatever he wanted was okay. So Elbert told him he had rather stay close to the plane, so let's go check out the barracks. Well they got out of the jeep and Elbert said, let's get a beer. They walked over and sat at the bar drinking a beer and talking to the bartender. To their left was a group of guys watching a movie being shown on a sheet hung for a screen, it was really quiet, except for the sound of the cowboys and Indians on the movie. Behind Elbert and the driver, were several tables and chairs, but they were all empty, nobody behind them. After awhile they were on their second beer, Elbert heard a noise like somebody grabbed one of the tables and was dragging it across the concrete floor. He turned and looked, but there was no one there. A few minutes later, he heard it again and again, there is no one there. Well, a few minutes later, he heard this CRASH, BAMM.   He turned and one of the tables had collapsed, apparently all by itself. Elbert looked at the bartender and he smiled and said: "Oh that is Bertha. " Elbert said: "Bertha? "

"Yeah Bertha is a Python snake, almost twenty feet long. She wrapped herself around the legs of the table and crushed it."

Elbert told the bartender to give them two more beers to go for the trip to Bangkok. His driver said: "I thought you would change your mind." If you're ready I am and they left.

As they came into Bangkok, all the buildings are decorated and designed like they have been for centuries, but this one building stood out like a sore thumb, it was the Bon Air Motel. It was owned by an American, married to a woman from Bangkok. They had the thing built, from plans of one just like it in California. Both his driver and Elbert stayed there. The next morning they went back and eat breakfast at that place they seen the python. Then he took Elbert to the plane. They had the plane back on the runway, but were only just starting to refuel it. You should have seen the rope they used. One end was looped and put over the elephants head and the other end, tied to the landing gears. They had cut logs and placed them in the trenches and pulled it right back up onto the runway. About that time, a convoy of trucks came up with barrels of fuel. They hand cranked all that fuel into our plane. It took hours to fill it up, so while they were doing that, they eat breakfast again.

Once they got fuel in it, they climbed aboard and taxied, as far back on the concrete runway as they could get and started a rolling take off at max power and they were airborne before they run off of the concrete part of the runway. Because we lifted off prematurely they were not climbing out at a great height and the trees at the other end of the runway were getting closer and closer. At the last second the pilot pulled the yoke back into his lap and we just barely missed the tops of the trees.

That place was top secret for a long time and later on, with the cooperation of Thailand and the U.S. That base became a fighter base and the runway was lengthened quite a bit. After the end of the Vietnam conflict it now has all the best of facilities. I think Thailand got the best end of the stick. America paid for it all, I am sure.

DARWIN, AUSTRALIA

During the night, they got a message to go to Darwin, Australia.

This was another one of those fifteen hours flights, and you can't imagine the boredom when it seems like everybody but you knows where we are, what we are doing, where we are going and when we are going to get there. Things happen and you sometimes wonder are you seeing what you think you are seeing? Like the time, Elbert looked up and seen a Chinese fighter on their wing tip. He hit the intercom button and asked if the copilot sees the fighter on the wing tip. He said yes, he was escorting them out of Chinese air space. Thank god, he didn't shoot us down. Elbert found out later they played dumb and they just sent them on their way. That could have turned ugly but it didn't. And to the best of their knowledge, they were not even in Chinese air space, but you don't argue about it when you can't defend yourself. It is apparent the fighter is talking to somebody he is so close you can read the writing of his name. That is if you can read Chinese. He rolled over the top of their plane and appeared on the other side of the plane for a while. He stayed with them for awhile and then disappeared just as fast as he appeared.

    The sun was getting brighter and hotter as their made our descent into Darwin. They refueled and locked up the plane. They left it secured by four guards and climbed into a bus that took them into Darwin to a Hotel.

    Later that evening as the sun had just gone down. A couple of them walked down the sidewalk looking for a bar when come up on a movie theater. They could smell the popcorn, and the movie was a western so they decided to go in and see a movie. They were sitting there and Elbert happened to look up and seen the most beautiful scene. It looked like they had a million lights in the ceiling and it appeared to be the night sky. He punched the guy next to him and told him to look at the ceiling. He did and about that time a plane flew across the sky. They looked at each other and then back to the sky. They were really looking at the sky and the stars. There was no roof in this theater. They started laughing and couldn't believe what they were seeing.

    Darwin was a mining town. Elbert didn't know what they mined, but that's what they said it was. He knew one thing they were in the middle of nowhere. It was more like a desert than anything. The wind never blew when they were there. He never saw any grass anywhere. And they walked from one shady spot to another. It was a sweltering hot and they sweated like nobody's business. They usually left early the next morning. They flew into Darwin several times, but never seen anything interesting to recall, except the movie theater, with no roof.

MEAT AND MACHINEGUNS

Well, it's homeward bound today, back to the Philippines. For almost a year or so he never ate anything off base in Japan because he just didn't like anything he seen. Nothing really looked good to him. But in the Philippines they were warned not to eat meat off base especially, from the street venders. Because you never knew what kind of meat you were eating. There was a variety of dog, cat, monkey, lizard, and Nutria, (rat).

One night they had been in town all day and now it was getting late and he was starving. They went to this place somebody had told them about. It was a two story bar. Upstairs, was for GI's from the base. And downstairs, was for the local people. As they got there and started up the stairs, Elbert noticed a street vender selling barbecued meat on a stick. It smelled really good and he was starving. He didn't care what it was if it tasted good. He bought one and it was great. So he spread his fingers and told him to put one between all his fingers then went on up stairs.

He ate several of them and was washing it down with beer, when all of a sudden the music was overpowered by machinegun fire. Everybody hit the floor. It was coming from downstairs, then screaming and the sound of a jeep leaving in a hurry. They were told to stay put by the bartender and waitresses. Then, they went downstairs, to see what had happened. They were told that there was someone downstairs that was running for some local office and his opponent had him killed. This was common and it happened a lot during election time. This is what Elbert means when he says they live a hard life that we have never seen. This happened again several weeks later in the little town outside the base there in the Philippines.

NATIVES ON MOUNT PINATUBO

On that mountain in the distance were primitive natives. The Chief proclaimed himself the King. You seldom seen any of them but you knew they were there and around. They were actually pygmies. Late at night if a plane was coming in or taking off, there was a guy in a pickup truck that would go out and ride the runway to clear it off of any animals like wild hogs or a water buffalo or whatever, especially these Indians. Well, he kept his windows rolled up because the natives would shoot the truck with bow and arrows and there were many times he would return with an arrow sticking out of the door or fender.

Often, if no planes were expected during the night, they would turn off the runway lights. And if they needed them on for some reason they would simply turn them on. Well, one night a plane showed up unexpectedly and the lights were turned off. When the pilot radioed he wanted to land they turned the lights on but only a few come on. They went out there to see what the problem was and found the majority of the lights were missing, the natives again. They didn't do it often but every now and then they stole the blue lights down both sides of the runway and then sold them back to the base. Elbert seen the King once in a parade and he wore a Generals hat, shirt, complete with name tag and medals. Can you guess what name was on the shirt? It was General Douglas MacArthur. And the King carried a swagger stick, given to him by the General, at the end of WWII. You see, these natives, helped rid the Philippines of the Japanese at the end of WWII. They killed and caused the Japanese a lot of trouble during the war.

AIRPLANE, ANNUAL INSPECTION

Everybody got excited when they heard their plane had to have an annual inspection. It meant they would have to take it back to Fort Worth, Texas and let them tear it all apart and put it back together again. And it would probably take them at least two weeks to do it. That meant they would be able to go see family. In its present configuration this plane had been in the air for almost two years, fifteen hours a day and really was fine but it was due for a major inspection.

Well, they just got word the answer was no. They couldn't afford for the plane to be gone and unavailable for that long. It will be inspected right there in the Philippines and done by their people. So they towed it to a make shift hanger made out of that temporary runway welded together to provide some shade and to keep the rain out, what little they ever got.

After two weeks, Elbert got called to come and help them tow the plane to a spot where they could run the engines and check them out. So, he climbed in to the pilot's seat to ride the brakes with another guy in the copilot's seat. Elbert turned on the master switch, so he could talk over the intercom to the man driving the Uke (tractor) pushing the plane out of the hanger. Elbert turned on the inverters for the instruments to indicate hydraulic pressure. The APU was on and the instruments indicated we had 1500 pounds of brake pressure. The UKE driver said to release the brakes and let's go. Elbert released the brakes and they started rolling backward out of the hanger. They moved backward and to the left in a wide arc until they stopped and the UKE driver said to set the brakes and he did. Everything seemed to be fine.

After about a minute Elbert heard from the ground, a voice that said: "Set the brakes." Elbert looked out the window and this guy has his hands cupped to his mouth yelling for him to set the brakes. Elbert hit the mike button and told the UKE driver to tell that guy the brakes are set. But he didn't answer back. About that time Elbert noticed the UKE has unhooked from the plane and is pulling away at a pretty rapid rate. Elbert looked back at the guy that had yelled at him and noticed he was walking beside the plane still yelling to hit the brakes. Elbert looked out front of the plane and it seemed if they kept going, they would run into an F-86 Fighter jet. It was hooked to a ground power unit with its engine running. The pilot was sitting in his seat with the canopy open, talking to a crew chief and did not see their plane headed for them.

Elbert kept hitting the brakes and he noticed the brake pressure had a gone to zero. He told the guy in the copilot's seat to grab that red handle and start pumping hydraulic pressure up into the system. Meanwhile, Elbert reached over his head and pulled the emergency brake levers. They were hanging loose with no pressure on them and they come down so fast they hit him on top of the head. Oh shit, they don't have any brakes what so ever and they are picking up speed getting faster and faster. Elbert grabbed the steering wheel and thought he was turning the plane to avoid the fighter in front of them.

But with no hydraulic pressure he wasn't turning the plane. The nose wheel was following the same track back into the hanger from where they started rolling, but now into the hanger. The elevation was almost three feet higher where they started rolling. So they were literally rolling down hill right back into the hanger. They missed the fighter jet and they never knew how close they came to almost getting killed. And the guy on the ground is now trotting at a pretty good pace, still yelling.

People in the hanger now see what is happening and they start running. Elbert told the guy in the copilot's seat that when he told him, for him to run for the hatch in the rear of the plane. It was in the floor right beside the seat Elbert normally sat in, when in flight. When Elbert could do nothing else, he told him to go, run, and he beat Elbert to his seat. Just as Elbert got to his buddy, his seat was facing the front of the plane so, Elbert grabbed him and sandwiched him between the seat and himself, as the plane collided with the engine stands and the ground power units and he could hear sheet metal tearing. Elbert thought, there might be a sudden jolt to a stop. But it was more like slow motion. When they stopped, they went down the hatch and out the back door to the ground. All of a sudden, it dawned on Elbert there was still power on the plane and the master power switch was on. So, he ran all the way back to the cockpit and hit the master switch, shutting it off and ran all the way back and out of the back door.

As he came out the back door Elbert met a General asking, what happened? Elbert quickly, looked up at him and said: "Don't ask me, I was just driving that thing." Well, that little comment came up in the accident inquiry. And Elbert explained it away, as emotion in the excitement of the moment.

Elbert got in a tit for a tat, with a Master Sergeant, about the brakes having to be released to pump up hydraulic pressure while on the ground. And one of the pilots came to his rescue and together they showed the court in the service manual Elbert was right, and the flight engineer, was wrong about the statement.

They found the UKE driver was at fault for disconnecting the plane without putting chocks under the wheels before he disconnected from the plane. Also the hydraulic man, he was half way through the inspection period when he had an emergency back in the states and left.

The replacement hydraulic man failed to bleed the air out of the system. That is why the instruments gave a false reading of 1500 pounds of pressure, when there wasn't any.

So, it took another month to fix all the damage, and Elbert got his flying time in on planes out of Base Ops. Making short flights here and there got his flying time in to draw flight pay.

RE-ENLIST OR NOT?

Well, it is time to re-enlist, or not. It has been four long years since Elbert joined the Air Force. He was under the impression that once he had four years in service. The Air Force would bring his vehicle overseas for him. He also understood that it he went home and got married, the Air Force would bring his wife back to Japan at no cost to him. So, he ordered a new Corvette from the factory and paid $500 down on it and made arrangements for a monthly payment to come out of his pay, to be sent to General Motors.

Janice and Elbert had talked about it and he was going to reenlist. So, he went over to Personnel at Clark Field and cheerfully said, I am here to re-enlist. And, to make sure everything was okay about my car and a new wife. Well, he learned things had changed or whatever but neither was they going to bring his car over there or bring his wife over there. They said, he had to have over four years in service when he originally went overseas.

So, Elbert looked him in the eye and said, "Let's make this perfectly clear, you bring my wife and car over here and I will re-enlist right now." He said: "Sorry can't do." Elbert said, "Well, I'll see you. I will be leaving and going home for good."

About three months later, Elbert landed in Hawaii and had a layover of several hours. He walked over to this giant gold fish pond. He stood on a small wooden bridge looking down at the same goldfish he had looked at two years earlier when he was there. Know how he knew that? They were orange, big and they looked at him like they remembered him. Suddenly, he heard them calling for his flight to San Francisco. He remembered hearing stories of GI's coming home from overseas and kissing the ground and at the time, he thought how silly that probably didn't happen. Well there might have been a pink elephant at the bottom of those steps, as he got off the plane. But his eyes were cast on the concrete dead ahead of him. When he got off the plane in San Francisco, he kneeled down and kissed the concrete. He didn't care how hokey you might think that was he didn't care if he held up the people behind him. He was through being embarrassed about things like that.

The reasons probably vary as to why different people do that. But let me tell you. The United States of America is like Disney World, compared to the rest of the world. Coming home from the Far East back then and especially the Philippines, you almost cry, you are so happy, to be back here. Elbert seen a bus that indicated it was going to Travis Field and he got on it and checked in to be processed out. He would have started walking east if he thought he could leave right then, but he still had a few days left on his enlistment and they meant for him to stay until the last minute.

The next morning, this Sergeant came looking for someone to clean the bathrooms, the barracks and someone to go to the chow hall for KP. Elbert simply ignored him, got dressed and headed for town. He got a room in a hotel and he stayed in town until the minute he had to sign papers and go home. He was not cleaning any barracks or peeling any potatoes. And he didn't.

Elbert put on a clean and starched short sleeve tan shirt, a starched and creased pair of pants and caught the bus to the airport in San Francisco. He had a ticket to Memphis, but he had decided he was going to Savannah, Georgia first. So he paid the difference in the ticket and flew into Dallas, Texas to change planes. The flight was long and he dozed and the more he squirmed in that confined seat the more wrinkled his clothes got. He had a long layover in Dallas and he paced and walked until he couldn't walk anymore. He slept sitting up until he couldn't sleep anymore. He went into the bar and had a drink or two then he slept some more stretched out on two or three seats until they called his flight to Atlanta. The flight from Dallas to Atlanta seemed like it took forever and he slept some more and now he hasn't shaved in a while. He had been through several time zones and his body didn't know if it was day or night. His hair was messed up from wearing a hat taking it off and on over and over he gave up on his hair being presentable. And he missed his connecting flight from Atlanta to Savannah. The next flight wouldn't be until the next day. So he wandered all over the Atlanta airport nervous aggravated, tired and wore out. He slept again all night sitting up in a chair in his clothes and now he had sweated in those wrinkled clothes.

The next morning he left Atlanta and about an hour and a half later he landed in Savannah and taxied up to the terminal. In 1964, the terminal was a one story small building, when he got off the plane he had to walk about 40 yards toward a gate in a fence and there were people there to meet their loved ones. There in the sunshine was this beautiful dark haired girl, wearing a light blue sun dress and smiling at him as he walked as fast as he could to hug her neck. They got his luggage and hurried to her car and went to her apartment.

He was starving to death and had kept saying, let's get something to eat but she insisted we would after he got cleaned up and got out of those terrible clothes. She ran bath water while he found some clean clothes and his shave kit. He looked into a mirror and seen he was really a mess. He was so tired and the hot water felt so good, he just wanted to sit there and soak for a few minutes and he called to her and asked her to come sit and talk to him while he just lay there and soaked. She did and they had their first quiet moment together in two years. After awhile, she left so he could get out and get dressed and they decided to go to her home in Cobbtown to see her folks and spend the night there.

Janice's folks were glad to see him. Her brother and sisters were there. And Janice's mother had a big meal prepared. Boy was it good to be home and eat food, that didn't come from a can.

MEMPHIS, TENNESSEE

The next day they loaded their clothes and left Cobbtown for Memphis. He needed to get home to see his mother, dad and brothers.

They drove straight through to Memphis and every so often, he had to add more oil to keep the red light from coming on in the dash board. Not once, had he thought to check the tires. Somewhere along the way, they picked up a nail and the first morning they were in Memphis, he had to change a flat. The spare tire looked terrible and the tire he took off was slick. He meant slick no tread and there was string or rayon hanging out of the tire.

Well, his mother said, she had connections at the Chevrolet Dealership in West Memphis, Arkansas. And for them all to ride over there and see what they might have. Well, his mother went to work on the salesman that she knew and had bought several cars from and they ended up leaving the dealership in a brand new 1964 Red Chevy Impala hardtop. Elbert planned to stay a few days and get back to Georgia, as they were going to be married in the church Janice had grown up in. They visited with all his relatives and said their good buy's to go back to Georgia and his family would follow in a day or so before the wedding.

BACK IN COBBTOWN AGAIN

They made it back to Cobbtown and one morning they all went to the church to clean and decorate the Social hall and the Sanctuary. The floor in the social hall was tile and needed to be cleaned so Elbert got down on his knees and went to work. He had cleaned the floor in a barracks in years past so he knew what he was doing. Boy did he impress the little old ladies of the church. They were all telling Janice, she sure had picked a wonderful husband. Boy was she lucky. Janice kept telling Elbert not to get the big head. But for years to come, they told him how he had impressed them by jumping on that floor and getting it so pretty.

WEDDING

His best man was Duane Carr. They had been roommates, back in Savannah, Georgia. Duane was from Needles, California. His wife's parents, Leroy and Lucy Grantham, had become family to Elbert and they all came to the wedding. Elbert's mother and his brothers were there and everything went so well. Except maybe, the ring exchange. When Janice went to put his wedding ring on his finger, there staring at them, was his High School Class Ring. He struggled to get it off and she put the gold band on but he kept trying to slip the class ring, on another finger but it wouldn't go on any other finger but about half way. He gave up and when they turned around, to come out of the church the photographer was taking pictures and you can clearly see that class ring was halfway on one of his other fingers.

After the reception, with everything they owned in the car, they left the church, and headed for Jekyll Island for their honeymoon. Their intentions were to spend a couple of nights and return to Memphis, Tennessee

HONEYMOON

However, when they bought the new car, there were some spots on the hood and they said they would fix them under warranty. But, to disconnect the speed odometer so there wouldn't be many miles on it. So, when they left Cobbtown after the wedding, anxious to get to Jekyll Island, Elbert was driving a little too fast. He didn't think anything about it but this became important on their way. They had so much stuff in the car, Elbert couldn't see out the rear view mirror. And halfway to Brunswick below Jesup , Georgia the highway patrol pulled them over for speeding.

Now get this, they have a new state patrolman and his boss riding with him. Because the boss is there, he has no way of letting them go. They give Elbert a ticket and made them go back to Jesup and pay a fine. Elbert and Janice both tried to pay the fine with new pots and pans, sheets and towels, but they wanted cash and cash only, now Janice hasn't said much during all this but about that time she says what if we don't pay you? I am in the process of getting her to hush and he leans around me and says: Well, little lady, it looks like you will be mopping floors for a few days, in jail. Elbert quickly paid him and Elbert thought Janice was going to hit this guy.

So now, they get back on the road and try again to get to Jekyll. They stay with traffic this time, to stay out of trouble. They finally got to the Wanderer motel right on the beach. They can hear the waves breaking as they come ashore and they can smell and feel the salt in the air. They check in and are told to follow the bell hop on his bicycle, to their room way down at the other end of the building. The building is built parallel to the beach, so every room is on the beach. They did and they are getting out of the car gathering their things to take up to the room. When Elbert noticed there are two state patrol cars, sitting in the parking lot and the patrolmen are watching the newlyweds getting ready to go to their room. They can just imagine the snide remarks being made whether they were or not. They haven't been in the room more than a few minutes when there is a knock on the door. Boy, it hit Elbert wrong, and he told Janice, I'll bet it's those state patrolmen coming up here to aggravate us because we are newlyweds. Elbert went to the door and jerked it open and said: "What?"

There stood the boy that had showed them to their room with a tray and a bottle of champagne. It scared the boy, and he said: stuttering, "Ah compliments of the house." Elbert thanked him, and he took off. The two state patrolmen were still down there.

They enjoyed their stay even though it was cut short, by their funds being spent on a speeding ticket. They enjoyed their walk on the beach, the swimming pool, the next day. They had their memories of Jekyll and their adventure. So after checking out they headed to Memphis, Tenn. Somewhere along the way up in the mountains they passed a log cabin Motel and thought that it might be fun to stay there. Janice didn't say anything but it ended up being a dump, so much for that. Elbert had wanted everything to be so great, for Janice sake. But things, just wasn't working out so great.

Upon arrival in Memphis, they planned to stay with his mother for a few days and look for a place of their own. Elbert went to see about going back to work where he had worked before going in the Air Force. And he came home excited, because they hired him back. Boy, it felt good to know, because he had done a good job before, they hired him again. Mr. Smith was still the Warehouse manager and he and Elbert had always got along very well. He very quickly started giving him assignments of a different nature, one right after another and he had become his mentor. After six months, Elbert was traveling all over Mississippi, Alabama, Arkansas, and Tennessee, auditing the jobber stores. Elbert was on a roll in gaining experience all thanks to Mr. Smith.

Janice had learned of a secretary job open at a furniture store and she got the job. They now had two incomes. They were doing pretty well but still didn't have any extra to speak of. It seemed like it took all they had, just to get by, till the next payday.

Elbert went to Mr. Smith and asked him if there was an additional job there somewhere, that he could work two shifts. He told him, he needed at least three hundred dollars a month. He told him to come see him after lunch and give him some time to check on something. Elbert said fine, and went back to work.

After lunch and before Elbert had a chance to go see Mr. Smith, he called Elbert to his office over the loud speaker. Elbert went into his office and he asked Elbert if he could be in Birmingham, Alabama by 5 o'clock. Elbert told him sure he could, if he left now. Mr. Smith shook his hand and said, you need to be there before 5 o'clock as tomorrow you will be the new Assistant Manager of the Birmingham warehouse there. Boy, he couldn't thank him enough and he ran to call Janice. He told her about the promotion and he needed the car to be there today. He would be back Friday night. Janice said: go, this is great, we will even be closer to Georgia now. So that following week end, they moved to Birmingham, Alabama. They lived in an apartment, up on a hill, on 4th Ave.

The warehouse was called Parts inc., in the Continental Gin complex. The whole place was owned, by a little old man that rode around in the back seat of a black Cadillac limousine, chauffer driven. He was a multi millionaire. He lived only one block from where Elbert and Janice lived in a huge three story, mansion with a curved driveway and iron gates. Elbert was standing outside the warehouse one day when he drove up and motioned for Elbert. Elbert walked over to him and he introduced himself. Elbert explained he had just moved to Birmingham and was newly promoted, as the Assistant Warehouse Manager. He then asked Elbert a strange question. He wanted to know, if Elbert needed any furniture, since he was only recently married. Elbert told him, they still needed a bedroom suite, for the extra bed room. He said, he had one and wanted me and the wife to come see it. He gave Elbert a card with his address on it and Elbert agreed to come see it that afternoon late.

When they arrived a maid let them in and took them to a sitting room. Shortly after, he and his wife, both are in their eighties join them and they had coffee and visited for a while. Then they took an elevator to a bedroom where they showed them this bedroom suit. It was huge and expensive they were sure. Elbert didn't recall the amount, he sold it to them for and they didn't buy it that night. Elbert's father had come the following weekend from Memphis to visit. He rode a bus from Memphis and back. Elbert and Janice were telling him about it and he insisted they let him pay for it. So, they went back and got it the following week. Elbert and Janice really got the impression the old couple were trying to do something good for somebody, specifically Elbert and Janice.

    After looking at the bedroom suit, Janice and his wife went back downstairs to visit, while he took Elbert out back to a shed to show him something. Way back in the far corner of his back yard was a small wooden building. He unlocked the door and they went in. He said to Elbert, working for another man is fine, but you will never get rich, working for someone else. You need to be in business for yourself, and he had a business that could be bought at a good price and Elbert could build a good business out of a small beginning. He began to open boxes of clear glass bottles, with nothing in them and with no labels. Then, he pulled out the labels. Then, he showed Elbert a box of full bottles, with a red liquid inside the bottles and the labels said: "Old English Furniture Polish." He then, gave Elbert a bottle to take with him and there were 55 gallon barrels of the material to stir up another batch of this polish. He would sell Elbert this business for just $250.00. Elbert just had to find the $250.00 first.

    Elbert and Janice went home and enjoyed talking with them and seeing inside a real mansion. It was something like you seen in the movies, very old and very high dollar. They had, to be in their eighties, and maybe their nineties. Elbert tried the furniture polish and it worked great. But, it left an oily residue and he could see that as a problem, as it would attract dust, he thought. Well, he didn't do it. But somebody did, because Elbert seen that same stuff in the same bottles and the same red color and it even smells the same. Elbert has seen it in furniture stores and hardware stores and variety stores, for years. It just could have been a fortune that Elbert missed and he will never know. Elbert still thinks about that from time to time, he really believes he made the right decision. But he will never know, will he because he wasn't much of a risk taker. That old man made his fortune and he was still working at it in his nineties. That is what it takes. You have to be a risk taker. If you never buy a lottery ticket, you will never win. If you never try, you will never succeed.

CHAPTER 6   1965 – 1968

BIRMINGHAM, ALABAMA

Birmingham was a dirty town. With soot in the air that settled on everything. There were several Steel Mills there, which left a haze over the city. Once they got used to it, they didn't think about it much. But Janice and Elbert were not used to the dreary days. She was homesick for Georgia and it all came to a head, when he came home and found her crying. She had washed clothes that day and hung them out to dry. When he asked her, why she was crying? All she could do was point outside, at the clothes. He went out to get them and found them covered in black soot from the steel mills. Well, they got by that crisis, and he went to work, the next day.

One of the salesmen that called on them drove up and Elbert watched him get out of a Cadillac Coupe De Ville. He was an older man, and he wore a hat, like Coach Bear Bryant, for the Alabama University Football team. Well, he came in and Elbert asked him, how do you sell enough nuts, bolts, washers and cotter pins, to drive a Cadillac. He smiled, and said, I don't sell a box of 20 I sell a whole display case and a display that can range from several hundred dollars, to several thousand. And when I replace a competitive brand, I might write an order for $20 to $30,000 dollars. You have to think big and you sell big. Well, later on, he made a comment about somebody that they couldn't sell a certain amount by a certain date. And Elbert told him he could. He looked at Elbert and said: "no way." Elbert told him, he would sell some dollar amount of his product by that date he had in mind. And all Elbert wanted was that hat he was wearing. He smiled and said okay, you're on. Well, Elbert did it. Elbert called every jobber auto parts store they had and wrote them an order for a new larger display than what they presently had. When the Dorman product salesman came by the next time, he already knew it because of the invoices already having cleared and he got the commission on what Elbert sold. He walked in and straight to Elbert's desk. He took off his hat and laid it on his desk. He said I want to shake your hand. You are a fast learner. Elbert gave him his hat back and said: I don't want your hat, I was just joking. The man smiled and asked what do you want? Elbert smiled at him, and said, your job. If you retire anytime soon, I want you to recommend me. He shook my hand and said you got a deal.

Well, after six months in Birmingham, one Sunday morning, Elbert and Janice are lying in bed reading the Sunday newspaper and Janice turned to him and asked, Can we go back to Georgia?

Sure, when?

Right now!

How about next weekend?

No right now today.

You mean forever?

Yes, I am lonesome for Georgia, and I want to move back to Savannah. He looked at her and said: Okay, get dressed. They jumped up, and took off for Savannah. They drove up to some friend's house they knew. It was Joan and Wendell West. They told them what they were doing and they insisted they stay with them until they could find a place. Monday, Elbert started looking for a job and found one by dark.

BENEFICIAL FINANCE COMPANY

This job was a chase man for a loan company. His job was to do several things but mainly to go and collect the payment for whatever had been financed. Now, he had no clue what this was all about, but he figured he would learn and we'll see. Well, he was given a card with a name on and an address. It said, he needed to collect $5, as this was two payments of $2.50 a month. So, he walked up, and knocked on the door, and a lady comes to the door. He asked was her husband home? She looked at him like he was a devil or something and asked what do you want him for? Elbert explained, he needed to collect $5 from him, for the Bible, he financed. All of a sudden, she took off and came back in just a minute. She unlatched the screen door and stuck a heavy box in his hand and said: "You can just take that Bible, he doesn't have any money and I don't want anybody else coming around here." Elbert is trying to get a word in edge wise to tell her he don't want the Bible, then she slams the door in his face. Now, he is standing there, with his mouth open, and holding this card board box, with one of those family Bibles in it. He went back to the office and told them what had happened and they laughed. The secretary said, she would give $5 for it. The manager said, SOLD. So just like that Elbert has made one lady mad, and two other people happy all in an hour or so.

So, He left the office and went to his next customer. He walked up to the door and knocked and heard a rough voice say, what do you want? It is dark inside and he is talking to this guy through a screen door. He can't see him, but he can hear him. Elbert ask, is Rufus so and so here? What you want with him, he says. I need to collect some money. I am from Beneficial Finance Company. This voice says he doesn't have any money. So Elbert told him that the manager said, if he doesn't have it, to bring him to the office to see the manager. It was quiet for a minute, then Elbert heard, what sounded like a seven foot tall, 300 pound man running at him and the screen door, so he backed up as this giant of a man is rapidly getting closer and about that time, a giant of a man came running through the screen door. Boards are flying and screen is tearing and Elbert is running up the street as hard as he can go down the sidewalk. Elbert was thinking to himself, I don't like this job.

Well, one day, the boss says, go get me so and so, and bring him back here, tell him, I want to talk to him. Elbert said, okay and he drove up to this little shot gun house, with a tall older man sitting on the porch. Elbert ask him, if he was so and so, and he says yes, he sure was. So, Elbert told him, the manager at the office wants to talk to you and I will bring you back. He says okay, let's go and he got in the car. Well, they are on the Bay street Bridge, stopped for a red light. Suddenly, he ask Elbert, who did you say wants to see me? Elbert told him Tom, the manager of Beneficial Finance Company. All of a sudden, he jumps out of the car, at a red light and Elbert am trying to get him back in the car. The guy behind Elbert is blowing his horn and Elbert liked to have never, got him back in the car. So he hurried on to the office and then this guy won't get out of the car and go in. So Tom comes outside, and talks to him through the window.

Then Elbert get these instructions, to go to this lady's house that had a couch recovered in pink vinyl material and Tom financed it. Tom says if she won't pay him, to call him. So Elbert went to see her and she is a big heavy lady and just as nice and friendly. So he told her who he was and what he wanted and she says she just don't have it, so he told her he would have to call the boss and she said, fine, call him. Well, Elbert was looking at one of those Lady Princess telephones and it was a bright pink to match her couch and the light glowed from beneath the part you put your fingers in. So asked her, could he use her phone? She said it didn't work. He picked it up and there was no dial tone, the phone was a dummy phone, just for looks.

So he went back outside to his car and called the office on the CB radio. The boss starts yelling over the radio for Elbert to go back inside and start putting a chalk mark on all the furniture. Tell her the truck is on the way and they are going to take everything with an X on it. Elbert listened to him and he is thinking, no way was he going to do that. So, Elbert told him, maybe you better come and do that yourself. He said fine he would, for him to wait on him. He drove up and got out of his car with a piece of chalk in his hand. He said, follow me. He walked up on her porch, opened the door and went right in, like he owned the place, and said: Gladys, I am through trying to help you. I have a truck on the way, and I am taking this couch and this table, he put a chalk mark on it and started for something else, when she reached in her boobs, and brought out $10 dollars, and paid him. Again, Elbert is thinking, Man, I don't like this job.

Well, it's starting to get dark and Elbert is driving down this dirt street, real slow, looking for a house number. Ahead, are 16 to 25 year old boys, playing basketball at night, under a street light. They move out of the way as he went by them, and stopped. The night is quiet and it makes the CB radio squelch louder, than it really is. The tall whip antenna on the rear of his car goes swish, swish as it swings back and forth. Elbert got out of the car, leaving the door open and walked up on the porch of a house and knocked on the front door. He can see through the lace over the glass part of the door, that there are two couples sitting there, but they ignore his knocking, on the door.

He went back to the car and called the boss on the radio. He told him they are in there, but they are ignoring his knocking on the door. The boss asked him if he had his big flashlight, and he told him yes, it was here in the front seat with him. He said, take it and go beat on the door, with it. That did it. Elbert told him, if you want somebody to bang on these peoples door, with a big flashlight, well, let me suggest you get in your car and come down here and do it, because he was going home.

The next morning, Elbert drove up to the office and where he was parked, the boss could see him out his window. He come outside and asked, what are you doing? He explained he was taking the CB out of his car, because he quit. He finished and went back inside and gave him the CB Radio. He walked out and never went back.

BORDEN'S DAIRY

The whole time Elbert was in the Air Force, Janice worked for Borden's Dairy, in Savannah, as the secretary to the Plant manager. So, when they moved from Birmingham to Savannah. Janice went to Borden's Dairy, just to visit to see them. The Plant manager hired her that day. By chance, the plant manager asks Janice, what is your new husband doing? Janice, told him he had just quit what he was doing and looking for another job. He asks her, would he like to have John Shaw's job? John was the Retail Route Supervisor and he was being promoted and would be moving shortly to North Carolina. So, when Janice comes home, she told him what the plant manager had said. Elbert went to see him the next day and he hired Elbert.

The morning he reported to work, they found out, the promotion for John, had been delayed, because the job he was going to wasn't available right then, but would open up very soon. So, they said, while they were all waiting for things to happen, and we have an opening in the door to door residential route. It would be a good training for Elbert to run that route until John was promoted. Elbert said fine, so he started driving a milk truck for the next six months. Boy, was that an experience.

There was this one house that he was instructed to just walk in the kitchen door, look in the refrigerator and make sure they had orange juice, cottage cheese, milk, etc. Replace anything they were out of and leave. On two occasions, he was putting things in the refrigerator, and when he turned to leave, there stood this lady at the kitchen sink, in some kind of black lace see thru night gown, that left little to the imagination. It was, all he could do to get out of there. He had heard all kind of stories about the mail man and the milk man, and the last thing he needed was for this to pop up.

Then, there was the lady that left him a note in an empty bottle, next to the screen door. He would drive up and run over to the screen door to get the note. As he reached down to get the note, this 100 pound English bull dog would come running and he could never stop. He would slide, on the smooth floor and his face which was already flat, ugly and full of slobber, would hit that screen door, and slobber would go all over Elbert. Not to mention, scaring the bee gee bees out of him. Thank god, the door was latched. He used to worry, if the latch ever broke, that dog would eat him alive. It was like that every time he went there.

There was a big house on high ground, facing the Savannah River out on Wilmington Island. There was long winding dirt leading to it. This little old lady lived there all by herself, and she had to be in her late eighty's. At one time, she and her husband owned almost the entire island. Some mornings as he came up the little dirt driveway, he would pass her working in her garden. She would be out there with a hoe chopping weeds. She was so frail she would squat on the row, while chopping and pulling weeds. She always left him a note on the refrigerator, telling what to leave her. She was real friendly and one day, he was admiring a giant grandfather clock in her foyer. He told her, he had always wanted a grandfather clock and hoped to one day, to buy him one. She looked at him and said: "You can have that one, one day, when I am gone. He didn't think anything about it and went on his way. A few months later, as he pulled up to the house, he noticed four or five Lincolns, and Cadillac's, with New York and New Jersey tags. He knew something was up. He went in the back door and met people in the kitchen. Elbert explained he usually checked for a note on the fridge and brought her milk and orange juice, etc. One of the men said, to bring some milk and orange juice. He went to the truck and got it and when he got back with it, the man said: Their mother had passed away. He also said: She left us a note that said she wanted you to have that grandfather's clock in the Foyer and you should come back later that day to get it. Elbert told them, he couldn't take that, he appreciated it but it had to be worth a lot of money, and besides, it wouldn't fit in his house, the ceiling wasn't tall enough. That thing must have been, ten feet tall. He really appreciated it, but he couldn't. The man asked if she owed him anything and he said no, I appreciate it but that was on the house, she sure was nice to him. Elbert thanked them and left.

    On a lighter note there was this German Shepherd dog at another house in a new subdivision that had tore up three pairs of his pants. He always left a half gallon of milk at the sliding glass doors from their kitchen to the patio. They had two cars parked side by side and the dog hid underneath one of the two cars and would lay in wait on him. It was terrifying every time he went there, the dog would let him get to the door and bend over, then attack him from behind.

    So, after the last straw he told John, his boss, to cut those people off. He said, no you can't do that. Elbert said, oh yes he could. They get no more milk from him. John said, he would ride with him and show him how to handle the dog. Elbert said okay. Well, they drove up to the house, and John asked him, where is the dog? Elbert told him, he didn't have a clue. But, he thought, he was under one of those cars. John asks if he have any of that mace. Elbert explained he did once, but the dog took it away from him weeks ago, and eat it. He really didn't eat it, but he took it away from him, and it didn't even faze him. John picked up the wire basket that normally carried six quart bottles of milk. He had that in one hand and the half gallon of milk in the other. He then, started for the sliding glass doors. Just as he set the milk down, the dog charged him. The dog took the wire basket away from him and chewed on his pants leg all the way back to the truck. Elbert is dying laughing, and John is red faced and out of breath, John then said: he agreed, they don't get any more milk.

When Janice and Elbert got married, Janice wore John's wife's wedding dress. Janice was now expecting, and John asked Elbert if he wanted a boy or a girl? Elbert told him a boy. John said, no you want a girl. Elbert said, no he want a boy. John said, no you want a girl. Elbert asked why do you say that? John said: Everyday when he came home from work, his little girl jumps up from what she is doing and runs to him saying daddy's home, daddy's home. His little boy could care less.

NEW HOME

One day Janice learned of a house in Savannah, that a lady from Cobbtown owned. They were looking for someone to assume their loan with nothing down, just assume the loan. Elbert and Janice went and talked to them and agreed to do it. Everything went smooth, and they were the proud new owners of a brick home, on Sheridan Drive, in Paradise Park, in Savannah.

Well, after a couple of months, the house note increased. When Elbert asked the bank about it, they said it had to be the insurance or taxes. That happened from time to time. But, a few months later, it happened again. Elbert went down to the bank and said: I want to know why the note increased. Again, they said, it had to be insurance or taxes. He said okay, which one. Well, they didn't seem to care, and said the information was in the vault and the vault was locked until like one o'clock. He said: fine, he would be back at one o'clock. At one o'clock, he was back and the man had the papers on his desk. It was insurance that had gone up and it did twice in seven months. It had gone up because Elbert supposedly had requested more insurance. He explained that was wrong, He had not done that. He ask where was this Insurance Company and the agent? They just happen to be on the next block, so he walked around there. To make a long story short, the agent was paid on commission. He made money every time somebody bought more insurance. So, he was forging people's signatures requesting more insurance. So, this guy was fired and they lowered the insurance amount and the payment. Elbert wanted him arrested, but they had already fired him when he asked about that.

JANET LYNN ALBERSON IS BORN

Lynn, was born with fair complexion, no hair and bright blue eyes wide open. Lynn was their pride and joy and now they were a family. Janice and Elbert had looked forward to this day. They couldn't wait until they had a child to hold and cuddle. To show off with pride, to watch grow up and enjoy. They had shopped and bought things. They had many friends and family to give them things and advice. They were ready and everything went well. Elbert remembered he was at work and a customer flagged him down and told him. John Shaw met him and let him go to the hospital. His mother was staying with them at the time, so she was with Janice at the hospital. They were all so proud.

XEROX

One day at church, Elbert met Terry Renfro in Sunday school at Bull Street Baptist Church. He asked him, weren't you in the Air Force? Elbert said yes. He asked him, if he would like to go to work at Xerox? Elbert had to ask, what is Xerox? He said: A Copy machine Company. He then asked Elbert if he thought he could fix a copy machine? Elbert told him, if he could fix an airplane in the desert or Alaska either one he thought he could fix a copy machine. He set Elbert up for an interview and to be tested at a motel downtown Savannah with Stanley Heaton. And they called him shortly after that and offered him a job in Brunswick or Atlanta. Elbert agreed to move from Savannah to Brunswick Georgia. So they went down there to look for a place to live. Moore homes, was a real estate company in both Savannah and

Brunswick. The owners were an older couple and Elbert assumed they would be good trustworthy people to do business with. They found a house they liked and went to see if they would swap their house in Savannah for the one in Brunswick. The Moore's explained, they would sell their house in Savannah and they could go ahead and move to Brunswick. Elbert said no, they wouldn't move into one, until the other is sold. Elbert explained they couldn't afford for an anything to go wrong and them be stuck with two houses.

    Well, one Saturday morning Elbert heard someone outside on their front porch. He opened the door and seen a painter painting the trim on their house. Elbert ask him, have they sold their house?   And he said, yes. Monday morning Elbert went to see them and was told they could move in the house in Brunswick now they had sold the house and they needed them to move. Elbert said great. So, they moved. After several weeks, Elbert asked, when are we going to close? Oh sometime soon he was told.

    Well, to make a long story short, Elbert found out too late, they had not sold the house in Savannah, they let painters move in it for awhile and then they moved and left it empty. They had let the painters assume my loan, and then they didn't stay there. And it was foreclosed on. Nobody, not Moore homes, or the VA loan people at the bank, contacted Elbert at all. It was over and done with, before he could do anything about it. Elbert learned a good lesson, Never Trust. Get it in writing every time, no matter what. Elbert was worried his credit was ruined but later, when they moved to Florida, the VA let him assume another loan , without any problem.

    CLORETTA LEIGH ALBERSON

    Our second daughter was born, Coretta Leigh Alberson. She was born with a full head of dark hair, olive complexion, and her eyes squinted closed. We now have two beautiful daughters. Lynn has a new sister to play with. Leigh was always into things and when Lynn felt bad, Leigh was the motherly type to fuss over her. Leigh would rub her and tell her it was going to be alright. They played together and loved each other as sisters and had the best time growing up. They looked after each other and Janice. They like to dress up and play house. Janice made most of their clothes and often dressed them as twins or very close to the same. They have always been a dream come true to Elbert and Janice.

SAPELO ISLAND

Elbert's job covered all of Southeast Georgia, so he traveled all day fixing copy machines. He even had a machine on Sapelo Island. To get there required a forty five minute boat ride. The island was owned by the R J Reynolds Corporation and there was a huge main house where the caretakers maintained an office, a huge conference room, and dining room. This was a two story mansion that was kept ready for visitors to stay overnight on a moment's notice. They would call Elbert a few days in advance of any big meetings and he would check out the machine to make sure it was running good. Elbert would take the boat over there in the morning, fix the machine in fifteen minutes and eat lunch with Mr. and Mrs. Stapleton in the big house. After lunch, since the boat didn't go back to the mainland until four o'clock. In an emergency they would take Elbert back in a speed boat, but he got wet doing that. He always took his golf clubs, just in case. He would go out behind the big house to the grass landing strip and hit golf balls from one end to the other. Sometimes, he would use one of their cars that stayed on the island and explore the island. There were wild horses there, deer and turkeys. They would just stand and watch you go by. He often walked on the beach passing time. Out and away from the big house, there were several cottages that were kept available on a moment's notice, for Scientist that would fly in unannounced. They would stay in one of these cottages sometimes for weeks on end doing research or just to rest.

There were some black residents that still lived on the island. Their children used to be schooled on the island, but in later years, they rode the boat to the mainland and went to school there. Elbert was told there were people born on Sapelo Island that had never left it for any reason. They originated on that island and were still living there in1965. Elbert and his family lived in Brunswick for a year and a half, but moved to St Simons Island, for a year and liked it a lot better. There was not the odor from the Chemical and Pulpwood mills in Brunswick. It was interesting to go there. They all give him tours of their Mill, showing him how they made different things. Hercules Chemicals Company had giant piles of pine tree stumps in their yard. He asked what that was for and was told they made dynamite and women's make up and even medicine from those piles of stumps. Being on the Coast, seafood was plentiful and available everywhere.

FIRST OUTING IN NEWLY ACQUIRED BOAT

Elbert bought a boat from Carroll Oliver and it took Elbert into many adventures, he wouldn't trade anything for the world. One day, his next door neighbor asked him, when are you going to take your boat out? Elbert told him, it had been so cold lately, he hesitated to go out on the water, but if it's warm this Saturday, would he like to go out and run around in it? He said yes, that would be great. So, Saturday Elbert and his neighbor take it to the Back River landing and put it in the water. They then head down the river that runs out into the sound, then take a short cut through the marsh, and back out into the sound again. Then, over to the Lighthouse at St Simons Island, then they head back.

The boat is running great and everything is great. Elbert seen these birds up ahead and told his neighbor to watch those birds he was going to make them fly. Well, just as he got to them it became clear they were standing up not floating which meant Wham! They had just run up on a sand bar. The water is two inches deep. Now they have to get in the water and push the boat off the sand bar. So, to keep their clothes dry to put back on later they stripped down and got out of the boat to push it into deep water again. Then they climbed back in the boat and put their dry clothes on again. Now, they are moving again. They made it through the marsh again but only at the last minute because the tide is now going out. If they hadn't gone through there when they did there would not have been enough water to get through. They made it back out into the sound again and went under the Sidney Lanier Bridge and started up the river behind Back Island when all of a sudden, they ran out of gas

They coasted up onto the island and stretched out the anchor rope up on the island. Then they started walking to the other side of the island, to the side that faces downtown Brunswick. Just as they get there, they met two young boys on the island hunting rabbits. Elbert asked them if they could borrow their boat to go get some gas and they said, sure just hurry back as it was getting dark. They paddled that boat over to a dock and walked to get some gas. At a pay phone, Elbert called Janice and asked her to come get them at the Concrete Products Dock, in town. He explained they ran out of gas and now had gas, but didn't have time to get back to the boat ramp before dark, so just meet them at the dock in town.

They rowed the boat back to the island and the boys were waiting on them. They give them their boat and thanked them for letting them borrow it. Then started walking back across the island to where they left their boat, but in the dark, they couldn't find it. The boys had put the anchor in the boat and pushed it out into the water, as a prank on them. Now they are stranded. In the dark they walked back to the other side of the island again. They seen across the water, Janice pull in the parking lot, and sitting in the car. Janice and his neighbor's wife were sitting in the warm car with the heater going and the windows rolled up. They couldn't hear them yelling for them. They couldn't see them either, across the water in the dark. Elbert decided to drag up some drift wood and build a fire, not only to get warm, but to get attention across the water. They had a five gallon can of gasoline and matches. So now they have this roaring fire and they are standing in front of it waving and yelling. Thank goodness, a security guard walked over to Janice in the car, to see what they were doing there. When she rolled the car window down, Janice and the guard, heard them yelling and seen the fire. The security guard called rescue and in the dark they heard this small boat coming to get them. It was going, putt, putt, putt, poking along. Their wives gave them no sympathy and they laughed at them. I imagine they looked terrible, wet, cold, tired and embarrassed but they survived.

Elbert had this big solid red flag in the flag holder on his boat and a lot of people thought it looked terrible but the next day, he went to the top of the big bridge in Brunswick, and looked out over the water and marshes. That is when he spotted that big red flag sticking up out of the marsh. He couldn't see the boat but he could see the flag and only he knew what it was. It had drifted back into the marsh and he walked in mud to get to it. But the tide had gone out and there was no water, to float the boat. So later that afternoon, he went back again and as the tide come in he was able to get it back to the landing and get it home again. Boy, don't you wish you had been there and then you would have a story to tell. Now isn't boating fun.

MOONSHINE

One day, Elbert had a call to go to Fort Stewart, to fix a machine. He was returning back to Brunswick, coming down highway 17 when up ahead he seen a black man with an arm load of buckets and things, starting to walk into the swamp. The man heard Elbert approaching, he turned and looked his way and just stood there, until Elbert got out of sight around, around a curve. Elbert thought that was strange, so he slowed down, then turned around to go back and see, if he could tell, what he was doing. When Elbert got back to where the man was he had disappeared. Then it dawned on Elbert. He was walking into the swamp to a moon shine still.

Elbert turned around again and continued on back to Brunswick. Well, as he came into the next town, the sheriff's office was right there on his left, so he stopped and went in. When he went in, a deputy was the only one there and he ask, if he could he help him. Elbert smiled and said he might be wrong, but, he thought he knew where there was a moon shine still. The Deputy never smiled and said: "Yeah? Where is that?" Elbert then told him and he handed Elbert a piece of paper and said, draw me a map. So Elbert drew him a map. The deputy said thanks, and Elbert left. Now you have to picture this guy, he was bald with a big scar on his face. He looked like he had been in a bad wreck, or a hell of a knife fight. Elbert thought more about it after he left, that deputy didn't appreciate that. Elbert wished he hadn't, even stopped, now. Anyway, Elbert went on to his next call. This just happened to be at the courthouse, in the next county. Let's not talk about what office it was. When he arrived, the ladies in the office ask him, what took you so long? So, he was telling them about the whiskey still and about stopping at the sheriff's office in that county and telling them about it.

The boss walked up and said come into my office for a minute. Elbert said okay, and followed her into her office. She walked over behind her desk and pointed at the floor behind her desk and asked. Do you see that? Elbert peering down at a wooden coca cola crate, full of coke bottles with caps on them. She asked do you know what that is? He said cokes? Knowing full well it wasn't because it was clear as water. She said no, that's moonshine. And the man you was telling about the moonshine, belonged to him, and he was the one to give her that. They not only knew each other, but were friends. Oh shit!!!!!

So, now Elbert is staring at her with big eyes and an open mouth when she said, you need to be careful who you talk to about something like that. She and Elbert became very good friends and they never talked about that again. These small towns are another world. In Memphis, nobody knew each other. In small towns, everybody is kin to each other, or married into each other families. Either way, everybody knows who you are and being a stranger you don't know anybody to speak of. So, you learn keep your mouth shut.

THE RENTAL CAR

Elbert had been with Xerox only a few weeks, and he had a fender bender in his car. He had a new company car on order, but it had not come in yet. So, he got approval to rent a car. They said, rent a cheap one. Sounded good to him, the only problem was, there were no cheap ones available. So, they give him a brand new 1966 Chevrolet, Red Convertible. Can you see the smile on his face? Elbert said, I guess that will have to do, with a smile on his face,

He was a cool cat, riding around, with the top down, in this resort community of Brunswick, St Simons, and Jekyll island community. But one day, he got another call in Fort Stewart and there was a short cut he took from time to time, that was a dirt road for about 30 miles. So, he lit out and he was flying down this dirt road. Every now and then, there was water running from one side to the road to the other. It wasn't but an inch deep, but as he hit these wet spots, mud would fly up and over his head, and it was landing in the back seat. He had no idea, until he got to Fort Stewart and seen the mess. When he got home, it took him hours to get it clean and he couldn't reach some of the places it went, like down in the hole where the white top folded up and when down. Every time he raised the top, there would be more mud on it. He eventually turned it in and never did hear anything from them.

Elbert and Janice made a lot of friends in Brunswick. There was the German lady next door, that baby sat for them and she was so nice. There was the man Elbert rented storage space for his work at the May Flower moving company, the man at the pawn shop, where he rented some storage space also. Then there was the man they rented from on St Simons Island, the people at the courthouse, Jurrell Roberts and his wife a school chum of Janice. They played cards with them and had some really good times. One day, Elbert's boss came from Jacksonville, to see him and they had a long talk. Elbert told him he did not want to fix copy machines for the rest of my life. He wanted to be a manager. His boss said: Well, then you need to transfer to Jacksonville, Florida, where you can see and be seen. So, Elbert did. Jacksonville, here they come.

JACKSONVILLE, FLORIDA.   THE DISTRICT OFFICE.

Right off the bat, the first thing they noticed was, it was hot there in Florida. The sun is even brighter, he guessed it was because the ground is white sand and even the roads are a lighter color than in Georgia.

They found a house to rent and they started moving in. Every one of the neighbors offered to help them at one time or another. That surprised them and it was great. The neighbor directly across the street walked over one day and he asked, "Where are ya'll from," meaning, hometown.

Janice said: "Georgia."

"Oh, where in Georgia?"

"South Georgia."

"Oh, where in South Georgia? "

She finally said, "a little small town, you probably never heard of."

He asked, "where is that? "

She is getting a little peeved at this and says, "near Metter, Georgia."

"Oh, what's the name,"

"Cobbtown"

He smiled at her and said, "Is that right? I am too. "He went on to say, he was born in Cobbtown but moved to Claxton and ended up in Florida. Wow, what a coincidence. Elbert told him, he was from Memphis.

The neighbor's two doors down was from a small town near where Janice lived and they became lifelong friends with them, Joe and Sandy Ennis. Their kids were playmates and went to school together.

Being from Memphis, when Elbert went anywhere, he dressed for the occasion nothing less than slacks and penny loafers with socks and a neat madras shirt. Well, in Florida, everybody wears a ragged Tee shirt, shorts and shower clogs. You can sit in the mall and watch people walk by and one may be poor as dirt and the next guy behind him, may be a millionaire with a 100 foot yacht. But they will both be dressed the same. Clothes, don't make the man in Florida or women either, it is so hot and sticky.

Lynn started to school and quickly seemed to grow taller and smarter. It was so much fun to watch the girls run and play, to learn to read, to draw and color in their coloring books. Janice made most of their clothes and often dressed the girls in the same style, color and material. Janice was good at sewing and loved doing it. And years later, they see a lot of things Janice made for the girls in pictures.

Time was really flying by and Elbert had been promoted several times. He started traveling a lot and even when he was home, he went to work early and stayed late. He give way too much of his time to Xerox, at the sacrifice of the time with his family, and especially, his children and rightfully so, they became more and more attached to their mother Janice, than daddy.

Lynn and Leigh both grew up playing sports and gravitated to softball. They both played on the same team, "The Eagles." They were both very good. Elbert missed more of their games than he went to see them play. And he regrets that more than you know. He was too wrapped up in his job. Why in the world, didn't he see that, but he didn't. He thought he was doing what he needed to, to get promoted again and to make more money, for his family. They didn't need more money, they needed him to be there to see them play to cheer them on, to hug them and smile at them, with pride, to go get an ice cream.

Elbert will never forget the first time he went to see them play. He arrived just in time and as he was getting seated. The coach came over to him, and asked if he would umpire first base for him. Well, Elbert is in a suit and tie with wing tip shoes, polished to the hilt. He had never umpired in his life. He tried to explain that to him but he would have none of it. So, Elbert took off his coat and tie and walked onto the field.

Well, here we go. The first batter is a little short fat girl that hits the ball and here she came running to first base. The ball is thrown and she is out by a mile. However, Elbert called her out verbally and loud enough for everybody to hear him, but the sign he give with his hands was she was safe. He had the signs mixed up. He kind of laughed it off, but the kid's mother had a few comments for him. Well, a little while later here came this same kid again, that he had called out, a while ago. And he called her out again. It was close this time and the mother yelled at him to get off the field. She said he didn't know what he was doing. He wondered, how she could tell. But she was partly right. But he ignored her. Well, the game goes on and on and wouldn't you know it, here came the fat kid again.

Well, it wasn't even close. She was out and he called her out again. About that time, he heard the chain link fence, rattling and he turned to see what caused that. When he did, he seen this 350 pound woman, hanging on the fence, yelling at him "I Will Kill You." This whole scene, reminded him of a Laurel and Hardy Cartoon. He had to laugh and that made her even madder. Lynn and Leigh thought it best, if Elbert didn't come to the games for a while.

Lynn and Leigh grew up close to each other. It was great to see they loved each other so much. Lynn and Leigh both joined the Cub Scouts and later, the Girl Scouts. Both took swimming lessons and were good swimmers.

BOB AND LYNN SMALLWOOD

Bob and Elbert worked together and became friends in 1969. Bob's wife, Lynn and Janice became great friends. Their kids were about the same age and in those early marriage years, neither of them had a lot. They eat at each other's house, and they eat out together and just enjoyed our friendship. They had a lot of good times and were very sad to hear, several years after Elbert and Janice moved to Cobbtown, they separated and divorced. When Elbert heard about it, he asked Bob, are you crazy? What he was referring to was, she worked for IRS. Elbert said, don't you realize, she will audit you every year for the rest of your life.

Well, they did it. The result was, she got the Cadillac and he got the payment book. She got half of everything else including his retirement.

Lynn, later on, years later, got breast cancer and after treatments thought it was over with , but it came back and eventually got her. They had a boy Brian and a daughter Sonya that are doing fine.

In 2011, Bob came to see Elbert and Janice, and he is doing well. It was great to see bob and to think back on those wonderful years when they were having children and trying to be successful. They really had some great times and some wonderful memories. Elbert and Janice was so glad they had them as friends.

MODEL A FORD 1931

One day Elbert stopped for a red light and he noticed this Model A behind a gas station. A few weeks later, he noticed it was still there. So, he pulled in and went inside to see if he would sell it but he said no, he didn't want to sell it. So, about two months later, he seen it still sitting there and he stopped and told the man, he didn't mean to bother him, but you never know, he might have changed his mind.
He said he was glad Elbert stopped. His pick up motor just give up the ghost and he needed $600 to get it fixed. Elbert told him okay, he would be back in a little while, he had to go get the money and some help.

Well, none of his buddies could be found, but he got the money from the bank and asked Janice if she would help him and she said fine. So the kids piled in and here they went with a tow chain.

The car had no brakes and they are on the service road of

Arlington Expressway and its 5 o'clock traffic. But Elbert hooked up the chain and told her to turn off the radio and lower the window so they could talk. That he would tell her when to speed up or slow down. So here they went and she took off like a bat out of hell. Oh shit, then she runs up on the red light and hits the brakes hard and guesses what? BAMMM. The light changed and she had just hit the brakes and bam he hit her and it scared her and she hit the brakes for a moment. BAMMM, they hit again and she takes off, because he is yelling at her and waving for her to go on, they are blocking traffic.

    Well, they got home as they only lived about 6 blocks away and she says, you care more about that old car, than you do about me. The kids are looking at us like a bunch of idiots.

    Boy, now he has this $600 car under the car port out of the sun and rain, but our new car is sitting in the sun and blazing heat. Elbert agreed to push the car as far back as he can and now, she can get her car under the shelter enough to keep her out of the rain and the car from getting so hot.

    This car sits there and he got it running and they are riding around the neighborhood, isn't that cool. The only problem now is, it won't stop. To stop, you had to shut the motor off far enough away that you could coast into their driveway. He got pretty good with that until one day he found a catalog, to order brake material, that he had to brad to the metal shoe. But he did it, and it worked great.

    Then, he found an older man, Mr. Kermit Yates in Cobbtown, that was an expert on model A's to rebuild the motor. And while he was doing that, Elbert found a guy, Mr. Anderson, in Collins, Ga., to paint the car and fix the only dent in it.

    So one day, Elbert went to check on the motor and as he was walking up, yet to see inside. He heard a Model A motor running. As he rounded the edge of the doorway he saw his motor sitting on a coke crate with a coffee can for a fuel tank, running. It was just sitting there in the middle of the floor. Mr. Kermit turned and smiled and said, she sounds good don't it. Boy, he wanted his car back from the paint shop bad.

    Elbert had this car for 31 years and had the best time riding the children at church on harvest day. He drove it in many parades. And put it on display in many car shows. But, he was fixing to have it   painted and new upholstery and then build another garage to store it and with retirement what it is, he needed to draw the line somewhere, so he hauled it to Knoxville, Tennessee and sold it.

He sold it to a couple that was older than him and they called his brother and a neighbor to come over and while Elbert unloaded it, they were pooling their money to pay Elbert. He didn't know or even think about how long he had had this car. But he turned over the title and on the back was the date he titled it. And it had been thirty one years. If he had not unloaded it, he would have taken it back home with him, but he had already unloaded it, so he just let it go.

Another of the reasons for selling it was he had just built him another car, that he could travel in to car shows off in other states. Distances that you wanted to stay with traffic and maybe air conditioned.

DECISIONS, TOUGH DECISIONS

Elbert really enjoyed the job he had. But he was getting pressure to consider advancement. Advancement meant a Branch Service Manager position. He was offered the Branch Service manager's job in Jackson, Mississippi. He looked into it and turned it down. Later he was offered the Branch Service Manager's job in Columbia, South Carolina. And he turned it down.

The girls were at the point, that next year, they will have to be bussed across town, into a neighborhood school of minorities. They were really worried about that.

Then, they also wanted a newer home. They loved their neighbors, but they needed a bigger home. When they looked into it, they found out it really wasn't feasible, right then.

Then, things started coming up roses. Roy Stigilich, the Service manager in Savannah, wanted to transfer to Atlanta. This would leave an opening close to Cobbtown, Janice's home. When they told her parents what they had on their minds, they offered to give them land, across the road from them to build a house on and help physically build us a new brick house, since that is what he did for a living. The schools were good. We would have a new home bigger than what we could afford in Jacksonville. And there was a job also with the same pay. Then Roy's transfer got delayed, which meant, Elbert would have to commute 140 miles one way to work.

They decided to do it. They sold their home in Jacksonville, moved into a trailer they owned in Cobbtown, and started building their new home. At the time, they had just lost their pet dog Danny, a Dachshund he died. They had a new pet dog named, Me Me, a poodle. And wouldn't you know it he got run over by a passing farmer.

Lynn and Leigh started school in Collins, Ga. This was the school their mother, Janice, went to and there was still teachers there, that taught Janice. It was no longer the high school Janice had graduated from, but now an elementary and middle school. Lynn and Leigh both graduated from Reidsville high School.

Lynn was good in school and after high School, went to Brewton Parker College in Mt. Vernon, Ga. This was a Baptist College. She did well, but after two years, she got to the point, she wanted her independence, meaning a place of her own and privacy. And she wanted a job, a source of income of her own. So she went off into the world and lived by her on rules, standards and expectations. Things didn't always go as she wanted and it showed in her comments and visible frustrations. You couldn't tell her a lot, because she didn't want to hear other opinions. Sometimes, because she knew in her own mind, she was wrong. But, she was going to do it her way or else.

Katie was her first child and a great child was she. Then Kayla was born, another sweet granddaughter. Lynn, after a series of different jobs, finally found her place with Georgia Southern College in Statesboro, Georgia. Lynn worked there for many years. Lynn met, fell in love, and married Obey Fail, and they had the sweetest little girl named Kaki. Kaci is the youngest and presently in 2013, in the eighth grade. Kaci has taken dancing and is a natural at it. She is sweet and loves her Grandma, Poochie (Janice)

Lynn could be the sweetest thing in this world and then at times you better get out of her way. No matter what, you had to tell yourself to let it go she really loves you. And she really did. You know it from the many times, she was a joy to be around, and the tender moments, she had.

    Lynn was diagnosed with Cancer and fought it for eighteen months. She finally lost her battle and passed away in 2006, at the age of 41. Without anyone knowing, she got Christmas Cards and wrote notes to her loved ones. She got somebody to mail them at Christmas time and to this day, Elbert is so proud of her for thinking of that. He read his over and over from time to time. He sat and stared at the penmanship and remembered her adult years. He sees in his mind and pictures of her as a child and he remembers the days she ran and played, kissed and hugged him. He thinks about the days she cried and cried, with a runny nose and ear aches and he couldn't do anything to make the pain go away. He thinks about the time she was in the hospital to have her tonsils out she was in so much pain. Again, he had to leave the room, as he felt helpless and he couldn't take away her pain.

    He thinks about their last trip to the mountains. She wanted their whole family to go off and be together. She loved the mountains. They had a great time. But in the group picture, you see healthy people and one lone very ill, weak person. He remembers on the way home, their air conditioner in their car went out and she rode with her daddy home. He enjoyed it so much. She told him to turn right and turn left, as he had never been the way she wanted to go. He learned she was taking him by things, she knew he had never seen and she wanted him to see them. She always hugged me bye when she was leaving and told me she loved me. She had a habit of saying, well, we have to go and she would stand up. Elbert always would stand and walk with them to the car. But she would start talking about something and linger, and linger and linger, until Elbert couldn't stand up any more. He would tell her, ya'll be sweet, but I need to go sit down. Then he would watch as she would linger some more. It was like, she didn't want to go.

    All her children have that trait now and he sees Lynn in each of them. They hug him and tell him they love him. He miss's Lynn. Part of him is gone and all he has is memories. Yes, he also remembers the times he should have been around more. He see's now, because he has lived long enough, to see the many things he should have done differently as a daddy. He just hopes she looks down and sees that he is sorry and that he loves her.

When Leigh was born, it was late in the night, or early in the morning. He remembers there was only one other man and Elbert waiting for the birth of their child. Wouldn't you know it, the other mans child came first. That left Elbert all alone, as he waited and he couldn't stay awake, so he dozed off and on. When at last, the nurse came and got him. She said, he could go to the window and see their baby girl. So, he hurried down the hall and a nurse was waiting on him holding Leigh. She was the opposite of Lynn. Lynn had light pink skin, no hair and wide open blue eyes. Leigh was red skinned and had a head full of dark hair and her eyes were squinted close. His first reaction was this isn't my child. But the nurse said yours is the only one just born.

In a day or so, Leigh was the twin of Lynn and Lynn loved her so. Lynn would hug her and kiss her and in time they were inseparable. They became the best of friends as they grew up. And in many ways Leigh was the more mature and level headed one. They each had their own personalities and began to assert their selves in different ways, as they got in their late teens.

Leigh eventually wanted to leave the nest and move to Savannah, just like her mother did as a teenager. Thank goodness, Janice did, or Elbert would not have met her, and married her. Leigh has always had a more bubbly personality of the two. Leigh has had fun every day of her life and today can bring enjoyment to the saddest bunch of dreary people you know. She lights up a room and you just want to be in her company.

After several years in Savannah, she learned of a job in Claxton, Ga. And if she got it, she would be better off financially and be closer to home. Well, low and behold, she got it. She has prospered greatly in this new company. She has always loved sales, and she could sell and Eskimo an ice box. She looks forward in going to work every day and has done really well with this company.

One of her childhood friends died and his house later came up for sale. So, she bought it. This is her first house and she has done wonders in decorating it. She has her own taste and Elbert questions it sometimes, but later he sees her objective and it really looks great. She is a terrific cook and has an inexhaustible amount of energy. She just can go on and on until he passes out. She and her mother are best friends and he means literally. They talk daily, multiple times and one can't go anywhere without the other. He loves to see them together. They talk as fast as they can and you would think, they haven't seen each other in weeks. Then five minutes after Leigh has gone they are on the phone again. What in the world can they find to talk about so much?

Leigh has seen and heard her daddy say how much he regrets, not being the father he should and could have been in past years. But she still loves him and she shows it in so many ways. God please, don't take her away from Janice and him. She is everything to them, everything in heart, mind and soul. She is a god send. She warms and brightens their very being and he hopes he never hurts her feelings, in any way.

Leigh has never had children. But she is one of those people that should have had five. She loves children so much. She would give anything she has, to help a child be happy. She has at times seen mothers treat their children extremely harsh, like in Wall mart etc. And she will quickly go to the defense of a child in a heartbeat. You don't want her to have to discuss this with you. Elbert would suggest you wait until you get home to abuse your child. She will knock you out. And all Elbert can say is: Go for it Girl. Love you. She will let you know at times, if she don't like your driving, she will tell you to pull over and she will drive. And when she is driving, you better wear your seat belts. Elbert loves her to death, he loves his Leigh.

THE STATIONWAGON

Elbert bought a Station wagon once and it was their pride and joy. The big deal was, the girls could stretch out and sleep on our many trips to Memphis or otherwise. They made pallets and really enjoyed traveling in this car. Janice and the girls were on this dirt road one day, and they had a big bowl of eggs, her grandmother had given her, to take to Janice's mother. As they approached the clay hill on that road, it was usually slippery, she was going a little too fast and wouldn't you know it, the car slid into the ditch. It all happened in slow motion and no one was hurt in any way. But the bowl of eggs went straight into the floor on the passenger side and they all broke. Well, most of them broke. This all happened, while Elbert was at work, in Jacksonville. They had it all cleaned up and was worried to death, he would fuss about it, but he fooled them. He could see the reaction they were expecting. He thought he said the right things, because he didn't remember getting anything thrown at him.

CHAPTER 7   1969 – 1973

XEROX MEETINGS

Thinking back on some of the out of town meetings he went to. Most of these were Region meeting's with a lot of management training, new programs etc. And, most of these meetings were conducted by "Gayle Tinsley." Gayle Tinsley was the Region Service manager. Hitler comes to mind every time Elbert heard his name. He was little in statue and probably had, that little man syndrome, he wasn't sure. But he was the ultimate fear manager. He had temper tantrums and you didn't want to be on the receiving end of one.

Elbert attended a Branch Service Manager meeting in Rochester, New York one time and he seen a side of him not normally seen. They were in a large room and the tables were set up in a "U" fashion. He asked a question and was going around the room seeking answers from each manager there. When he pointed at this one fellow, Gale didn't like his answer and all of a sudden he reared back and threw a magic marker across the room and hit this guy in the chest with it. Needless to say, he didn't like the answer the man give him. You might be wondering, why Elbert is referring to him as Gayle, instead of Mr. Tinsley. Well, they were on a first name basis in Xerox all the way to the President and CEO. Well, when he seen that, he thought to himself, he better not do that to me, I will go after him, job or no job. I won't put up with that.

Several months later, Elbert checked in at a hotel in Atlanta and went to the bar to see if any of the other guys had checked in yet. It was dark when he entered the room and he paused to let his eyes adjust. Out of the darkness, a voice said, "Elbert come sit over here." As he approached the table, wouldn't you know it, Gayle Tinsley, (little Hitler) was sitting by himself. Elbert sat down and just knew, he would probably fire him right there for something. But, you know what they had one of the best conversations. Elbert got to know a different side of him and he learned he was human just like him. He just wanted everybody to do their job and do it to the best of their ability. He explained something Elbert never thought of. Elbert had learned discipline in the Air Force, but there were a lot of people that had never had any discipline. They had never had to stretch for something, go the extra mile to achieve anything. Elbert understood then, something he had heard many times. Never judge anybody until you have walked a mile in their shoes. He had a lot of responsibility and he couldn't afford to hope you did your job. He was paid, to expect you to do your job.

CHANGE IN THE WIND

Well, there was always change in the wind and we all met in Atlanta for a review of the new programs for the coming year. After listening to several speakers on the subjects they were responsible for. Here came Gayle Tinsley. Well, he explained the world would end tomorrow, if we didn't go and do just what was required of these new programs. And even more. To show and or prove to him, we were committed and understood what was expected, WE WERE EXPECTED TO BRING A BRICK OUT OF THE WALL OF THIS HOTEL TO THE MEETING TOMORROW. We were dismissed, until 8 am the next morning.

Well, some went out to eat and whatever, but those that knew Gayle Tinsley, went immediately to find a brick, me included. Around back there was a wall around some Electrical units that was there to hide the ugly appearance of them. Well, wouldn't you know it, a truck had backed into it and knocked some bricks loose. So Johnny Persall, Frank Mulkey, and Elbert got them a brick and a couple of extras in case somebody we knew needed one. Then we went out to eat somewhere. We took care of business first.

At 8 am the next morning, everybody had a brick setting on the table in front of them, except Gayle Tinsley's staff members. Yep, he told them to leave the room, and don't come back without a brick.

Well, about 9 o'clock, the Manager of the Hotel and another man came into the meeting room wanting to know what was the meaning of these people tearing up the building? Gayle introduced them to the managers and then explained why we did this and he said he would pay for any damages. The manager of the Hotel said oh I wasn't worried, you will pay for the damages or you will go to jail. He smiled and left. To this day, they don't know if all that was a set up or not. But he never asked for a brick again.

SNOWED in at DULLES AIR PORT IN CHICAGO

Trying to get back home, from a meeting in New York, Elbert got snowed in at Dulles. There was about ten of the managers from the south and they all knew each other. Some were from Miami, Tampa, Jacksonville, Birmingham, etc. Somebody decided to pull up some seating around a table and play poker. Somebody produced the cards and everybody started digging for their change. They had been playing for about an hour, nickel, dime, quarter limit, when somebody said let's raise the limit to a dollar, five dollars. Well, the ante got raised and now there was several hundred dollars in the pot. The change disappeared, and now the green stuff, is laying out there, for everybody to see. Every now and then, Elbert looked up and different people were watching them play cards. Then, yep, here came the law. He looked up and there he stood. Elbert thought oh shit we are going to jail sure as the world. Now, that normally is the time to run but where are you going to go, they were snowed in. The officer wasn't saying anything and it dawned on Elbert he couldn't take us down town they were snowed in. Elbert looked up again, and he smiled and said, don't worry about me, just don't try this when we aren't snowed in.

L-1011 DELTA FLIGHTS

All the Branch Operations Managers had to fly to Dallas once a month for Region meetings. So, they all made their flight arrangements to meet in Atlanta, and fly an L-1011, that way they could reserve the upstairs all to themselves. It took six to reserve the upstairs and they got their own stewardess. They had the best time on these flights. The stewardess even kissed them as they were leaving. Well, everybody, but Elbert. Elbert noticed her name, on her name tag, and it was Bible, but he will never tell.

LAKE GENEVA, WISCONSIN

It was summer time and not cold at all. The place was a resort, right on the lake. They had big bowls of popcorn in the lobby and they were welcome to take it out to the lake and sit in lawn chairs and just enjoy the lake. There was also ducks, walking around everywhere, along the edge of the lake, and they would come right up to you, if you tossed them popcorn. Well, one day, one of the guys, got the idea, to pour beer all over the popcorn. Yep, you guessed it. It was hilarious. These ducks got drunk and would keep coming back for more and then run off and fall over. We probably could have been arrested.

The next morning, Elbert was reading the local newspaper and an ad caught his eye. It said If the owner of said property didn't cut the weeds, consisting of rag weed, and, MARIJUANA, by a certain date, the city would do it at his expense. Elbert went to the desk and asked the man behind the counter about it and he said, it was a wild weed that grew everywhere up there. It had no bad properties in it. Like the one that was smoked.

So, with that bit of news, let's go play golf. Now, this was an experience that was out of this world. They teed off, and the first hole was 200 yards out in front of alright, but it was down the hill about a thousand feet. Then the next hole was way up there near a ski lift about 1500 feet up and only 200 yards away, out in front of them. The wind was blowing so hard them had to take their hats off, because they couldn't keep them on their heads. So after three holes, they decided to go play poker, until it was time to eat again. The first playboy Club was built in Lake Geneva and they went by it but no one in our group was a member, so that left us out.

RODCHESTER, NEW YORK

Elbert attended a week long Management Development Meeting and the first morning, as they all sit around a conference table. They had to stand up and give their name and title and where they were from. Well, when it came to Elbert, and he said Savannah, Georgia. Elbert noticed this one guy, from New York City, seemed to think it was funny. So, Elbert ask him. Did he say something funny? He said: Grits, do you eat grits? Elbert told him yes and from that moment on, he referred to Elbert as grits. It was grits this and grits that, for a week. Elbert let it slide and didn't say a whole lot about it.

Then one day, they were discussing affirmative action, and he said: Hey grits, I'll bet you have a hard time hiring a black person. Elbert said no, I have nine black people out of 31 and I hired the first female black technician in the corporation. And the person I left in charge while I am in this meeting, is a black person. He didn't have anything else to say then.

Then, on their last night there, they all went out to eat together at a Steak and Ale Restaurant. Elbert went to the rest room and used the urinal. He then, started for the door, when he heard this Yankee from New York say: "Hey Grits, up north, we wash our hands after using the rest room." Elbert turned to him and said: "DOWN SOUTH, WE DON'T PEE ON OUR HANDS." Elbert then turned and walked out. Before the door shut behind him, He heard clapping from the other people in the place.

DODGERS, WINTER TRAINING CAMP, FT LAUDERDALE, FLORIDA

There was a big meeting down there and at night, there wasn't much to do, so they played a lot of poker. One night, they had been playing for hours and they set a limit of one in the morning to quit and get some sleep. Just as they were getting up from the table Bobby Smallwood came walking in, in his pajamas. They ask him, what was he doing up running around in his pajamas? He said: his roommate was snoring so bad, the lamp shade was vibrating, and he couldn't sleep. He was looking for a couch or somewhere else to sleep. He carried on and on and told them to follow him and listen to this guy.

So, they all walked across the parking lot, seven of them, to Bobby's cabin. They opened the door and walked in right up to the bed within inches of this guy sleeping and snoring. You should have heard it. This guy snored the loudest, they had ever heard. And the sound vibrated the lamp shade violently. This was unreal. They didn't know where Bobby slept that night, but Bobby got his own room, the next day.

Twenty seven years, as a manager, and going to meetings out of town, left many memories, and he could go on and on, but he better quit with these comments. It's good to be home in my own bed now.

THE BOSS WANTS TO GO FISHING IN MY NEW COMPANY CAR

Elbert's boss, Russ Schneider says, let's go fishing Saturday. Elbert said great, let's go. Elbert went and picked up Bob Viets and then went to pick up Russ Schneider. As they were standing in his front yard his neighbor walked over and Elbert learned, she knew Janice, Elbert's wife from Cobbtown. They both were from Cobbtown, in Georgia. Helen Calloway was her name and they were friends for years, before she passed away.

Now, Elbert had just got a new company car, a 1968 Ford. And Russ wants to put the boat in the St. Johns River on Hecksher Blvd. Elbert explained , it's too shallow, to launch my boat, let's put in at Mayport. No, it had to be Russ's way. So they drove all the way around to get on the other side of the river. He may not be right, but he is the boss. Elbert learned that a long time ago. You can argue about it, and do it, or you can, just go ahead and do it.

So they get there, and Russ is guiding Elbert back into the river, to unload the boat. He keeps saying come on back, come on back. Elbert looked to his left and seen water, he looked in front of him, and there is twenty feet of water in front of him. Russ says, okay you can pull out now, so he did. When he got out, he noticed the water line on the car, and said: I bet you, there is water in the trunk.   He raised the trunk lid and there is $4000 dollars worth of electronic parts floating in salt water which means, they are ruined.

Elbert looked for a drain hole, and there is none. So, he took a screwdriver and a hammer to punch a hole for the water to drain out, while they are fishing. Now, that is done, they pile in the boat and push off into the river. The current is strong today and is pushing them down river and the motor won't start. No battery.

There is a long pier sticking out into the river and it looks like they are going to drift down to it, which is good. Then, they can walk back to the car and get the battery. Elbert climbed up on the pier and walked all the way back to the car, got the battery, and walked all the way back, to the boat. He hooked up the battery and cranked the motor, and they head out into the river. All of a sudden, his boss says, he need bait, can you pull up over there, to the Mayport boat ramp, for a minute. Elbert could have killed him. That is where he wanted to put the boat in, in the first place, and they wouldn't have had all these problems, if he would shut up, and listen. But, again, he is the boss.

As Elbert turned the boat to head that way, the boat motor is turned about 30 degrees and the steering cable breaks. Now, they are approaching the middle of the river and he can't steer it. They look up, and see a huge ship bearing down on them and he is going out on the outgoing tide at a pretty good clip. Then he blows his horn at them sitting directly in his path. If they don't move pretty soon, he will run right over them.

Bob Viets, got on one side of the motor and pushes with his legs, on the motor, to turn it and Russ gets on the other side and pushes with his legs and between the two of them they steered them out of the way of the ship.

So, Elbert fixed the steering cable and now they have been on the river, a good hour and a half or more, and this isn't fun. It's funny now, but then, it called for a cold beer, maybe two. They got Russ some bait, and Elbert got the steering cables fixed and off they go again. They didn't catch anything that day but Elbert remembered getting a performance appraisal that said, he needed to take better care of company property. (Meaning his car) He showed his true colors that day.

THE BOSS WANTS TO GO FISHING AGAIN

Elbert's boss wanted to go fishing. He wanted to fish the Inter coastal waterway as it goes through St Augustine, Florida. Elbert told him he still didn't have his car tag. And if the law catches him they will give him a ticket. He said no sweat, with the boat behind the car nobody can see if you have a tag or not.

Elbert told him, he can't afford to get a ticket and Russ said, if you get a ticket, he would pay for it. So here they go and they fished all day and had a good time. Now they loaded up and head for home. Yep, wouldn't you know it, the Florida State patrol, pull him over and got this big expensive ticket.   Now, Russ starts with just put it on your expense report a little at a time and call it parking expense.

VISITORS FROM ENGLAND

Across the street from Elbert and Janice was another neighbor, Gene usher. Gene's sister, Peggy and Jerry, lived directly across from him. Gene's wife, Lynn, was born and raised in Peterborough, England and had the cutest English accent. They met and fell in love, when Gene was in service, overseas. We got to be good friends. He used to be an FBI agent, but retired now. If you had ever seen him somewhere, you wouldn't have guessed in a million years, what he did for a living.

One day, Elbert learned Lynn's parents were here in Jacksonville, visiting and would be here for a month. Every day, when Elbert came home from work, her father would be sitting in the front yard, in a lawn chair with a large, ice tea glass. Elbert thought it was tea he was drinking. But, he learned later, it was bourbon. Elbert walked over there one day and met her parents. He was so nice and wanted to know what Elbert did for a living. He told him and invited him to ride with him one day, to see what he did. Elbert enjoyed hearing all about England. He said he had a little car it was an English Ford nothing like the big cars in America. Elbert asked him about their home and he explained in England, you put your name on the waiting list and when they call you, you build on to the end of a row of houses. When you are through somebody adds on to your house, then another and another.

Elbert had to go to St Augustine, to an aircraft plant to fix a machine, and he rode with Elbert. Everything excited him. He was fascinated that we have street lights even out on the highways. We have sidewalks, and curbs, and gutters. He would look and point and say look at that. What is that? Things we take for granted.

BOATING AT NIGHT DOWNTOWN JACKSONVILLE, FLORIDA

Elbert lived in Arlington, in Jacksonville for nine years. The St Johns River wasn't but a few blocks from their house. He kept his boat ready to go on a moment's notice, to go fishing, skiing, or just riding around. His aunt bertha came from Memphis to visit and she had seen the lights from the bridges of Jacksonville shining with their reflections from the water at night and said that must be pretty from the water. Elbert had never thought of that so he asked her would she like to go out in the boat and see the lights? And she said oh yes let's do that, can we? He said sure. So, he got the boat and they went to the boat ramp about four blocks away, and here they go.

Everything is going great and the sights were beautiful, all of a sudden the steering cable broke. The steering wheel was useless. Nothing to do now but fix it, number one thing to do, is keep Bertha calm. You see she had polio when she was about 14 years old. And she wore this heavy steel brace on one leg. Elbert quickly found his flashlight and tied the cables back together and they were good to go. There was only one more problem, now. He had wrapped the cables backwards and now when you turned the steering wheel to the right, the boat turned left. So he had to quickly learn to steer the boat the new way until he could fix it correctly. They got back to the dock without further ado, and everybody has another story to tell about Elbert's boat.

SURF FISHING

Elbert's boss was an avid fishermen and he fished with several of the guys that he worked with. One Saturday, as a group, they decide to go surf fishing down the coast, for whiting and one of the guys, knew of a great place to fish in the surf. Since he knew about that, he also knew about the bait and beer joint, that was on the way. So, they stopped and that is when it started with the beer. Well, they shot pool, had a few drinks, bought stuff for sandwiches and headed for the fishing spot. Now, Elbert is in the back seat, with a jar of Mayo between his knees and the mustard in his crotch, the bread being squashed between three of them in the back seat of a brand new Ford LTD. The guy driving was up from Orlando and he had the car about a week. Elbert fixed the driver the sandwich he wanted and went to hand it to him. Did I mention he is driving? He turned to reach for it and was trying to tell something to one of the other guys in the back seat and all of a sudden, they left highway US 1 and went flying into the sand dunes, running a good 60 miles an hour. Now, they come to a stop and everything is fine. No problem, everybody is fine and the car is fine too. But they are now 50 feet, off the road in powdery sand at least a foot deep and headed the wrong way.

So, they sit there drinking beer and eating their sandwiches. When they finished that, they got out. People are going by and laughing, some are waving and they wave back. But nobody stops to help. "Ain't Life Grand." Well, they pushed and pushed and managed to get it turned around, headed the right way, but that is all.

WELL GUESS WHAT? A state patrolman stops and from a distance he asked (fifty feet away, I might add). You need any help? He wanted to call them a wrecker. They said no but thanks they were okay and they will be out shortly. So the patrolman leaves. Thank God!!! Well two hours later, here the Patrolman comes again, with the same offer. And again they said no thanks. Well, two more hours go by and here the Patrolman comes again with a wrecker. The state patrolman left again. The wrecker guy pulls them out and wants thirty dollars for pulling them out. They didn't have thirty dollars between them. So, they ride in the car, and follow him back to the station. They talk the owner of the station, into holding their brand new spare tire, until they can bring him the money. Are you laughing yet?

So, they call it a day as it is dark now and they haven't wet a line as yet. So they all go home with a new story to laugh about and they are sun burnt to a crisp. Don't you just envy the manly life?

COOKING OUT WITH JOE AND SANDY ENNIS

Joe and Sandy came from next door and suggested they grill out together that afternoon. Janice and Elbert said great let's do it. The kids can play and they can just relax and enjoy the afternoon.

There was a meat Market just a few blocks away, so Joe and Elbert went to get the meat. They got this idea to buy one big monster steak and grill that one piece of meat. Elbert said, it sounded good to him, let's do it. So, they got the coals just right in the grill and put this monster piece of meat on to cook. This meat is the same size as the grill, and they could just barely close the lid.

Elbert had pulled his boat trailer into the front yard and he is working on the wiring of the lights. Joe is watching the grill. Then Joe got a long distance phone call and he went to the phone. Joe thought Elbert was watching the grill, and Elbert thought Joe was watching the grill. Both of them were deep in thought in what they were doing and every time Elbert looked up, Joe was checking on the meat.

Well, when Joe got off the phone, he heads for Elbert's house and he sees this giant plume of black smoke coming from the grill. Elbert looked up to see, Joe running up to the grill and smoke is rolling. When he picked up the lid to look at the meat, it was black as smut and that monster steak as big as the grill, is now the size of a hamburger. It wasn't funny. This was those early marriage years and money wasn't plentiful. The only thing to do was, go get more meat. Joe and Elbert got in the car and Joe said, stop at Jax Liquors I think we need a beer. And they started laughing. They got more meat and they both sit in a chair and stared at it until it was done. Those early married life years didn't mean you could burn expensive meat up on a grill.

COLLEGE

Elbert had thought about college but he had to be honest. His interest was only in the light of the GI benefits from being in the Air Force. One day, he learned that Xerox would pay him to go to college at night. He thought that was great to know. In talking to some other guys he worked with they all had recently gotten out of the Navy or the Air Force and as a veteran, the government would pay for them to go to college at night. So, Elbert with that recent interest and knowledge was seriously considering going to college at night.

Then he got word of a Class Reunion coming up in Memphis. So, with his family, they headed for Memphis. After the reunion, they went to Corky Ireland's house. He had this beautiful new house, and a Baby Grand Piano, and he began to play the piano. Elbert was amazed that he could play so many different songs without the music. Elbert paid for piano lessons for his children for eight years. And to this day neither can play a note without the music in front of them. One day, Elbert walked by the piano in his house and his daughter was playing something. He casually asked her, to get down on the Boogie Woogie and she looked at him like he was crazy. He asked her, why are you looking at me like that? She said, she had to have the music. He was shocked.

Anyway he asked Corky, how do you play everything and anything that people ask for? He smiled and said, he had paid his way through college playing in bars at night and mostly for tips you learn pretty quick when it is to your advantage.

Elbert remembered what he said and when he got home, he registered at Jones College in Jacksonville, Florida. He also registered with his corporate office and as long as he made A and B's Xerox paid his quarterly charges. The school took care of the veterans benefits, and he got a check quarterly from the government also. I think some might call it double dipping. I call it smart and good management. He had two people paying him to go to college and he was clearing $181.00 a quarter. A pretty good deal I would say and pretty smart to take advantage of that. He would have been pretty dumb, if he didn't.

Elbert finished after four and a half years of going from 5:45 pm to 10:15 pm three nights a week, with a BS Degree in management. He got a nice raise and promotion out of that also. And he says thank you to Corky Ireland for his words of inspiration. Corky ever knew what he told Elbert that night or how it inspired him to go home and go back to school.

HUMPHREY'S GOLD MINE

All over Jacksonville, Florida where Elbert and his family lived for nine years as you entered any neighborhood. You would see at each house a family car, a boat, and a Beach Buggy. The boat varies, sometimes it is a fishing boat, or a ski boat, or a sail boat, or a sure enough big cabin cruiser. Now, if there is a Beach Buggy, it more than likely was, a souped up volkswagon, without its body or a homemade beach buggy.

Elbert's boat was a combo ski, dive and fishing boat, used regularly for four years of fishing and four years of scuba diving. His Beach Buggy was a 1950 Plymouth frame shortened five feet and had a shorter wheel base than a volkswagon. This thing had two seats and a small bed to haul a cooler with food and drinks. And the wheels were 11 inches wide with 15 inch tires.

Behind the Mall, there were sand dunes called Humphreys Gold Mine. It was just like the desert, with giant hills. It was a few miles long and a few miles wide. There was places, they would get a running start and climb a sand mound two stories high. Sometimes, they made it, and sometimes, they didn't. When they didn't, they were in for a twenty foot backwards ride, down the mound. Because they rolled backwards, as fast, as they went up, trying to climb it. And that is if, they were lucky. If they were not lucky, they flipped upside down and rolled sideways down the hill, they were trying to climb.

Then sometimes, the hill might be shorter and when they hit the top they went flying through space because the other side of the hill went down just like the other side. Sometimes, they thought it would be flat up there, then when they got there, they learned it was straight down all the way.

Elbert eventually took it to Cobbtown and used it as a hunting buggy for years until the motor blew up, and now it sits in the woods as a reminder of days gone by, the good old days when he was younger and somewhat crazy.

If his mother only knew, the half of it she always said he would never live to be 20 years old.

ORAL SURGERY

One day, Janice, his wife had a tooth that was killing her. So he asked around at work if anyone knew of a good dentist that they would recommend. He learned of one, on Riverside Drive, that was good and they made an appointment. So here they go to the dentist, Elbert, Janice and two little girls, Lynn and Leigh. They got there and they take Janice right away. They told Elbert, that it will be at least two hours so he might want to take the children to a park or something. It was pretty and warm outside, so they go walking. And all is going great for him and the girls. They even stop and get an ice cream cone. So, at the appointed time, they went back and checked in, the nurse told him, she is ready, for him to pull around back to pick her up? Now he is thinking, why was he pulling around back? As he came around the corner of the building, he sees two nurses leading and helping his half asleep wife, down a ramp to the car. He got out and went around and opened the passenger door and he got a good look at Janice. She has gauze hanging out of both sides of her mouth and she is barely conscious. She got seated and the door is shut, so off they went, headed for home.

She is sick to her stomach as they had put her to sleep with gas. And cut out four wisdom teeth.   He had no idea what they were in for. He thought she would get one tooth pulled and everything would be okay. He got her home and in the house and to the bedroom, as she can hardly stay awake. So he and the girls eat some lunch and the girls went into the back yard to play. After an hour or so, Janice came into the den and said, for him go on back to work, she and the girls would be okay. So, he called in and they were really getting backed up, so he said, he would go take one call, and be right back. He was gone a couple of hours and when he returned and walked into the house. Janice was asleep on the couch, right where he had left her and the girls were in the den sitting in the floor quietly making mud pies. You should have seen the mess.

Janice woke up and said, why did you let them do that? She didn't remember telling him to go on back to work. And he shouldn't have listened to her. What was he going to say? She was right.

SCHOOL BUSES

The lady across the street had 2 or 3 school buses that she contracted to the board of Education. She drove one and her husband drove one, and she asked Janice if she would drive one for her. Janice started out being her substitute until both of their girls were in school.

Then, she was home alone all day and really wished she had something else to do and to make a little extra money. She ended up really enjoying it.

DISNEY WORLD OF ORLANDO

When they moved to Jacksonville, Florida one of the first things that came to mind was Disney World. The kids were at the right age to enjoy it so they went a couple of times and would tell their families back in Memphis, Tennessee and Cobbtown , Georgia about their trips. And they invited them all, to come see them as they had plenty of room and would love to have them visit.

Well, they had lots of visitors and they ended up taking everyone to Disney World. It was fun to see the smiling faces and to have been the ones they enjoyed it with. Today at their age they show them the way to get there and wave to them. They tell them to have a good time but it is too much for their bad knees.

They have really had some great times and seen exciting things. They wouldn't take anything for the happy faces on the children. Walt Disney has brought happiness to almost six generations. Can you imagine how many people have been there.

BIG MAMMA AND BERTHA

One summer, they come to visit and stayed a week or so in Jacksonville, Florida. During their stay, both wanted to go to the Beach and to swim in the ocean. Now Big Mamma, his grandmother on his father's side, is about five feet tall and in her 70's, but she waddles down to the water's edge and eases into the water letting the wave's splash against her. After a while he heard her laughing out loud and yelling weeee. She is now out almost shoulder deep and the waves are breaking over her head. The waves are almost knocking her down and she is having the time of her life.

The kids are playing and having fun. They had a couple of those lawn chairs that are made for the beach. They sit you down low close to the sand. Bertha wanted to get into the water so bad, she asked if Elbert would carry her out there and sit her down in one of those chairs so the water would come up around her legs? He said sure and took a chair and got it situated in the water. Then went and carried her to the chair.

After a while she squirmed out of the chair and was just sitting in the edge of the waves. The waves would come rushing in and her bad leg would go where ever the water wanted it to go. And she just laughed saying look at my leg. Bertha had polio when she was 14 and has worn a brace on her bad leg ever since. Since she couldn't get the brace wet we had left it in the car.

When we got home everybody had to have a bath to get the salt water out of their hair and the sand out of their pants. Janice helped Bertha take a bath and she came out of the bathroom laughing saying Bertha must have had a pound of sand in her bathing suit. That was one of the times, they really had something to talk about, when they went home.

Years ago, back in Memphis when Elbert was a little boy, they went to Big Mamma's house a lot. Big Mamma, liked Watermelons and every summer they got one and she would cut it in half and kept it in the refrigerator. They would come in from playing outside and she would give us cold watermelon.

Elbert and his brothers could crawl under her house and one day, he and his brothers crawled under there, to see what they could find. Eggs, they found eggs. Big Mamma heard them under the house and came calling them, to get out from under there.
They showed her the eggs and she said they were rotten, do not break any of them or they will stink. Yep, they had to break one just to see if they stink. They threw them in the ditch and did they stink!

Back in Jacksonville, before they went back home to Memphis they wanted to go to Cobbtown and visit with Janice's family. They had a big mobile home there, on her father's farm that they stayed in, when they visited so they went to Cobbtown that week end. Her daddy picked tobacco that week end, so they got to see how that was done. And they got to ride the tobacco picker. They even let Big Mamma, drive it. This tickled her to death.

Bertha, not to be out done wanted to drive the tractor. Bertha had not experienced a lot of things, like that. Having polio and wearing a brace on her leg had prevented those kinds of things. So, Elbert put her on it and got behind her and off they went across a field then down a dirt road and back across the field and back to the house. She laughed and giggled and chuckled all the way. You should have seen the smile on her face. She had the best time.

Just as soon as she could she got on the phone and called several of her friends back in Memphis to tell them she had driven a tractor. Not ride one, but drove it.

Big Mamma and Bertha liked to come see Elbert and Janice as they let them do so many things they had always wanted to do.

VASECTOMY, MY FRIEND RON

Our neighbor, Ron Callahan, and his wife Linda were good friends ours and still are, 45 years later. Well, Ron mentioned one day he was going to have a vasectomy. Elbert just happened to be home that day when he came home from surgery. Elbert seen him hobble into the house and he joked to Janice about it and he seen Linda drive off. That meant Ron was home alone. Elbert decided to play a prank on him so he gave Ron time to get nested and he called him on the phone. It rang and rang and rang and all of a sudden this weak sad voice said: hello. No telling how far he had to walk to get to the phone.

When he answered, Elbert said: Hey Ron he didn't really have anything important but since you have nothing to do maybe you could just stand there for the next hour while told him about this girl he knew. YOU DON'T WANT TO KNOW WHAT HE SAID TO Elbert. He swore vengeance on Elbert.

VASECTOMY

Well, Elbert decided to have one too. So it's all set for Friday, at five o'clock in the doctor's office. Elbert got there and there are no patients and the nurse came out to the waiting room to get him. She took him to this room and said strip from the waist down and the doctor will be here shortly. So he was sitting on the table with a sheet over him and freezing. Now here came the doctor and nurse. They left the door open and Elbert can see all the way into the waiting room and there is a lady in there running a vacuum and if she looks in his direction she will get an eye full.

The nurse says to lie back and she steals his sheet. Now everything is staring at everybody present. The doc tells him he will feel a pinch and did. The doc tells the nurse something because she gets this piece of tape to tape things out of the way. Well she didn't need much tape.

About that time one of the other nurses sticks her head in the door and says good night, I am gone. Okay have a good weekend, they answer. Then, another nurse sticks her head in and then another. Elbert was about to tell the nurse to go outside and see if there was anybody else that wanted to see what they were doing, but he didn't.

He felt the doc pull on something and Elbert raised his head to see what the Doc was doing and the nurse asked did you feel that? Elbert almost lost it, he said yeah real serious like, he told her when he pulls on that down there my head keeps coming up. She almost believed him. The doctor looked up smiling and looked at her.

Elbert then told her he hoped the doc wasn't going to do him like he done hogs. She looked at Elbert and said: Hogs? Elbert said yeah, we cut the male hogs sometime before they get to be 70 or 80 pounds, so they will get real big and heavy before market. Now the doctor is listening and knows what Elbert is talking about and he is smiling.

The nurse looks at the doctor and asked what is he talking about? And he said to Elbert, to tell her. So he told her they slit the sack and squeeze the gonad out and cut if off and throw it in the dirt and the other hogs eat it. Elbert thought she would croak. She had been holding the tape down and out of the way but her hands went up to her face and she said: Oh, you have got to be kidding me.

After a few minutes, the doc said: all finished you can go but we will need a semen sample later to make sure all is not working anymore.

Elbert left and headed across the Mathews Bridge to get home as usual. As he approached the toll booth it dawned on him, he didn't have a cent to his name. He went through ash trays and everything but no quarter. He gave the lady his business card and told her, he just had an operation and before he could finish she said, right you look like you just got up from an operation. She was just being funny, and Elbert couldn't help it, he laughed too. She then said: you can make a u turn and go back like he had come. And bring a quarter the next time. So, he did what she said, and went the long way home. A week later Elbert took a sample of semen put it in a jar in the refrigerator and dropped it off at the doctor's office the next morning. The nurse felt the cold jar and asked, who told you to put it in the refrigerator? If there were any live sperm it is dead now, laughing.

But, guess who called Elbert ten minutes, after he got home. When Elbert answered the phone, Ron said: In between laughing, he said: It's payback time!

BROKE ANKLE

Sometime in 1970, Elbert had been painting his house and was almost finished. All he liked was the ceiling of the front porch and he would be through. If he could just get that done then next Saturday he would be free to fish or go scuba diving. So it is Sunday morning and he decided that while Janice and the kids are at Sunday school and church, he could get that painting done and he would be all through.

So after they were gone he got a tall bar stool. He then poured some paint into a roller pan and rolled the majority of the ceiling. Then all he had left was to do the brush work. He had the radio on and turned up loud playing some 50's music. He was painting away and having a big time and just a little more and he would be through. Well, the music was great and he was singing and dancing on top of that bar stool with the roller pan in one hand and a brush in the other.

He didn't know it but the bar stool legs were uneven. He was rocking and didn't think anything about it but the stool was walking towards the steps of the porch. All of a sudden he is falling through the air and he tried to stick out his left leg to catch his fall when he heard a loud pop and he is laying there with paint all over him, the porch and the steps. He tried to get up but pain shot all over him and his ankle. He looked at it and it looked like Dagwood. There was as much space behind his leg as there was in front. It was dislocated for sure.

He looked around but there was nobody in sight, nothing to do now but yell and holler. None of his neighbors heard him. A man on the next street over heard him and came around to see what was going on. Then here came his next door neighbor. He's funny. He says to Elbert you want a beer? To him if you just had a beer that will make everything right, Elbert said yes though and he sent his daughter to get him a beer. When she returned, the feeling was starting to really hurt now. The pain is so great he became sick to his stomach and the smell of that beer made him say take it away I don't want it. Someone else asked Elbert, do you want some water? He said yes and that was better. Someone called an ambulance and here they came, lights flashing and siren going.

They wrapped his leg and put it in splints and put him in the ambulance and away they go. At the hospital, they put him in this little room on a bed and he is lying there watching what is going on in the main room. He could see a wall phone and several people went to use it. But, everyone that used it got paint on them from where the ambulance people had got it on the phone. They all would look for something to wipe their hands. Their neighbor went to Church and got Janice. Now, here she comes and looks down at me and says. If you had gone to church, none of this would have happened. Again, she was right. Why is it, they are always right?

They put him to sleep and put everything back where it was suppose to be, and said, come back in a week and if anything has moved we will have to operate on it He is feeling sorry for himself until he seen the guy in the other bed that is all broke up and they can't fix his broke leg, until other things are better.

Well, a week later, they x-ray it and now, they want to operate on it. Elbert ends up with a big three inch screw holding on one of the knots on the side of his ankle. Now, he has a different roommate, a young boy and every day the girls from school come to see him and he raises the sheet to show them something.

Well, one day he turned over on his side and the sheet is pulled up and he is showing him his backside. And the stump where he has had one leg removed. Elbert motioned for a nurse and she covered him up as he was asleep. Elbert no longer felt sorry for himself. Later that day, here came another group of girls and he is over there showing himself to them and having a ball. He kept a grin on his face the whole time they were there.

NASSAU, BAHAMAS

Janice and Elbert won a trip to the Bahamas for a week and they flew there. As they were flying in to Nassau the water below is a beautiful blue and so clear. They land and get checked into the hotel and have a restful day of sightseeing. That night there was a banquet and a short business meeting. Xerox, had to get the tax write off. The next morning, they had a short business meeting for the men and the ladies went to a fashion show.

They got out earlier than the women so they are standing around waiting as usual on women. One of the men spotted the hallway leading to the Casino. So they wandered down there and wow. It is huge and has everything you see in the movies. This was a first for Elbert and he stopped at a slot machine and started putting in quarters from his pocket. Wouldn't you know it the machine went wild and gave him a double hand full of quarters back with bells ringing and lights flashing.

Elbert noticed in between each slot machine was a stack of cups and they were for him to put his winnings in. He picked up one and filled it up. Within a few minutes he had another cup full of quarters. About that time someone yelled the ladies are coming out so they wandered back to meet them. As Janice walked up she asked, where did you get those? Meaning these large plastic cups Elbert was holding one in each hand. He told her they walked into the casino while waiting for her and he started playing this slot machine and this is what he won.

Now you have to know something, Janice Elbert's wife, is a diehard Baptist and you don't gamble. Never, except when you win a trip to the Bahamas. And as long as momma, daddy and the preacher was home in Georgia.

She says show me and he gladly led the way. Now the fever has hit him and he is worrying, has somebody got his machine? He quickly led the way, because he quite frankly thought she would fuss at him for playing the slot machines. And now, she wants to know where that machine is.

He found the machine that he had been playing and was paying off and Janice asked how does she do this? He showed her the more coins you put in means you win more than if you play one coin. So now, she is putting four quarters in at a time and the machine is dumping coins out like crazy. Pretty soon they now have five cups full of coins. A cup held forty dollars. Five times that means they are rich.

Then she reaches for one of the cups, Elbert is holding one in each hand and one in the crook of his left arm. This is good, listen to what happens next. Elbert said to her, do you know what day it is? She thinks a minute and says Sunday. He asked her do you know what time it is? She looked at him and said, I might add, while pulling the handle to spin the wheels, she says ten o'clock.
And if we were at home right now, where would you be? He told her to get her own cup.

He told her, let's not push our luck, let's take our winnings to the room and count it later. Let's go shopping and sightseeing for now and they did. They worked out a routine that worked great for them. They would start with $20 and if they filled a cup they stopped and went shopping. If they lost their $20, they quit and went shopping. Every time they won money they took it back to the room and put it in a basket with a lid. They wanted to take it home and let the kids count it. But the basket wouldn't hold all the quarters and it was heavy so they cashed the quarters in. They brought home $270 in winnings. This was a fun filled week and they really enjoyed it.

MALAGA, SPAIN AND MOROCCO, NORTH AFRICA

Elbert won another trip this one was to Spain for a week and this was nice, in it's own way. But they like to have starved to death. First of all every meal was served in courses. What that meant was, they would be at the table for the next two hours. There was no speeding them up. At each place serving there was the round ball of bread and butter. Now this ball of bread was hard enough to break out windows. Inside of it was soft and very good and the butter was good also. In front of the plate, were two bottles of wine a red and a white, if you wanted more they would bring you more.

The first meal they eat, not being a wine drinker Elbert sipped maybe a small wine glass full of the white wine. The more he drank the better it tasted. So after a week of these two hour sit down and wait for something to eat meals that was half raw, he was drinking a whole bottle of wine at every meal. Nothing, they ate was cooked well done.

Everything appeared to be seared or warmed up but after a few days they were getting hungry for a hamburger.

The first morning they were there they went for breakfast it was fine no big deal except for coffee. Elbert among others, asked for coffee and the waiter looked at him like what? Elbert said coffee, black, No cream. So, the waiter left and came back with milk in a coffee cup. No, no, said Elbert, coffee, in a cup. The waiter left again and came back with hot milk, in a cup. Now, everybody is watching now and smiling at what is going on. Elbert told him no he wanted coffee, not milk. No milk. Elbert said, Agua, hot, in a cup. Well, he brought hot water, in a cup and Elbert give up. That is where Elbert started drinking wine for breakfast, no longer a glass or two, but a bottle at each meal.

After a few days, they signed up for a side trip, to Morocco, in North Africa. They rode a tour bus to the airport and right up to this plane. They got on this plane that was built in 1947, mind you. It is a, C-47, commonly referred to as a "GOONEY BIRD," in the Air Force, and flew to Morocco.

When they got there and got off this, old, loud, rattle trap, of a plane. They ride another tour bus, to the Casbah. They are told, before going in, to hold hands with your wife, or loved one, because, if you get separated, you may never see your wife again. She could end up in a harem. Now since this was in 1970, everybody there was in their middle to late thirty's. So, they took them seriously. Today, they probably wouldn't have to worry. But, they still heard some jokingly say good riddance and do you promise? And the guy with the straight face says, I am not kidding you, it is common. Boy, they latched together, the whole time they were there, in the Casbah.

Once they were finished shopping there. They gathered up as a group outside. Then here came the men with their camels to give the women a ride of course for a fee. Elbert laughed, you should have seen these ladies that wanted to ride a camel. They went up to this guy and give him whatever it was to ride and then stepped up on a stool, to climb up on the back of these camels. About the time she would throw a leg up the camel guy would put his hand on the ladies butt and push them on up. The ladies all squealed and their eyes got big and their mouth flew open.

After that experience they went to the Sultan's palace, for lunch. The Sultan had just recently built a new palace somewhere and moved. There was no telling, who owned this place, now. Where we ate there was no menu. They ate what they brought them. It consisted of a bowl of something that looked terrible. With all the jokes about what they ate over there the rumor started around that it was rat soup or camel soup. Regardless, about the only thing anybody ate was, the bread and butter. An Arabic band played music that a belly dancer danced to. She was about the age of my grandma and looked silly, dancing out there, bare footed and barely dressed, behind skimpy see through clothes.

They flew back to Spain, and went for a Barbeque Cookout at a ranch that night. And that was really the only well done food they eat while there. It was really good food. They had a whole hog, cooking on a spit, when they got there. They all pigged out and stuffed themselves.

COFFEE

The next day, they went shopping downtown Malaga, Spain. Everything was going great. Elbert walked by a doorway that he looked in and seen, it was a small grocery store. And on the shelf, way back against the back wall, were bottles of, Sanka instant Coffee. Elbert yelled, to everybody to look what he found, they bought all the instant coffee the man had. The first thing they done, when they got back to the hotel was go to the snack bar and order a cup of hot agua. They all made them a good hot cup of coffee. They had not had a cup of coffee for three days. When the waiter seen what they were doing, he smiled and said: Ahhh Sanka, we have Sanka. They thought about killing him right there.

On the way to Spain on the plane everybody was excited laughing, talking, walking around, drinking, partying and having a great time. They served cold sandwiches for a meal on the way to Spain and a lot of people didn't eat hardly anything. They were drinking mostly.

But, when they boarded the plane to come home half the people were sick from something they ate while there, but not everybody. They were all tired and ready to go home. Once in flight, you could have heard a pin drop. Nobody was saying a thing. It was quiet. Then they brought out those sandwich plates again. They were eaten so fast, some even ask for an additional one.

Elbert had occasionally picked up a bottle of white wine some people didn't drink and brought them home. They had a New Years Eve Party and Elbert broke them out. They tasted terrible. He had let the corks dry out and they turned into vinegar. So that was the end of that.

THE GREAT DANE

Once home. Dick Krebs and his wife invited Elbert and his family over for dinner one night. They had gone with them to Spain also. Dick and Elbert, worked together for years. When Elbert got to their house and rang the door bell. They were standing there, with their two little girls in front of them, when the door opened wide and this giant of a dog suddenly appeared and licked Leigh in the face. She was looking at this dog, eyeball to eyeball and it all happened so fast, there was not any time to yell, scream, or holler. They all stepped into the house and visited for awhile and then moved to the dining room table. As they were sitting there eating. Leigh had forgotten about the dog and all of a sudden the dog walked up to her and his head was level with her plate. They didn't remember the dog's name but he just stood there and looked at her. He didn't bother her or her food. They assumed he just liked her. Leigh never forgot that and talks about that to this day. He was a Great Dane.

GRILLED PORK CHOPS

Bobby Smallwood and Elbert worked together, and their families, had become great friends, and are today. Bob and Lynn invited them over, to grill out, one night. Elbert had never even thought about grilling pork chops, but they were really good. Lynn, bobby's wife had a great recipe for Lasagna and Elbert's wife still uses that today. It is the best, they have ever eaten and everybody that has tried it, really likes it.

Lynn was also an Elvis Fan, really, big time. Elvis came to Jacksonville and they all went to see Elvis. Lynn had got her a ticket that put her on the front row. She was a teenager again and had the time of her life. The rest of the two families, were several rows back, and they had as much fun watching Lynn, as they did watching Elvis. Well, as Elvis would occasionally throw a scarf, out into the crowd, Lynn jumped up, and got one, he had just wiped sweat, off his brow. She quickly tied it around her neck, in tight knots and she wore it for the longest time, to show everybody. Well, when it came time to take it off, she couldn't get the knots untied. Janice and Elbert laughed, till they hurt, listening to her tell the story, of her and Bobby, trying to get it off. They were a lot of fun and we did a lot of things together.

Then one day, they got a divorce. Elbert and Janice were really sad for them than they were for themselves. They had been married for years, but they parted ways, so sad. Several years later, Lynn got Breast cancer, and died.

AL BURKHARD

Al is a passionate man and has a love for animals. Jerry and Peggy Hendricks also friends of Elbert and Janice, lived across the street from them. They had a Weimaraner, with pups. Al just had to have one and he loved that dog. Al named him, Bruno. Bruno was a good name for him. Everything went fine for a while. Then one day, Al got the idea, to close in his screen porch. He worked at it for some time and it really looked nice. Then one Saturday, he left Bruno at home and went scuba diving.   He had a great time as usual, and it was late when he got back home.

The next day Al came to work and you could tell he had something on his mind. So, Jim Highley got him to tell them, what was on his mind so heavy. Bruno had got mad at being left home alone all day. So Bruno eat about four sheets of expensive paneling, the door facing and was well on his way to eating the door. Now Bruno is a big dog but when Elbert saw the damage it looked like there might have been six big dogs in there. Boy was that dog mad.

Al called Elbert one day and asked if he would help him pour some concrete on his driveway. He told him sure he would be there the next day bright an early. When he got there, Al had already framed it up so all he had to do was smooth the concrete when it comes out of the truck. Now this is about seventy feet long and two foot wide strips, for his car tires to ride on. No big deal. After a little while, here came the concrete truck, and he backs in and starts dumping concrete. Well, they poured the first long stretch and started to pour the other one. Elbert ask the concrete man, to hold up and let us smooth what he has poured. But, he says, he's in a hurry he has to get back and get another load and be somewhere by a certain time. Well, what are you going to say? So they poured the other long stretch and the truck leaves. So they go back to where they started and now the concrete is setting up and they can't get the rock to settle and leave them with a smooth finish. Yep, you guessed it. Al now has the ugliest driveway in the neighborhood. You can't roller skate on it and you can't walk on it bare footed. It really isn't funny though.

 Another time, Elbert drove up to Al's house and he was cutting grass with a riding lawn mower. Elbert had never, rode one so he ask him to let him try it. He said sure just be careful. So Elbert started across his lawn and when he got to the other side, he realized there was no neutral. So to back up you just pull the lever back and it suddenly slams into reverse and it throws him back and the front comes up and the next thing he knows is, he is laying on the ground with this riding lawn mower still running and the blades are now up in the air like a helicopter and all he could think to do was push it to the right, and throw myself to the left and he did. Al, come running and the lawn mower landed up right and still in gear, it's now headed for the shrubbery. As dangerous as it was and they could have got hurt bad, they were laughing so hard you would have thought they were drunk as cootie brown, but they weren't.

 Al, bought, a 1964 Corvette split window Sting Ray. He had it painted and new upholstery. And one day he offered to sell it to Elbert for $1500. Elbert didn't have the money, nor any use for a sporty car like that. The insurance alone was out of sight, it was so high. But, if he found a ragged one barely running, and needing to be totally rebuilt from the ground up, it would be worth $25,000 today. And totally restored, it would be worth at least $100,000. That is one, hard to find car today.

 Al had a buddy from New York visiting and Al needed something from the store. So, he asked his buddy and Elbert to go get something from the store. They did and were headed back to Al's house. Al's friend wanted to drive Al's corvette and Elbert was just along to show him where to go. On the way back, he is flying down this road and they are talking, when all of a sudden it dawned on Elbert that there was a sharp curve up ahead. It was too late to tell this guy and they went into the curve sideways and slid off on the shoulder of the road. The car was leaning so much that when Elbert opened the door, he fell out into a ditch. There seem to be no damage so he carefully pulled back up on the road. Elbert jumped in and they went back to Al's house. When Elbert got out at Al's house and walked forward something hit him in the knees. He looked down and seen long tassels of Johnson grass sticking out from the tire and rim. The tire had pulled away from the wheel and grass was now stuck in it.

Al had a brother named John that lived in New York. There was as much difference in Al, and John as daylight and dark. Everybody knew Al was from somewhere, but not necessarily New York now John, you knew, he was from down town New York City. He had the colorful language, and expressions of a New Yorker. He owned a Deli, and Elbert enjoyed being around him. Elbert laughed at him and it probably annoyed him, but he never said anything. John, Al and Elbert went into a fast food place and Al says Elbert what are you going to get? Elbert was looking at their sign hanging up there, and said he didn't know, he might try this or that. And John explodes. Anxiously he says, "Spit it out, pick something. If you come to my Deli, and I point at you, spit it out what you want. I don't have time to dilly dally around with you. If I point at you twice and you don't say what you want. I say to hell with you and you don't get waited on. "

    John was not used to the down home lazy way we order a sandwich down south. He later sold his Deli and bought a cab. He tried that for a while but he didn't like being robbed and mugged so he sold his cab and retired to Florida. John is gone now but Elbert liked john. He like Al, was one of those people of northern persuasion that you liked.

    Al had another friend in New York that he had known all his life. Warren was his name. He was a liquor salesman. He and Al, both being single booked this cruise for a week or more and they had these visions of what it was going to be like in the movies. They could just see 500 single girls that were probably school teachers or secretaries just looking for a wild vacation.

So they get on board and they are asked do you want to eat at the early servings or the later servings. They thought, oh let's go to the early serving and they did. When they walked in to eat breakfast, the youngest person in the room was in her sixties. They had booked a cruise full of retired older people.   There were not more than a few women their age.

So, every time the ship stopped at a port of call, they were the first ones off the boat and when it was time to leave that port, they were the last to get back on the boat. When they got back home and Elbert learned of their stories. You could see the disappointment in his stories. Al said he would never do that again.

Al was the Bachelor's bachelor. Al was single and loved it, Elbert thought. Well, it was more than that. Elbert had known Al, for years now. But, out of the blue Al said he was going to New York this next week end. Just a casual statement, and Elbert said hey Great, Vacation?

Al said no, he was going to get married. What? What did you just say? Al smiled and said, yeah, he was going get married. Elbert thought to himself, he has got to be kidding. What do you mean? He knew Al was from New York, but he had not been to New York in years and he is going to get married, just like that? Who is she? Why hasn't he said something, before now? What is going on? Is he crazy? The whole time, Al is smiling and looking at Elbert like it is no big deal. Well, he goes off to New York and came back in a week or so and invited Elbert and Janice over to meet her. She is beautiful, with personality plus, she never meets a stranger, and she can cook like a chef in an Italian restaurant.   They had a beautiful daughter and stayed married a couple of years, before they parted ways. They are the best of friends to this day.

JIM HIGHLEY

Jim was another of Elbert's best friends and they worked together for years. He and his wife lived a block from them and they had a little boy. Both he and his wife were from Ohio, but you would never know it. Well, Jim and his wife would come over and if they didn't come to their house, they went to theirs. But after several years Jim came to him one day and told him, they were getting a divorce. Elbert said you're crazy, no don't tell me that. He said yes, that's what they both wanted. Then, he threw out the killer. They were to see the Judge Monday and they wanted him to be a witness for her. Now he knew they were crazy. Elbert said, you have got to be crazy, he can't do that. He knew too much. He can't sit there and tell them people stuff, no, he can't do it. Jim said, no, we want you to do it. You don't have to say anything to speak of. The judge will ask you, can you verify these statements to be true and you just say, yes your honor. Oh hell, this is killing Elbert. He is wondering, does either of them realize what they are doing? So, Elbert finally agreed. So, now he comes up to Elbert with the real kicker.

Jim knew Elbert was renting the house they were living in. They have been looking for some time and wanted a house in the neighborhood, where they lived. So Jim said, we want you and Janice, to assume our loan and buy our house. Just assume the mortgage, with nothing down, just move in, when they move out. He told Jim, he couldn't do that. He would give them as much as he could, but he didn't have hardly anything to pay them. Jim kept saying, no you can have it we want you to have it. So, after talking to Janice, they agreed to assume their loan, with nothing down. Jim's wife and son went back to Ohio, and Jim stayed in Jacksonville. Elbert rounded up $400 dollars and one day, he give it to Jim and at first, he wouldn't take it, but he eventually did.

SCUBA DIVING, ARTIFACTS and PALENTOLOGY

One day, when they were out fishing in salt water, they met a lot of good people and one of these mentioned Diving in the rivers of Florida. Finding all kinds of things from Colonial days, to Indian Artifacts and strange things, like Mastodon teeth, and Mammoth teeth and Camel teeth.

Well, they heard about Scuba Lessons and they checked into it, Jim, Al, and Elbert. They took the training course and graduated with flying colors. Then they started buying pieces of the gear they needed, some new and some used. These things are a little expensive, so they didn't just go buy all of it at once. They were certified by (FSDA) Florida Skin Diving Association. Later, they got certified by PADI and then another certification after that. So they did the smart thing and got the training before killing themselves.

Well, one day, Elbert was getting a haircut and the barber's name was Bob Slagle. Elbert noticed over in the corner, was a Dive Suit hanging on a clothes hanger and he asked Bob about it. Bob told him, it was for sale and at about a third of the cost new. He knew Elbert had been taking lessons and he asked, did Elbert have a wet suit yet? Elbert said no, but he sure needed one as it was cold at the time and he was going to the Santa Fe River this weekend. Bob said, well, if it fits go ahead and take it and he could pay him later. Elbert said okay and took it with him. Well, he was anxious to try it out and it was a top of the line model with a purple velvet interior which made it easier to slide on and off. It fit like a glove and he was a happy camper.

Elbert later bought the boots and the hood to complete the outfit. Someone suggested they ought to start a Dive Club. So they printed up some flyers and spread them around at all the dive shops and boat places. Wow they had a great turn out and they started a club. The name was the Jax Reef Sounders. They set the rules and requirements such as you had to be certified, as we wanted no part of someone getting hurt. It was too easy to get hurt or even killed, if you didn't know what you were doing. They designed their patches and had them made, to put on dark blue jackets and boy did they look sharp.

They met and developed friendships that have lasted to this day almost 50 years. As a matter of fact, Elbert recently had Jim, Al, and Ronnie Hall come to his house and spend the night talking about old memories. They spent two days and almost all night laughing and remembering things from so long ago. A lot of our old buddies have passed now and that was the sad part.

Bob Slagle the barber was a diver and he even joined our club. He went with them to the Santa Fe River, outside of Ft. White, Florida that first Club Dive. They set up an underwater obstacle course and they started out at one point then swam to the next and the next following directions like a map.

Elbert suited up in his new wet suit, put his air tank on, fins and mask and started into the river. He found all of the arrows up to the eighth marker and could not find the ninth arrow. In looking for it he got tangled up in a tree limb underwater and couldn't get loose. At the last minute, he took off the tank as that was what was caught and swam to the surface. He got one of the other guys to go get his tank he had left on the bottom of the river. Bob said: he would get it and he did. Now they are sitting there on the tail gate of a pickup truck, talking about what happened and bob said.

The last guy to wear that dive suit should have been as smart as Elbert was. Elbert asked him what do you mean, he smiled and said: the last man to wear that wet suit, drowned in it. Elbert said: What? What did you say? He started backing away and Elbert ain't smiling. You have got to be kidding me. Don't tell me that. Are you for real? Bob started laughing and said: no. He was just kidding you. Boy, he had him, then Elbert started thinking, he's just telling him that. So, Elbert asked him who did the suit belong to? And he told Elbert and he verified it later, the suit was too short for this guy in Jacksonville, that had a fence company and he had just bought him another one and left it with Bob , to sell to some diver that come into his barber shop. Elbert liked Bob okay, but he never did get real close to him because of his sense of humor.

Many of the following weekends for four years, they dove in the Santa Fe, the Suwanee River, the Ichetucknee River, and several springs, like Blue hole and others.

Every trip had them leaving Jacksonville, at 5 am in the morning, and ending, with them eating at Sonny's Barbecue, in Lake City , Florida, getting home after dark. They would be worn out from being in the water all day. And usually they ended up with ear aches, until they learned to put hydrogen Peroxide in their ears, and flush with alcohol when they got home.

Every time they went to the river, they would find something that astounded them. On one of the trips one of the guys found a whale's tooth. They didn't have a clue, as to what it was, until one day they met a professor from the University of Florida and he had written a book on the hunting points and tools used in the Paleolithic period of time. They found things that they were calling arrow heads and yes much later in the history of the world these same size points were arrow heads, but from the period of time they were made and used. There was no such thing as a bow and arrow back then. That point was a spear point. Some of the points they found were dated as far back as 9000 years old before Christ.

They found Mastodon and Mammoth teeth totally different teeth and huge in size. But many, with the enamel still attached. They found leg bones and one with a point buried partially in the bone. That is how some of this was dated. This river is a hundred and fifty miles from the ocean. And even today divers can still find shark teeth in it. How is that possible? Well thousands of years ago, the whole state of Florida was covered by water. And when the water receded Whales and Sharks, were trapped and died miles from the ocean.

This, you may really find hard to believe. But the area known as the state of Florida at one time had more camel in it than is in the world today. The rivers are full of camel teeth. This explains why they found camel teeth in the Florida River's. This hobby of Scuba Diving started a study of paleontology by Jim, Al and Elbert for years. If they heard there was a lecture somewhere they all attended it. They became a very knowledgeable Club of divers in the Jacksonville area for quite awhile on paleontology. They still find it interesting today. Sometimes, Elbert has said, he wished he had been a scientist. You know like "The Raiders of the Lost Ark" to travel the world researching everything unknown. They even mapped the bottom of the rivers and noted exactly where things were found. In Florida many of the rivers have limestone bottoms bright white and smooth as concrete that reflects sunlight. From the bank it looks like dark ice tea but from the bottom it looks like somebody turned on an overhead light. And three months ago, this side of a river would be covered by five feet of sand but today the sand has now been moved to the other side of the river. They would dive in a spot two or three times and think well they have found everything here. Then come back a month later and find even more. The reason was more had washed out of the river banks. The river is constantly changing it gets wider sometimes and narrow another.

There are holes or pockets everywhere on the bottom of the rivers. They always swim up river along the bottom and with one hand hold on to the bottom against the current while the other hand is fanning the water over one of these pockets. And all of a sudden an arrow head will flip up out of the pocket no telling how many years it has laid there. They then deposit it into a net type bag. When they get out later they can look at them more closely.

Well one day Elbert was watching the guy next to him on his right. He has his left hand holding onto the bottom of the river and he is looking to his right and down, fanning over a hole. He didn't see it when it happened and he didn't even feel it at first. But a snake that was just floating along the bottom of the river hit his arm and wrapped itself around his arm three or four times. Elbert was trying to get his attention when he finally seen the snake. Elbert noticed, he shut his eyes Elbert could see through his face mask. About the time it takes to count to three. The snake let go and floated on down the river. They both went to the surface and floated back down river to where they had got in and got out.

Elbert ask him what were you doing when you shut your eyes. He looked at Elbert and said: he was praying that when he opened his eyes again, the snake would be gone. Because if he was still there, he was gonna fill my britches up with you know what and die.

MOTORCYCLE UNDER THE BRIDGE

One day they seen a sheriff's car stopped on a bridge and he is looking down at the river. They stopped and ask what was going on? He said they had arrested some guys that had stole and disposed of a Honda Gold Wing motorcycle by dumping it in the river but he couldn't see it. Elbert told him, they were divers and would check it out if he wanted and they did. Come to find out there were two motorcycles down there. A pretty new big one and another that had been there for a year or more. The deputy give Elbert a business card and he wrote on the back let him go one time he then signed and dated it. Elbert never got to use it he lost it somewhere.

OLD FORT WHITE

Old Fort White was a town that disappeared years and years ago. It had been so long that all the old people that knew where it was had already passed away. The stories were that there was a river crossing in the middle of town. That meant it was on the river's edge. They found a guy that had been looking for years and he had a metal detector. Elbert told him he had a boat that they could work off of along the river. He said Great he had this place he wanted to try but the only way to get there was by boat. So they went and found located the town. The metal detector went crazy and they all suited up and got into the river. What Jim, Al and Elbert wanted, was in the river. They figured with years of wagons crossing the river in the same place there had to be things that fell off wagons or was thrown away or washed downstream. They were looking for guns, bottles, dishes etc.

At first they went up stream and found nothing what so ever. Then they got fresh tanks, and went down stream. There they found a lot of things. Elbert has a water pitcher made of crockery and at first he only had the biggest part. But he kept going back and in about the third time he dove on that spot. He found the missing two pieces. Now it is all there but some of it was buried and some of it was exposed, so part is shiny and the other part is dull but he loves it. Because it has been broken, it isn't worth a lot, but as a keep sake of an item found like it was, it is a very valuable piece, as a keep sake.

WEEKENDS AND VACATIONS, IN COBBTOWN

They lived in Jacksonville for nine years and they enjoyed it in many ways. It was close enough to home that they spent many weekends in Cobbtown especially during the summer. Occasional visits were fine, but Elbert was sure, Janice's parents would have liked to take a nap once in a while but couldn't because here they come with two children and a dog. So they found a three bedroom Mobile home reasonably priced. They bought it and set it up on her dad's old home place. Now, they could come and go and not disturb somebody trying to work and rest when they could.

QUAIL HUNTING

All the men in Janice's family were hunters of Quail, Dove primarily. When Quail season was in they would walk behind a quail dog, all day long and come in late in the afternoon with plenty of birds. They would clean the birds and Mrs. Gertie, Janice's mother, would cook them. Some fried and some in gravy and rice. After quail season, Dove season would come in, then they would find a good spot and sit on a stool, waiting for them to come flying into the fields we had surrounded with friends and neighbors.

Buddy Nail Janice's brother was only 14 at that time. He hunted with a single shot 410 gauge shot gun. Elbert used a 12 gauge shotgun and he would out shoot him four to one. He was and still is a natural.

One day, Buddy drove up and they were standing out in the driveway, talking. They had been looking up at a bird way up there in the sky. He was almost out of sight he was really only a black dot. Somebody told Buddy, they would bet him he can't hit that bird up there. He took his deer rifle with a scope on it and pointed it skyward. He pulled the trigger and it took a second for the bullet to get there but he hit the bird and it came down like a helicopter. Yes he is good. Now Odis Janice and Buddy's daddy was left handed he did everything left handed. It was amazing to watch him drive a nail with a hammer left handed. Elbert couldn't do it. He shot pool and a shotgun left handed. And he didn't miss either.

THANKSGIVING

One weekend, Elbert and his family went home to Cobbtown and his father in law, Odis said, come and go with him. Elbert loved him like his own father. It was cold outside and Elbert bundled up and followed him to his truck. He got his 22 rifle and they walked to the hog pen. The hogs come to them thinking they were going to feed them. Well, he looked them over and picked out the one he wanted and shot it right between the eyes. It dropped like a rock. He then got the tractor and put the boom on it. They then got the hog and brought it to the back yard. They got a 55 gallon barrel and dug a hole big enough to put the end of the barrel in the hole at a slant. Then they filled the barrel with boiling water and dunked the hog into the hot water. This loosens the hair on the hog and they clean it of all his hair.

Then they hung it upside down and remove the innards. Then they lifted it up on a big table and cut him up into the pieces they wanted. The other pieces were to be ground up into sausage. The skin is chopped up into small pieces and deep fried in a big black pot for pork skins. Some are turned into chitlins, the bacon is sliced on a meat slicer, the hams, are taken to a meat place that will salt cure them. The feet are pickled and the brains will be fried and eaten with scrambled eggs in the morning.

HOMER

Jean, Janice's sister, lived in a small town outside of Atlanta, and nearby, was a stock market.   Jean like to go, every once in a while and one night they bought a bull. This bull was no more than a calf.   They drove up to Odis and Gertie's house, the next day. Jean got out and opened the back door and out   come this bull no bigger than a dog. Odis had agreed to take him and feed him out and one day they would sell him for a profit. Well he got bigger and bigger and bigger and he acted more and more like the bull that he was. You didn't want to get close or turn your back on him.

Well, Elbert and Janice were asleep one night and something woke Janice and she woke Elbert up. She said Homer is outside our bedroom window. What that meant was he is out of the field he is suppose to be in. And more important if he goes behind their house he might fall into the swimming pool.

So Elbert jumped up out of bed in his Jockey shorts and barefooted, he went running out the back door around the house to run homer back across the road. It is pitch black dark and Homer is pitch black, Elbert can't see him and he is yelling, to scare Homer back across the road where he is suppose to be.

Elbert didn't scare Homer at all until Elbert ran into him and fell down. Now Elbert is on the ground under this bull that weighs three thousand pounds and might step on him or the family jewels any minute. He is stomping all around Elbert and finally Homer ran back across the road.   Odis met Elbert at the gate and they get him back into the cow lot. Odis said don't you think you ought to put some clothes on, laughing at Elbert. Elbert told him he was going back to bed.

Well, one morning Odis shot Homer and they took him to an abattoir. Then they brought him home and put him in the freezer. Now Janice, their two girls and Janice's sister, heard the shot and knew what it was and they seen Odis and Elbert drive off with Homer on a trailer. They didn't eat meat for months. All the women turned vegetarian for a while.

SNOW IN SOUTHEAST GEORGIA

One morning in Jacksonville, the phone rang and it was Odis in Cobbtown. He called to tell them it had snowed and it was 4 inches deep. All the roads were closed so don't even think about, coming home for the weekend. They said okay, and hung up. Then, they all jumped up, to get their clothes together, and get on the road up there. It was a hundred and forty miles, but they got to Reidsville, Georgia and it wasn't but fourteen more miles but when they got within 5 miles of Cobbtown. They seen the road turn white with snow and they made the tracks in the highway coming into Town. Odis was in town and he threw a snow ball at them, when they drove up.

They had never, in 33 years, seen 4 inches of snow in Cobbtown , or since then. They were so glad they didn't listen, it was beautiful. Had they stayed in Jacksonville, and seen the pictures later, they would have been sick.

JOHNNY NAIL FARM

This is where Janice father was born and raised. Her Grandparents and a uncle, had lived in the old house for years. Well, right down the road, one Saturday they were picking tobacco. Grand pa Johnny Nail and another older man Mr. Woods was standing in the middle of the dirt road looking up at something. So Elbert walked over there and asked them, what are ya'll looking at? Without looking down and still staring Mr. Woods said: That plane way up there. Mr. Johnny said: I would hate to be up there in that thang. Mr. Woods calmly said, I would hate to be up there, and not be in that thang. Both of these men were in their late 80's, close to 90 years old. Elbert wished he could have videotaped that conversation. They were so serious and they never cracked a smile. You had to be there.

That tobacco barn caught fire and burned up with four rooms

full of tobacco. It happens from time to time that while cooking the tobacco it sometimes gets so hot that it burst into flames.

One day, Elbert heard the chickens squawking and looked in the chicken yard, and there was Keith and Kenneth, Janice's nephews, chasing the chickens. They were little hellions and they would   chase a chicken until the chicken would drop dead from heat exposure. Grand pa would raise cane   and holler at them.

The last Sunday in February, every year, they would have a birthday dinner for Granny Nail and her twin sister. Her maiden name was Tucker and the whole Tucker and Nail clan would come to the home place and eat out in the yard. There would be tables set up with food covering 40 feet at least. All this would be in the side yard under big trees. Years later, they moved it inside the Community house in Cobbtown and it still goes on, today in 2013.

CUTTING HOGS

Almost every farmer had a sow and a boar hog, and would raise a litter of pigs to sell some and to eat some. Well, when the pigs got close, to being a number one hog, they would hem up the ones that needed to be cut. Then Odis, and Elbert, would hold them, while Mr. Vonyer, talking a mile a minute about any and everything, would use a sharp knife, to slice the hogs nut sack open and squeeze the nut out, and cut it off. Then spray the incision with a purple medicine and turn him loose. Now, he would get to be a big, fat, heavy hog, and bring a good price at the market. Then they would catch another one and do it all over again. Mr. Vonyer, was a neighbor and also kin. It seemed like, almost everybody, in Cobbtown, was kin, some way or another.

GARDEN TIME

Every spring, Odis would always plant a big garden. There were five children in Janice's family and now they are all married and they have children. So it takes a lot of garden to feed all these. They all, any and everybody in the family that happened to be around, helped to get the ground ready and plant. Also to pick it when it was ready and help can it for the coming winter months. There was corn, potatoes, tomatoes, squash, cucumbers, peas, butter beans, okra, ford hooks, (big Butterbeans)   and from time to time, other things. Since they all lived off, in other towns and states, they could only help on weekends but that was greatly appreciated.

And in those early married years it was a blessing when they went back to Jacksonville and they had some vegetables and meat from the freezer to take home.

NEIGHBORS

Neighbors were like second families. Neighbors were always there for you when you had celebrations and sadness, when you needed help bringing in a crop, a garden, cutting hogs, or killing a hog at thanksgiving. They came and helped you do anything and you went and helped them also. Sometimes there would be money exchanged but very seldom. Mostly you helped your neighbor because you wanted to but also because you cared for them and knew one day you might need their help.

First of all you knew your neighbors because they had been your family's neighbors for generations. The farms all around them, belong to people, Janice, was raised up with. She called some of them Uncle and Aunt. Most everybody is friends or relatives in their community. Only recently have some people moved into their community that have no roots here.

MOONSHINE

Yes there has been moonshine. Elbert doesn't know of any today, but back in the 60's. If you were out quail hunting there were places you just didn't go to hunt. You went around that wooded area over there let's go this way instead. And there were three different houses that you could go to and get as much as you wanted.

Elbert's boss, back in Jacksonville, was originally from Austin, Texas and he asked him one day if he could get him some moonshine. Elbert told him he didn't really know but he would ask around. Shoot, the first person he asked told him where to go. He went and got him a gallon and took it back to him. That was in 1972 but as late as 2006 Elbert don't know about today.

LEEDIE AND BAD WEATHER

Leedie and Ernest Collins were their neighbors and lived just up the road within sight. They were an older couple. If you looked out the window while washing dishes in the kitchen you could see their house up the road. There was a corn field between their houses and one day Elbert looked out the window and noticed there were two rows of corn that somebody had cut, the tops out of the corn and those rows of corn were a foot shorter than all the rest So now Leedie can see all the way across the field to Elbert and Janice's house and vice versus. Leedie like look and see what they were doing and if they were home or not, but to also look after their place while they were gone or for any number of reasons.

Now Leedie, was afraid of Lightening and Thunder. If a storm came up, ie thunder or lightening, you would see Leedie coming down the road with her apron and bonnet on. She would visit until the storm passed. Yes they were kin somewhere in the family tree, more like an aunt and uncle, but older. Ernest was too old to go hunting quail with them, but he had him some quail traps in the woods and he eat as many as they did, if not more. And he never had to buy shells for his gun.

Through the years Janice's family helped them put up corn in the freezer and kill a hog around thanksgiving time and they helped in return..

HAND FISHING the GATOR LAKES

Elbert, Odis, Ernest, and EJ, went to the gator lakes to seine some water holes after the river went down leaving fish in shallow places. Elbert's job was to walk across the hole in the middle, holding up the seine so fish didn't jump over the net and get away. When they got to the other side they put the fish in a croaker sack. When the sack got full they would come out go home and clean them.

Well, they had left their truck near a fence and when they came out to it. They had to climb the fence to get to their truck. Well they piled into the truck and went to the house after a long day. The women folk were waiting on them, sitting on the porch, in rocking chairs. Talking about any and everything, after a while, one of the ladies asked where is the fish? Let us see them. Everybody looked at Elbert and he thought to himself, did he put them in the truck, after he climbed the fence? No, he had left the darn things on the ground and forgot them. Elbert jumped up and took off. Sure enough there they lay he picked them up and hurried back to the house.

    Odis had worked hard for those fish He had gone under water reaching up under this big tree into the hollow part of that tree to get some of the fish. You could hear them flopping and he would come out with one after another. Elbert had held the sack so he could drop them in and one of the times he come out from under water he had a snake in his hand. He threw it out on the bank and Elbert said: Okay that's enough let's go now, laughing. They all laughed at Elbert but they didn't go them. They were ready to fish for more saying the snake is gone now.

    The first time Elbert ever went to the gator lakes, they had already gone early Friday morning. Elbert didn't get there until almost dark. They had left rags tied to bushes leaving Elbert a trail to follow to where they were. When Elbert at last parted some bushes, there they sat, with a fire going and fish frying in an iron skillet, right at the water's edge. They had set out trot lines and they worked them all night taking fish off of hooks and putting more bait on. They made hush puppies and eat fish almost all night. You could shine a light out across the water and you could see a red pair of eyes looking at them motionless in the water. It was strange but they stayed away from them and except for the red eyes they didn't ever see a gator at all. The next day after they had more fish than they could carry, they loaded everything up in a boat, then they each got a corner of the boat and walked three miles back to the truck.

    SKEET SHOOTING

    One day Buddy Nail and Al Sikes said, let's go shoot some skeet. Elbert said great, let's go. Elbert was ready. Elbert had bought him a new 12 gage shot gun with an aluminum frame and it was a skeet gun. It was lighter than a browning and he could walk all day long shooting quail. Now Buddy and Al Sikes are the two best shots Elbert knew of. He couldn't hold a candle to them.

    Elbert thought maybe he could hold his own or maybe even out shoot them on the skeet range. Wrong...... They were out shooting him and he had just finished a round when the owner's wife came walking up and asked Elbert how he did? He told her there must be something wrong with his gun as they were out shooting him terrible. She asked if she could shoot a round with his gun? He said sure, and watched as she hit everything she aimed at, she out shot Buddy and Al, and with Elbert's gun. She finished and handed Elbert his gun and said there isn't anything wrong with your gun winked and walked away.

MEANWHILE, IT'S TIME TO GO BACK TO JACKSONVILLE

They enjoyed every minute they spent in Cobbtown. And they enjoyed Jacksonville but Janice and Elbert had already decided if they ever got the chance they would move in a heartbeat. Until they sold their house in Jacksonville, Janice and the girls would go ahead and stay in the trailer in Cobbtown and get the girls settled into school. Meanwhile Elbert would go back and forth on the weekends.

ST. AUGUSTINE, FLORIDA

One of the biggest reasons Al, Jim and Elbert became the best of friends was they got interested in fishing and then their interest changed to Scuba Diving. Elbert had a boat and almost every weekend they went fishing somewhere. Sometimes, it was surf fishing. Then they started fishing for drum. They went to St. Augustine for years and fished the intra coastal water way. After a while, they knew where just about every drum hole was for 40 miles. Then, there was usually the winter time that they trolled for blue fish. They really had some good times and Elbert will tell you of some of them. Almost every time they went out with this boat, something happened, that made it memorable.

One of these trips started out, with the air temperature at 21 degrees and snowing, in St. Augustine, Florida. Elbert's boat had a top and side curtains and an open back. So as long as they kept anchored into the wind they were okay temperature wise. His boat was an 18 foot fiberglass hull with a 75 horse, Mercury outboard motor. The sides were high and he really liked it because kids couldn't trip and fall out. Anyway they are out there and he knew it was going to be cold, so he brought a small grill and set it on metal and three quarter inch plywood under the dash close to where his feet was when he was driving. It was full of charcoal Briquettes and the heat from that was keeping the inside of his boat comfortable. Everything is going good and they are even drinking cold beer even though it is 21 degrees. Well there is another boat load of their friends that they knew from work out here with them. They pulled up along the side of Elbert and their teeth are chattering and their lips are turning blue. They said they were going in because they were freezing. Elbert looked over on the bank and seen a 5 gallon bucket. He told them to go get that bucket, put some sand in the bottom of it and come back. They would give them some charcoal and they would have a heater like them. They liked the idea and went and got it. They came back and Elbert helped them get a fire started in their bucket. They then pulled away about fifty yards and went back to fishing over a drum hole. Elbert had forgotten all about them.

Well all of a sudden they hear people yelling and they look to see what the commotion is all about and it's them. Thick black smoke is rolling out of their boat. It looks like they were on fire so Elbert quickly pulled the anchor and headed over to them. As they approached them they pitched that bucket overboard. You should have seen them. They looked like raccoons and it was hilarious. The bucket they were using was an old paint bucket and the dried paint on the inside caught fire and they had flames and black smoke rolling. They give up the ghost and went home. See what he meant, if Elbert put his boat into the water something happens, to talk about for years to come. That was 37 years ago.

OFF SHORE SPEAR FISHING

One day the guys wanted to go off shore and spear fish so Elbert said okay. They load his boat and fill all the gas tanks. They have plenty of food and drinks and the weather is beautiful. They had not been off shore in Jacksonville to spear fish before so they didn't know where the reefs were or wrecks etc. So they just decided to head out and stop every once in a while then one of them would go to the bottom and see what was there and they did. The first two times they checked there was nothing but a sand bottom and no fish. Elbert had two gas tanks and they both held the same amount of fuel. So he had planned to run off shore until the gas ran out and refuel and start back in. Well, the first tank ran out and the motor quit and he changed fuel tanks. When tried to start the motor again it wouldn't start.

So he opened the cooler that had their food and drinks and

said, let's go ahead and eat something and it will start in a few minutes. One of the guys says what are we going to do if it won't start? Another guy says, aw it'll crank and the other guy says, he's just like the Captain of a ship trying to keep everybody calm. They ate and drink then they shot the bull for awhile and Elbert knows as soon as the fuel system gets under pressure it would fill the floats in the carbs and it would crank. So he said well let's try it and vooorrmmm it started up and we headed back in. The lesson they learned was find out where to go ahead of time.

WEST PALM BEACH SPEAR FISHING TOURNAMENT

Al, Jim and Elbert were members of a Scuba Diving Club and the club decided they would go to West Palm Beach, Florida and enter this Tournament. So, they went down there, a day earlier and they are riding around with all the equipment, to show them the bottom and help us find a reef with lots of fish. Well, they found what they were looking for so they suited up and went down with tanks into 100 feet of water. They all had been certified by FSDA, PADI and NALI Certification. Ronnie Hall shot a huge Jew fish but it wasn't dead. When Elbert swam up to Ronnie, he seen Ronnie has the steel leader wire wrapped around his hand. Then all of a sudden the fish takes off and that steel leader wire cut into Ronnie's hand down to the bone. Now, they have blood in the water, which attracts sharks, if any are around. Al, and Jim, together, shoot the fish again and killed it.

About that time Elbert's tanks warned him, he was out of air, and he had to immediately start ascending or else. Elbert then noticed it got dark all of a sudden and he could hear a big powerful noise. What he was hearing was a ship passing over his head moving along empty and his propellers were half out of the water and making that noise. He had to start up so he headed the opposite direction the ship was headed, by doing that, when he got to the surface the ship would be gone. He surfaced and their boat come to them and got everybody in the boat but the fish. He was so big they couldn't get him in the boat. So, they tied a one inch rope through his mouth and out his gill and towed him to the dock. When they got there they got the fish up onto the trunk lid of a 1966 Ford and they rode all over West Palm looking for an ice house that could weigh this fish. They finally found a place to weigh it and it weighed 266 pounds. They took the fish back to the dock where they stood the fish up like it would swim through the water and carved one inch steaks off him. It was pretty white meat and we filled their coolers before throwing the skeleton back into the water for the crabs and people to gawk at.

The next day, they lined up and they shot the gun. Fifty boats raced for the ocean and their favorite fishing spot. Elbert's boat was nice in it's own way but there were cigarette boats with airplane engines that passed them and ran out of sight. They didn't even come close to some of those guys that had been doing that all of their life.

KEY MARATHON, FLORIDA

The first of August every year the Lobster season opened in Florida. And Elbert and his dive buddies were all there for five years or more. They took the wives and children one year and they had the best time. The Atlantic Ocean was on one side of the highway and the Gulf of Mexico was on the other side of the highway. Either side had the prettiest water you have ever seen. All the diving they did was snorkeling, as the water where the lobster was wasn't but chest deep so they pulled an inner tube with a cooler on it. They would grab the lobster then drop him into the cooler and when they filled the cooler, they would empty it into a bigger cooler and go again.

One day, Elbert rented a small boat with a canvas top to provide shade, and took Janice and the kids out into the Gulf. They stopped and he told them to watch this nickel as he dropped it over the side. They watched it all the way to the bottom. It hit the sand on the bottom and a little plume of sand come up when it hit. She asked how deep is the water? Elbert said, it isn't deep, go ahead and cool off, he didn't think it was even over her head. Well, she stood up and jumped in. She went down and down and down , then she shot to the surface saying you tricked me it was deeper than she had been led her to believe. He then told her the water was 65 feet deep right where they were. You could look down and see all kinds of colorful fish swimming all around them. That water was beautiful down there.

Elbert looked up and seen a rain squall was approaching from the west, so they headed for the inlet, to take the boat back. He was afraid they would not make it before the rain hit, and they didn't. He kept staring at the inlet and focused on it. Just as they got to the inlet, it disappeared in the rain. Both sides of the inlet, was rocks. He thought please don't let me hit those rocks. He slowed and kept going and he went right up the middle of that inlet. Whew, that was close.

CAY SAL, BAHAMAS

One of the guys in their club knew of a guy named Chubby Winters at Key Marathon that they could charter, to go to Cay Sal, in the Bahamas. So they chartered his boat, for three nights and four days. They all met up at his boat, at nine o'clock one night and headed out to sea. Elbert looked up at the wheel house, of this 45 foot boat and Chubby is guiding them out into the ocean and deep water, following marker lights on poles in the water. After about an hour or so everybody is looking for a place to stretch out and get some sleep. They won't get there until after the sun comes up. They are headed for Cay Sal, in the Bahamas. It is a very small island and mostly rock and only one small sandy place in the middle of nowhere. Elbert, Jim, Al, and Ronnie, walked up to the bow and stood talking as they headed out into total darkness with no horizon. They were looking at the stars and commenting how clear it was and it looked like you could reach out and touch the stars. Ronnie said ya'll turn around and look at the wheel house. They turned around and Chubby had put the boat on autopilot. At least they hoped he had because he was in the process of helping this beautiful naked blonde climb up onto a bunk behind the wheel. Then Chubby followed and turned out the overhead light. Elbert commented, he hoped they don't run into some ship out here somewhere hopefully we are past the north south sea lanes.

As Elbert understood it, Chubby was single. Owned a night Club in Key West, had his own air plane, this boat, and drove a Corvette. Elbert said: "I would say he had it all." As the sun was coming up the next morning, his girl friend fixed them all a good breakfast. They were told, they didn't have to bring any food, as whatever they shot spear fishing or caught, is what they would eat. All they had to bring was something to drink. He would provide a salad to go with each meal and the fixings to go with   fish, lobster, crab, or conch.

Since they were in Bahamian waters, spear guns were not allowed. They had to use what is called a Hawaiian Sling. It is a long spear with a rubber band attached to one end of it and you hooked the rubber part on your elbow and push it back stretching the rubber and holding it tight in your hand. When you see a fish, you point and release the shaft and you spear a fish.

They were on this boat for three nights and four days. Diving all day and some at night. Now, that is an experience. Here you are in the middle of the ocean and it is pitch black dark. You have no idea if a Barracuda or shark is right next to you. Elbert tried it, but that just wasn't for him.

The water where they were anchored was 45 feet deep. It just wasn't deep enough to use our tanks, so they were free diving down to the bottom. Elbert couldn't get to the bottom the first day or so. But he finally, got to where he could dive to the bottom with just a mask, snorkel and fins then come on back up. But those guys, that had been diving all their life. Would go to the bottom, swim along the reef for a minute or so shoot a fish and slowly come on back up.

One day Ronnie and Elbert swam over to the island and they could see one lone building with bullet holes everywhere. They were told do not get out of the water and go on that island as it was against the law. US Law was once you set foot on it you had left the US and needed a passport to come back to the US. So, by staying off it, they didn't need a passport. And every day at daylight an air force plane flew over. Why? Because if Cubans had come to the island during the night, trying to leave Cuba. The Cubans would kill them right there. And Chubby said, if a Cuban gun boat come by and seen them on the island they often shoot first not knowing they were Americans.

Elbert watched as some of the guys brought up, a bunch of Conch shells he had never seen how they got the meat out of a shell. They took their knife striking it and knocking off the pointed top leaving a hole in it. They then took a fork and twisted the meat out that hole then they deep fried it and chopped it up in a conch salad. It tasted a lot like chicken and it was very good.

You live and learn, as Elbert had taken a case of coke and a case of beer with him on this boat. Both foamed up every time he tried to drink either from the salt water in his stomach he had swallowed diving. It got to where he was swapping two cokes or two beers for a glass of water or white wine. The guys that had gone on these type trips in years past always brought a case of water and a gallon of white wine.

Chubby mentioned one day, that out in front of the boat about a hundred yards was a ledge, where the water went from fifty feet deep to 3000 feet deep. If we haven't ever seen anything like that they ought to go over and take a look. So they suited up with their tanks and swam over there. It was fascinating. Elbert swam out over the ledge and the water turned a dark green, and you couldn't see the bottom. You also had the feeling you were falling, even thought you wasn't, you hurried back to the ledge.

After that, they went back to the boat and got something to eat. Then Ronnie and Elbert swam over to the island. They were looking at some holes, looking for Lobster, when they noticed a shark coming their way. They had their spear guns with them, and while they held onto the island ledge with one hand, they kept the spear guns pointed at the shark until he swam out of sight. Just as they started back Elbert noticed a shark on the bottom just sitting there. Ronnie said it was a nurse shark. It is the only shark, that doesn't have to keep moving, or it will drown. They swam down there and they touched it. The shark's skin is like sand paper. It finally swam on off somewhere and they went back to the boat. Just as Elbert got to the boat, he felt something tug at his fin and he thought somebody like Al or Jim, was playing around but when he turned, it was a barracuda and he had bit his fin. He looks scary when you see him under water. He will sit sideways to you, with his mouth open and just stare at you.

During the day, they never saw another boat or anybody. But at night they could see the lights of Cuba off in the distance. Elbert had the best time and he would love to go again sometime. Just to go and be there. But he thinks his diving days are long gone. He sold all his gear and it has been thirty seven years since he has been in the water. Elbert is so glad he experienced Scuba Diving. It was a great experience and a wonderful world never seen by most people.

CHAPTER 8   1974 – 2013

One day it was pretty in Jacksonville and they were building new houses a block away behind where Elbert and Janice lived. Janice and Elbert decided to walk around there and look at them.   They had been thinking about buying a new house. They loved the location and neighborhood so they walked up to the model home and met the saleslady. They liked the model home and asked about it and the price. The home wasn't any larger than what they had it was just pretty and new. They were paying $80 a month. So with that in mind Elbert asked, if he paid $10,000 down how much would the payment be? She figured for a minute and said: "$400 a month." Elbert smiled and said, "Well thank you but he am not going to move a block away, move into a house with the same square footage and pay $400 a month instead of $80, thank you "and left.

They had a house plan they liked and they had ask Janice's dad how much it would cost to build it. He said $29,000. Now this is 1975 and the house is 2200 square feet and brick. Janice's mom and dad said, they could have a half acre across the road from them, on the corner of the dirt road and the paved road. They sold their house in Jacksonville and made $13,000 and told her dad, they were ready to start. He went to work shortly after that. Janice's dad Odis had two helpers, Houston Holland, and Terrell Williams. Then, he called in Mr. Vonyer, Janice, called him, Uncle Vonyer. Then, Janice and Elbert helped on the weekends.

They moved in just before school started in 1975. This was the best move they had ever made.   The girls were of the age and knew how to swim, so they had an in ground pool, 18' by 36' installed.   This brought the grand total to $34,000 dollars for house and pool.

THE COMMUTE OF ALL COMUTES

After selling their house in Jacksonville, they had moved to Cobbtown and were staying in a rental house in town while building their home. Elbert still worked back in Jacksonville. It was tough getting up at 4 o'clock in the morning and leaving at 4:30. It was one hundred and seventy miles to his office, yeah, that is three hundred and forty miles a day. He usually got home at 8:30 pm. Elbert usually stopped in Blackshear, Georgia and had toast and coffee, but had to leave there by 6 o'clock to get to the office by 8 am. You might ask, why did he do that? The answer was, he lived where he wanted to live, and he worked where he wanted to work. He bought a New 1975 Chevrolet Vega, primarily for the gas mileage. He put a hundred and forty one thousand miles on it, before selling it. Then he bought a 1977 Ford Pinto. There is no telling, how many miles he put on that. Then he bought a 1979 Ford Courier. He put an extra gas tank in it to be able to buy lots of gas when it was cheap. However this made him a bomb going down the road hauling fifty gallons of fuel.

For the first year, he went back and forth every day. But the second year, he taught Electronics two nights a week and he stayed in a motel. That way, he only made three round trips a week.

He carried a tape recorder that plugged into the cigarette lighter and he had his mail for the day, so he would read a piece of mail and dictate a response, then throw the mail onto the dash, until he was through and when he got to the office, would give his secretary the tape and she would start typing letters and bring them to him for his signature. Their system worked very well. I guess, it was a miracle he didn't run off the road, into the bushes, on the side of the road.

Back then, he smoked cigars and somebody figured out how many gallons of gas he burned and how many cigars he smoked and they put it on the Bulletin Board for laughs. That was 504 cigars, if you're counting.

Back then, he had a CB Radio in his car, just in case he needed it and it was fun talking to all the truckers etc. This was before cell phones existed. He learned there were people Home Bound. He never thought about that but these people had CB Base Stations and spent a big part of their life just talking on the CB. They were home bound, confined to beds, or wheelchairs, or no car, or what have you. This was their freedom to talk to somebody and hear what was going outside around them in the world. They knew more about what was going on in the world than he did. He learned from them what the politicians were saying or doing, as they listened to the news all day long, while he was running up and down the road and at work.

There was the trucker he met at the intersection of Highway 121 and U.S. 1 every morning. They talked all the way to Jacksonville. And there was the trucker he met coming out of Jacksonville every night on my way home. He smoked the same brand of cigars that Elbert did. One night, Elbert told him he would be stopping up ahead to get him a cigar and the trucker said just pull over, he had a whole box and he did. He came running up to Elbert and shook his hand. They got to meet for the first time in a year of talking to each other every day. He gave Elbert a hand full of cigars. Elbert hasn't seen or talk to him now in 33 years.

SPEEDING AND THE NEW STATE PATROLMAN

One morning, Elbert was 4 miles north of Blackshear, Georgia and running about 75 miles an hour, when he went by what looked to be a state patrol car sitting on the side of the road with his lights off. After passing, Elbert looked in his rear view mirror and he seen his lights come on. So, he just eased off the gas and pulled over and waited for him. Elbert got out and met him at the front bumper of his car and Elbert could smell the paint burning off the motor, of a brand new patrol car and Elbert thought he probably was a new patrolman. He was right. He had his ticket book in his hand and he was ready to write. He filled out the ticket and held my license and said: "follow him." So, he did.

Well, they pulled into the parking lot of the courthouse and there was only one light on in the building. Elbert waited, as the patrolman went to the door of the sheriff's office and found it locked. Elbert thought, hey this is great, maybe, he will let him go. No such luck. The patrolman then, started for the jail, next door. This was that red brick two story building next door, that served as the Jail down stairs and the sheriff lived upstairs.

The patrolman knocked on the door and talked to someone and in a minute or so here came this guy with no shirt on, no shoes or socks, walking with the patrolman, in his starched and pressed clothes and shiny patent leather shoes. It looked like Mutt and Jeff, in the comics.

The patrolman motioned for Elbert to follow them and they walked to the sheriff's office. This half naked man sat in the sheriff's chair because he was, the sheriff. He looked at the ticket and the patrolman left Elbert with the sheriff. The Sheriff then looked at my driver's license and seen Tattnall county on it. He looked up at me and said: How is old Romey Waters doing these days? Romey was Elbert's sheriff. Elbert told him, he had seen Romey yesterday and he was going to play poker with John Albert Strickland and that bunch. He laughed and said: that will be so much for the ticket Elbert forget how much it was. Elbert told him he didn't have the cash, but he could write him a check. But he wouldn't take a check. So, Elbert told him, he would be back through here tonight, and he would bring him the cash then. He said fine and kept his license. Elbert asked him, what if he got caught again and with no license. He just smiled and said tell em, I got em. Elbert smiled and said okay and left. That was the only time he got a ticket in the 140,000 miles he commuted. He got pulled over one other time, but he let him go with a warning.

NEW JOB IN SAVANNAH

The Field Service manager in Savannah, Roy Stigilich,

transferred to Atlanta. Elbert was the Branch Service Operations Manager for the Jacksonville branch and this left them with an opening for a f Manager in Savannah. This was just 70 miles from Cob town, not a hundred and seventy miles. This could be the opportunity of a life time, if Elbert wanted to step down. Normally you want to move upward but this time he was considering moving to a lower management level. He discussed it with his manager, and he didn't want him to do it. He said he was being considered for a promotion to Jackson Mississippi as the Branch Service manager. Before he made a decision on Savannah, he and the Region wanted him to consider the Jackson Branch. Elbert checked into it and decided no, he would not move to Mississippi, he had rather move to Savannah even though it was backing up professionally.

Well, the Region approved his going to Savannah. Elbert didn't know it at the time, but there was a reason they did that. After got into Savannah after a while, he got another offer, and it was to except a promotion, to Branch Service Manager, in Columbia, South Carolina. Well, Elbert drove over there to see what the drive was like and it was a hundred and fifty miles from Cob town. Elbert told the Region the only way he would accept it was to commute. They said no they wanted him to move to Columbia. Well three months later they offered again and said he could commute. He told them no, as it was just too far to commute and he wasn't going to move thanks but no thanks.

Now that, he was situated in Savannah he got to keep his salary, which was greater, than the job called for. And his commuting expenses were considerably reduced, so he actually got a raise out of the deal. While 70 miles commute one way might sound long to some. He would be home in no time, because it was a straight shot and all expressways at 70 miles per hour and no red lights. A lot of the time he was home before some others that lived right there in Savannah.

When you commute long distances for years on end you get bored with the same scenery etc., so you start looking for shorter routes and maybe easier routes. Well, there was another route that involved in going through two other towns, highway 204/280. One of them was Claxton, Georgia and Pembroke, Georgia. Going that way, might have been a mile or two shorter, but it was two lane black top and if he got behind a school bus, it could take forever.

One of the good things about working in Savannah was there was the mall, or Lowes that he could run by, if needed, before heading home. So he had all the advantages of the big city at his finger tips. After selling their house in Jacksonville, they started moving things, little by little.

THE PIANO

Elbert's mother in law Ms Gertie as they affectionately called her had gave them a big upright Piano, for the girls to practice on. It was early one morning and Odis his father in law let Elbert use his truck, to haul the piano to Jacksonville. Elbert arranged for friends to meet him and help him unload it in Jacksonville. It started out pretty good, but soon turned into the trip from hell.

He no sooner than got fifty miles down the road and it start a misty rain. Now it is cold, it is winter time and the roads are wet but no problem yet. On down the road he was coming into Blackshear, Georgia. He was not doing more than 45 MPH, and he seen this 1951 Chevy sitting in this Liquor store parking lot , waiting to pull out into the highway. Elbert seen him and was watching him, thinking to himself if you are going to pull out do it now but he just sat there. Just as Elbert got too him, suddenly, he takes off and pulls out in front of Elbert. Elbert swerved to the right and hit the brakes, but the weight of the piano and truck, kept him sliding across the muddy parking lot on into the front yard of the man's house next door and finally stopped. The Piano had leaned against the back window of the truck and broke it, now cold air and rain is coming in on him.

Elbert looked to his left and the 1951 Chevy is slowly poking along towards Blackshear.   Somebody opened my driver's door and there stands a drunk, and he is saying he seen the whole thing.   Mr. So and so pulled out in front of you and look at him go, leaving the scene. Elbert was so glad to hear somebody seen what happened, but wouldn't you know it had to be, a drunk stumbling drunk and he has one eye looking one way and the other looks the other way, it kind of makes you wonder what he seen. Anyway, Elbert wrote down both men's names and headed on into town. On the left, was a Chevy dealer so he pulled in there to get an estimate to fix the back glass? Once he got that he used their phone to call the Sheriff. When Elbert told him what happened, he ask where was he now, and he told him. He said: you left the scene of the accident. Elbert said: yes, he was in pursuit of the man, and he didn't want to cause him trouble, but he wants the money to fix this window. If he won't pay him, Elbert wanted him arrested. He told Elbert to go on to his house and if he won't pay him, to call him again and he would talk to him.

So, Elbert found his house and he come to the door. Elbert immediately felt sorry for him. He was an older man wearing a three piece suit, living in a huge house by himself, and drunk. He invited Elbert in and Elbert told him he was the man he ran off the road at the liquor store. Elbert wanted the money to fix his broke window. He said let him call his insurance man, so Elbert stepped back outside. He came to the door again and gave Elbert a card with the address and Elbert went to the insurance office. The insurance man was nice and said it was sad. He was a good old man, but he stayed drunk and had a wreck about once a month. He wrote Elbert a check and Elbert thanked him and left. Elbert put cardboard over the hole in the window, and at least kept dry and warm for the rest of the trip. When Elbert got back to Cobbtown he had a story to tell and a check to pay for the damages, so all was not lost and all's well that ends well.

THE CAT

Elbert went by himself to Jacksonville to get the last load, clean up the house and bring their CAT. Elbert should have said mountain Lion.

Elbert locked up the house and casually, slowly, walk over to their cat. He is huge he is beige in color and is really a nice cat that has always been one to let you pick him up. But, not today! Elbert thinks he knew what was coming. So after about thirty minutes of begging on Elbert's part, and sitting still for almost fifteen minutes, so he would come to him. Elbert had him in his arms and he opened the driver's door and the cat starts to get squirmy, so Elbert jumped in and shut the door. Alright! Mission accomplished. Wrong! Things are not alright.

Elbert started up the car and started up the street and the cat is running across the dashboard, across his left shoulder to the back seat, across the back seat to the other side of the car and around and around and around. It is alike a NASCAR Race with a lot of left turns.

Now, Elbert is getting to the Matthews Bridge Toll Booth, and he is going to have to let the window down, to throw coins in the thing a ma jig. So this has to be timed just right and with arms flailing to keep the cat away from the window. Elbert quickly throws the quarter into the air and it sailed into, "Thank God", the chute. Now, in his effort to get the window up real fast, his elbow is caught, he is trying to watch where he is going, while climbing the bridge, and hit the window button with his right hand to lower the window enough to get his left arm free to raise the window again, and not let the cat get away.

Alright! Elbert made it out of town and he is flying down U S 1 highway on his way. He had the best of intentions of stopping somewhere and using the bathroom shortly, but the CAT hasn't slowed down, he is still circling the inside of the car at about 20 MPH.

Well, Elbert is starving to death, and the cat has stopped and is just resting and looking around. So Elbert said to himself, when he gets to the next town, he will get him a hamburger, and go to the bathroom. Alright, so Elbert had to look at the cat and the cat starts running again, Oh NO, now what? So Elbert has to drive on past Hardees hamburger place and continue on home. Well, Elbert finally pulled into the driveway, and the cat stops too. Elbert opened the door and said Go, you wanted out, now is your chance. About that time, Janice and the girls came running to the car and the cat shoots out of the car like a bullet and the last they seen of him, he was running a hundred miles per hour down the road.

About three or four months later, they thought they seen him, but he wouldn't come to them. And they saw him once or twice in the next year or so. Then, they never saw him after that.

MR. JOHN CROTHERS

Sometime in 1979, while traveling home to visit family in Memphis, they stopped at an outlet Mall, south of Nashville, Tennessee really to stretch their legs and to get out of the car for awhile. And, if the truth was known it was just another Mall, but the story was they needed d to shop for new shoes to match something or other.

Anyway, Elbert does not shop very well so his job is to walk the mall, down one side and up the other. And if there is an upstairs, walk that too. There has been time's Elbert has walked these monster Malls and returned to the designated place to wait for the girls and Janice is still only ten feet from the door they came in right where he left her an hour ago. The girls, Janice, Lynn and Leigh, pick up, touch, and try on, three hundred items and then buy the first one they touched. Why do women do that?

Elbert was told to go sit and wait at the shoe store, so he did. He learned a long time ago, you can argue with them and do it, or just go ahead and do it, so he went to the shoe store. He walked up and was looking in the window. The cashier was ringing up the sale of a pair of shoes for a man that was looking down at the moment but then he raised up and their eyes met and locked on each other. Elbert couldn't believe he was seeing, who he thought it was, it was Mr. Crothers, his High School Principal from back in Memphis. They both motioned to each other and he came outside and they shook hands and then he hugged Elbert. Elbert had not seen him in 20 years.

They found a bench and sit down and talked for over an hour. This was one of those times Elbert was glad, Janice and the girls, were not in a big hurry to get back on the road, as it give Elbert a few minutes to visit. Janice and the girls came up and he was able to introduce his wife and daughters to one of the men Elbert had always admired while in those school years. He was one of a few people that Elbert always wanted to be proud of him and to know, he had done well in life.

He was with the State of Tennessee Board of Education and Chairman of a team to bring a huge Nuclear Atom Accelerator to the State of Tennessee. He lived in the suburbs of Nashville and really liked living there. He asked about mother, as she was the only Cafeteria Manager he had at Kingsbury. He and mother had been friends and he had advised mother on several occasions. Elbert had been, one of those occasions, more than once.

They all walked out to the parking lot and he walked all the way to our car, it was almost like he didn't want us to leave. Mr. Crothers is part of the reason, Elbert had been recently trying to locate friends that he had special memories of and hadn't seen in thirty, forty, or fifty years. He lived another 13 years after that chance meeting and Elbert never seen him again. Elbert always felt like, he should have looked him up several more times and he regrets it today that he didn't. This is an example of one of those cases where everybody has lived life way too fast, without stopping to smell the roses.

That chance meeting and short visit, was the only real mature conversation Mr. Crothers and Elbert ever had on a man to man level. All others were a student talking to his principal. There was a big difference where he could see and feel the respect he had for Elbert and how proud he was Elbert had made something of himself. Elbert was a manager, with a major corporation, managing multimillion dollar budgets. This was a far cry from the student he knew in 1959. The skinny boy with the Brylcream and Duck tails, in his hair, that he paddled 20 years earlier.

OUR NEW HOUSE

It took three months to finish their house and for the next 37 years, they have been in another stage of their lives. The concrete says 1975 and there are the hand prints of our children. There is a saying, that to build the perfect house, you have to build at least two and just maybe, three, to get it right. Janice and Elbert thought out everything and did a great job, except for one thing. Elbert wanted a carport, wide enough to park two cars, with all the doors wide open and be able to walk around them, with an arm load of groceries.

So, he told his father in law, to put the wall right there and he did, now on the other side of that wall, just mentioned. Was Janice's utility room with the washer, dryer, and a third bath? Elbert bought her a built in ironing board that folded up into the wall and she was excited about that. The only problem was, when she opened it and brought the board down it hit the top of the washing machine.   This room also had a small cabinet with a sink and a door going outside to the pool. So, for 37 years, Elbert has heard about this wall, everyday.

At the time they built the house, Elbert had the inside walls of the carport bricked, so in the event they ever decided to close it in, they would already have three walls finished and only have to build one more, with a triple window and a door. So, after he retired, he did just that. But, this left their cars, in the hot sun so he built a three car carport and attached it to the end of the house. Now, they could come and go rain or shine and not get wet coming or going.

NEW SCHOOL FOR THE KIDS

For the girls, Leigh and Lynn, after moving, then a new home and now a new school. One of the exciting things about this new school for the kids was. This is the same school where their mother went to school when she was a student. Janice had walked these same halls. Some of the teachers, that taught their mother, were still in the community and were more than past teachers, but really true friends.

EVERYBODY, SEEMS TO KNOW EVERYBODY, THEY REALLY DO, BECAUSE MOST ARE KIN.

Everybody Elbert met, spots him for a new comer to the community. And they all ask. Who are you? Elbert tells them he is Janice's husband, and they look at me like, who is Janice? He then says Poochie's husband. And then the smiles come and they say, you don't say, well I am so and so, tell Poochie you seen so and so. People that have known her all her life know her as Poochie, a nickname that stuck from an aunt, years ago.

The majority of the people in Cob town are Sikes. And yes, they are all kin. Janice's mother was a Sikes. Janice's mother and Elbert's mother, was both born on July 2nd. They were both School Cafeteria Managers for years. Both born and raised in the country. Janice's dad was a farmer, a brick mason, a carpenter and a builder of houses, churches etc. Her sisters all left the farm and now are all back in Cobbtown. They have had many great times when the family gets together. They get together and cook, usually fish, at Joyce and Carroll's pond house. One of the first things Elbert built, right after retiring. They get together at Thanksgiving at Elbert and Janice's house. Then at Christmas time, they all meet up at Buddy and Ellen's house. Then, New Year's day, they all eat at Joyce and Carroll's.

Odis and Gertie have both passed away now. Poochie's mother

and father have truly been a blessing in our lives. Odis was really more of a best friend to me, than a father in law. And they had many, wonderful times at their house, the home place. They have eat, played and had many wonderful times, as a family.

Buddy, Poochie's brother has stayed around Cobbtown all his life. And he had a twin sister, Betty that had moved to Jacksonville but now is home and living in the home place. Jean lived all over the southeastern part of the country but finally moved back home to the Johnny nail farm, her Grandparent's on her Fathers' side. Joyce lived off in Jessup and Jacksonville for a while but moved back to the home place, next door to Odis and Bertie. And Poochie, after awhile in Savannah, Brunswick and Jacksonville, moved back to the home place across the road from Odis and Bertie.

VOLUNTEER FIRE DEPARTMENT

Right after Elbert moved to Cobbtown there was a fire or a series of fires that made the community aware they needed a new fire truck. The one they had was a 1949 Mack. Half the time, the thing wouldn't start and when it did, half the time, it wouldn't work. The community was growing with nice new brick homes going up, people moving back home, after going off into the world to make their fortune. There was several high dollar investments being made and they needed a better fire department. It was a bad feeling to be first to the fire truck and it wouldn't start.

So, they got together and recruited more volunteers. They selected a Fire Chief and called in the Forestry Service for advice. They advised the newly formed group to get their people formally trained and by doing so, their homeowners insurance would be cheaper. They quickly found the right people to help us start a formal fire department. They got the City to help, the Forestry Service, and other fire departments like Metter and Reidsville. They got the state people to help get them on the right track to obtain grants, to purchase new equipment.

The Army, at Fort Stewart, loaned them a fire truck, which they used for years. And Elbert became the Training Officer initially. They all went to every fire school available for several years and got formally and officially certified as fire fighters. Then their homeowners insurance went down. That was great. The more equipment they bought and more training they got, the more their insurance in the community, went down, again and again.

They started a campaign to get some of the younger generation to join and be trained. That proved to be the right thing as they were even more energetic than these charter members were. The mayor and councilmen got behind it through the years and they now have a fire department that is second to none. This new generation has done a beautiful job. After 25 years on the fire department, Elbert finally hung up his fire suit, as the new generation could run circles around him. It was time to get out of the way and let them do what they had been trained to do.

Elbert might add, in thinking back. This same charter group had just started a new Lions Club. And the majority of the Fire department was also the Lions Club. They were all church members of the Baptist, Methodist, or Primitive Baptist Churches. So often, if they had a fire call during church, all the churches lost their men for a while to fight fire. And Elbert might add also most everybody had known each other all their life. And at that time, they all knew where each other lived, so they got to their house pretty quick. And they saved many buildings, barns, fields, animals and people and homes. Elbert is proud to say he was a Fireman.

LIONS CLUB

One day in Sunday school our class all being about the same age wanted to start something like a Jaycees or something in our community. Someone suggested a Lions Club. Several people knew others that were Lions and they ask them to come and tell them about their organizations.

They put out notices everywhere in town, for anyone interested and they met with the Metter Lions Club and some others that explained how to get started. They started with 28 people which became Charter members. Poochie's dad Odis and Elbert became Charter members.

One of their first projects was to raise money to help the Blind was to sell Barbeque Chicken Plates. Odis and Elbert, borrowed some wire racks from somebody and they built a temporary pit with concrete blocks and charcoal and they cooked chicken half's starting early that day. Their intention was to sell plates for supper later in the day. But, they had set up in the middle of town at the red light right next to the highway. Well the smoke and the smell of the cooking made most of the traffic pull over and they sold those plates starting before lunch. They sold so many plates, that they had to go get more chicken and more charcoal. Now wouldn't you know it, it starts a misty rain. Thank goodness, it wasn't enough to put their fire out, but just enough to keep them wet, tired and smelly. They kept cooking as long as they kept coming and they made a fortune on their first project. The community really came out and supported them.

They had a great club going and they all were the best of friends. The community supported the Lion Club and Elbert had the time of his life. Elbert served in every position there was at Club level multiple times. And he went on to be everything you can be except District Governor. Elbert had to draw the line somewhere and that was it. So, now he had only recently moved to Cob town and he had been a part of a newly formed Fire Department and now a Charter member of the Lions Club of Georgia.

After 28 years Elbert slowly let a new generation take over and he supported them and helped them cook pan cakes and sausage when he could. It was an Honor and a Privilege to be a part of a community, state and worldwide organization and work with his friends doing good worldwide things for those with sight and hearing problems. Thank god these men and women exist.

CHURCH LEAGUE SOFTBALL

One day in Sunday school, someone mentioned getting up a softball game within the church. If they didn't have enough for two Boy's teams, they would make it mixed teams and play each other. Everybody liked the idea and they talked it up for awhile and the next thing they knew, they were on the way to Claxton, Georgia, to play Eastside Baptist Church in softball. They had a makeshift field. They played on a Sunday afternoon and everybody had the best time.

Cobbtown, had a ball field, but it had never been used to speak of and it was grown up in weeds and the fence was in bad shape and it didn't have dug out's nor even bases or a pitcher's mound.

So, Elbert asked Ray Archambeault, one of the city councilmen if it would be alright for the church to use the ball field? He said it was a mess right now, but if they wanted to use it, it would be fine.

So, a bunch of them went down there and cleaned the place up and cut the grass. They ask the church to give them some money to have some softball recreation. And they did. They had enough to buy bases and balls. So, they started playing every Sunday afternoon and the word got out, they had a team and some of the local churches, wanted to come play them. They eventually, had a meeting and they decided to start playing a schedule. Well, before you know it, other churches want to play and they started playing on Saturday and Sunday afternoons. Then they started drawing a crowd. The older folk started bringing a lawn chair to sit and watch the games.

Elbert made a drag to smooth the dirt part of the field and he cut the grass every Thursday and eventually someone bought them some grass seed. Then someone, give them water hoses and sprinklers. Then James Hensley and T-Mar Durden donated the money for a six foot fence. Georgia power and the county paid for lights and Byron Smith brought his crew and equipment and installed the lights for our field. Then Danny brown helped build dugouts and a bathroom for boys and girls. Then the city bought bleachers and Danny Brown and his buddies come and built roofs over the bleachers.

Then, Elbert started building a concession stand and an announcer's booth. Elbert got Danny Brown to lay the block and one day Elbert was just starting on the upper part when Mr. Tommy Brown drove up and volunteered to help him. That was a blessing as Elbert had never cut rafters before and he showed Elbert how. He told Elbert to stay up there and he would do the cutting and hand the rafters to him. Tommy and Elbert put a roof on that building before dark. Mr. Tommy was as good as they came, at being a carpenter, a Christian and a man.

Elbert traveled a lot in his job and someone told him if he went to Wrens, Georgia there was a place up there that would give them, the white powder to put the lines down at the ball field. So he went up there and asked around until he found that place and got a truck load of 50 pound bags that lasted all season. Elbert went every year and got more, for fourteen years.

It became the norm for him, to once a week, cut the grass, drag the infield, and put down the white lines and bases. He then opened the concession stand and made sure the sound system worked and got hot dogs cooking, and turn on the lights. They had three games on Thursday night, three games on Friday night and four games on Saturday night. They started having crowds of people coming from as far away as fifty miles to watch and play in these ball games. They had thousands coming.

Then, if Elbert wasn't pitching, he was umpiring or running the concession stand. And after all that, it was then time to shut everything down, lock up and turned out the lights. Did I mention he did the schedule also? And this was for fourteen years. So, now he was part of Softball, a fireman, a Lions Club member, and he had the best time of his life.

Read on for more, we are just getting started. Up until recently or the past few years, Elbert has been allowed to be a part of this community to the extent unimaginable in other places he has lived. Living in a small town and community where everybody knows everybody is unbelievable. The population is 341 or 370, something like that. If anybody dies, we go to the funeral home tonight and the funeral tomorrow out of respect and we feed the family at the church. This is the most caring community he has ever lived in.

Elbert had a heart attack in 2006, so like others his age, they are gradually being replaced by the younger generation. Some of those older than him have already passed on. Some of those were the best friends he ever had. Elbert has laid down the softball playing. He has laid down the fireman duties, he has laid down the Lions Club. He has laid down his carpenters tools and he has retired from his work at the Xerox Corporation. He has done his last Scuba Diving. Elbert only has a few more Car shows to go to. And he will lay that down also.

Elbert love's his Church, but he may retire as a Deacon soon and leave it to the younger generation. Elbert grew up and found friends he never knew he had. He found friends he had not seen or talk to in 50 years. He lived long enough to tell them he loved them that he missed them and he cared for them. He has lived long enough to find out some he revered, are unworthy. Some he trusted he has learned it was misplaced. Some he thought were a friend, he learned they were not. He has lived long enough.

He has listened to some and what he heard is they haven't lived long enough. This might be the definition of Wisdom. For some have Wisdom, and their hair seems to be white, silver or gray.

CHURCH AND ELBERT

ELBERT grew up in church. As a child he attended the Bethel Assembly of God church in Memphis, Tennessee. The pastors were Brother Frank Massorino and his wife, Sister Iris. Sister Iris is the sweetest lady he has ever known. She lives today in 2009 he learned recently. As a child, was in awe of the preaching seen. He never grew to understand a message, but he got the message by how they loved the Lord and how they loved you and me. Brother Frank was an extrovert preacher. He talked fast, he talked loud, and he ranted and raved. He sweated, People rolled in the floor, others shouted and waved their hands. Yes, they scared him to death. So, sometimes, the preacher's son and Elbert would sneak out and hide behind the bushes outside and wait for church to be over.

Elbert visited other churches and learned they were not all the same. He learned that there was some he was more comfortable in and he didn't want to go back. But it didn't matter what he wanted, he was a kid and would do as he was told. There were other churches that he was eager to go back to. Those were the ones, where he didn't cringe and sit wide eyed. The ones where he understood the sermon, he didn't always agree with his conclusion, but he always assumed, he spoke what the Lord would have him to say and have him to hear. Later in life, Elbert learned some were messages were from the lord and some were not.

The lord he knows is a loving lord. He loves him and knows his heart. He forgives and Elbert's name is written in the book of life. That on Judgment day, some may receive his favor and his blessings more than Elbert. But Elbert will be there, he truly believe's.

In the Philippines, when Elbert was in service. Elbert was walking down a road late at night all by himself, and the sky had fallen all around him and the stars seemed to be close enough for him to touch. The Lord and Elbert had a talk. It was one where Elbert listened to him tell him where he was going wrong and showed him the light and the path to happiness. His life changed that night.

He came home, got married and went to Bull Street Baptist Church in Savannah, Georgia. Then, one Sunday, a message being preached hit him like a ton of bricks. It so affected him that it was on his mind all week long. He couldn't wait for Sunday to hurry and get here. He had decided that if it was meant for him to join this church at this time, he would make him walk that isle and join that church. At the end of the sermon, he knew. He said to himself, they would always sing two verses at the end of the service. He mentally, said to himself, if they sing a third verse, he would join that church. He will give himself to the Lord. When they started the third verse, he let go of his wife's hand and walked down that isle. He wanted to be baptized. He felt his love and he has tried to be that man ever since. Has he been that man, the Lord would have him to be? No, he has sinned, he failed, and he has been tempted and tried. He has failed.

Does the Lord still love him? Sure he does. He does not love the sin, but he loves the sinner. Does he forgive me? Sure he does. He forgives you and him.

In Jacksonville, Florida his family, went to Arlington Road Baptist Church. Every church he has ever attended, he learned something that has stayed with him, ever since. This, he wanted to say, and he wanted you to hear him.

One Sunday, on their way to church, Poochie said to him, they needed to stop on their way home and get milk and bread. He said okay, no problem. During the morning service, the plate came by him and he reached in his pocket and he only had a $20 dollar bill. So, now he was thinking, could he maybe take some back, so he can stop and get milk and bread on the way home? Then, he thought, no don't you do that, give the $20 and forget it. So, he did. It didn't even stay on his mind. They got in the car and headed for home. Janice said, don't forget to stop and buy milk and bread. Elbert looked at her and said: "I can't" and she said: "why not? " He said, "I only had a twenty dollar bill and I put it in the plate. " She didn't say anything for a minute and then said, "No matter, we'll figure out something. " When they got home, there sit a friend of his that owed him $400. Now, you might say, oh that was a coincidence. Well, He'll be honest and tell you, he did to at the time. But that was sometime around 1974. And the last time it happened just like that, was in 2008. And it has happened several times in between. Believe me, trust in the Lord, and he will provide.

One Sunday in Jacksonville, Bob Harrington, come to our church and preached a revival. He was known as the Bourbon Street Preacher. He became known, as the Preacher who went into the bars of New Orleans preaching. He might not have changed New Orleans very much, but at least he tried. He was terrific and people was walking the isles and he eventually left us and went on to another church somewhere. Elbert later learned, he came to their church, but they had to pay him a lot of money to come. That bothered Elbert for a long time. If he was so holy, how could he charge some outrageous price and make a profit on the word of God? Elbert knew he had to make a living, but there was a lot more paid to him than a living. Elbert chalked it up to one of those things he didn't understand but who was he to suggest he was anything else but what he said he was. Then later, Elbert heard he had left the Ministry, with all the money and took his secretary with him. Now twice, he has caused Elbert to question a man of the cloth. Elbert learned then, that there were those that were not of the cloth that would have you believe otherwise.

Then moved to Cobbtown, and he joined the Cobbtown Baptist Church. He had heard many preachers and one day, he was asked to allow his name to be nominated as a deacon in 1977. He thought about it and said okay. If this is to be, it will be and if not he could understand it just wasn't to be. Well, he became a Deacon. He went to many deacon meetings and helped to solve many problems of the times in the church and a multitude of other little things.

Then, his world blew up and fell apart. A called meeting occurred and the problem presented.   In addition to that, a solution was offered. The solution was, to take a pastor out of the pulpit. Now up until now, on Judgment day, Elbert only had to answer for himself. Now, he is thinking okay, how do we know these charges are true? So, he sat and listened to others. Then, it came down to a vote of what to do. So Elbert said: "When I die, and I am standing before the lord, what I don't want to hear is. The lord saying to me, Who do you think you are, taking one of my pastors out of the pulpit and preventing my word from being spread? And especially if I don't have any proof. So, I will tell you now, if you have nobody to be a witness, I will vote we go home and forget it. Two deacons, immediately said: My wife is the accuser. I said, okay, as a deacon, I will take your word that he is guilty. And if he is not, it will be on your head. And with that, he voted for dismissal.

Then another devastating blow occurred in the pulpit. This time, the law was involved. There was an arrest, a trial, and time served.

Then, another occasion that caused a split in the church body and a long time negative effect on families and members alike, because another man of the cloth, claimed to be one thing and he ended up being another.

Elbert has lived long enough, to see things that it took time to understand. So much we see happening around us at the time, we only think we understand. It takes years to put all the pieces together to be able to understand. That is why older people seem to have greater wisdom. They have lived it and know for a fact, what the truth is and what supposition is. They know what to stand up too.   And when to walk away and let a sleeping dog ly.

The greatest lesson Elbert has learned in his life is the lord doesn't need his help. The lord works in mysterious ways. If you study the bible, you will understand. We are saved by Faith and Faith alone.

OKLAHOMA STREET ROD NATIONALS CAR SHOW

One Thursday morning, Elbert got up and got dressed to go to work as usual. He wasn't in any kind of hurry as everything was going like it was suppose to. All his employees were busy at work and he had no messages which meant no complaints from customers or his boss.

He stopped in town to buy gas. Now, this is not, just a gas station. The owner, Buddy Collins, is also the mayor of Cobbtown. He is also the only Mechanic in town.

It was close to 8 o'clock and several of the older men in town, had come up and was sitting on the Dead Pecker Bench already. Elbert got the usual hellos, Hi Ya's and what's up comments. And Elbert told Buddy to charge the gas he had pumped. He filled his truck up and paid once a month. It was not uncommon to have a bill of $400 a month, but Buddy liked it that way and it was fine with Elbert too.

About that time, Elbert's cell phone went off and it was, his brother Wayne. He was in Oklahoma City to install some computers at the main post office and was staying at the Residence Inn out close to the Fairgrounds, where they were having a car show. Wayne was calling to tell Elbert about it and to tell him to come on out there and he could stay with him. There were 20,000 old cars there, every color you could imagine with big chrome plated Engines and fancy interiors.

Elbert told him he would think about it and let him know something later in the day. After he hung up the old men sitting on that "Bench" had heard everything Elbert said. They started on him. Why don't you go? You don't do anything, anyway. Now you have to understand these old men. They were farmers that worked from daylight to dark and anybody that wears a suit and tie, and don't go to work until 8 o'clock and quits work at 5 o'clock. Well, in their eyes they don't do anything. They just don't know how hard it is to talk on the phone all day and sit in meetings and ride the roads all over the southeastern part of the U.S.

Elbert decided to drink another cup of coffee with them and the more he thought about it, he finally said: Why not? Elbert called Charlie hall, his right hand man and told him he was taking off for a few days. And, he needed for him to look after things while he was gone. Charlie said, go on and have a good time. So, Elbert went home and changed clothes, loaded his truck with his things and took off. Elbert blew the horn as he passed the old men and they waved. Elbert headed for Atlanta, Chattanooga, Nashville, Memphis, Little Rock, and finally stopped for the night, in a rest area, about 50 miles from Oklahoma

City. He slept until the sun woke him up and he went inside and freshened up, shaved and changed clothes.

As Elbert pulled into Oklahoma City, he seen the fairgrounds and since Wayne was at work, Elbert went to the car show. He walked and looked until about 4:30 that afternoon and left to find the Residence inn, to wait on Wayne to get off work. Elbert found the Residence Inn on the street Wayne had mentioned and described. He said, he could sit out front and watch the cars coming and going to the car show. And he was right. Elbert parked and seen they were cooking hamburgers with all the trimmings and potato salad and drinks in large plastic cups. Elbert had stayed at Residence inn's before and knew this was for their registered guest and since he was staying as Wayne's guest, surely he was welcome to a burger and a drink. So, he helped himself. Elbert set up his lawn chair in the front lawn so he could see the cars and Wayne would surely see him when he got off work.

After awhile, Elbert went back and got another burger and a drink. He then returned to his spot and was having a great time. Then, Elbert began to wonder, where is Wayne? Was he working late? Had Elbert missed something? Had he come home and Elbert missed him?

Elbert decided to go inside and ask the desk clerk to ring Wayne's room. He looked and said: he had no Wayne Alberson registered. Elbert told him Oh No, that can't be he had called me yesterday from here. Maybe the room is registered to the Post Office. He checked and said no. He was sorry. Elbert give him a blank stare and asked: Is there another Residence inn on this same street, or somewhere around here? He smiled and said: oh yes, about four blocks down the street. Elbert ask him, could you call them and see if he is registered there? He said sure. He called and Wayne came on the phone. Elbert told him he would be right there (Laughing out Loud)

When Elbert found him, Elbert told him he was at the wrong Residence inn. Wayne had a barbecue sandwich in one hand and a drink in the other and he asked have you eaten yet? Elbert told him he had been sitting in a lawn chair on their front lawn, for the past three hours and he was full. Elbert had eaten two cheese burgers, potato salad and two drinks at the other place. He didn't need any supper.

Wayne is rolling on the ground laughing saying, No, you didn't. They are both laughing like idiots. They had a great time and seen at least one of every kind of car ever made before 1949. Elbert got up Monday morning and when he went to work, Elbert headed for home. He drove nonstop and it took 25 hours. I guess you could call him, a spur of the moment kind of guy.

STREET RODS

In 1992, Elbert's other brother Neal called him and wanted him to meet Neal in Louisville, Kentucky for the National Street Rod Association Car Show. There were three of Elbert's buddies, Carroll Oliver, Doug Allen and Johnny Pearsall that wanted to go so, they drove up there. WOW, there were fifteen thousand cars that were 1948 and older, painted every color that you can imagine with big chrome motors. Elbert got so excited, that he decided then when he got home, he would build him one of these cars, all this on the first day of being there.

The second day he was there, he was inside the main building going from one vender to another, collecting catalogs and talking to the venders about different things. Suddenly, someone came in the building yelling, if your car is parked so and so, it is going to be flooded if you don't move it. Elbert went to the door and looked outside and it was a solid wall of water. When the rain storm was over, 900 cars had been flooded. They got soaked moving cars and getting them to higher ground. One young couple said they had spent money they shouldn't have, on their car and she was crying. They had a 1932 Ford roadster, baby blue in color and beautiful even although it was almost covered in water. They were up all night draining water from the motor, transmission, rear end, and inside of their car. The last time Elbert seen them, they were going down the road.

When Elbert got home from seeing all those beautiful cars he started looking for a motor to build. He found a 1979 Chevrolet and bought it from Wallace Jarriel and he towed it home for Elbert. Elbert pulled the motor and transmission and sold the rest for junk. He took the motor to John Moore and got him to rebuild the heads, bore it and turn the crank. While Elbert was there one day, he met Eddie

Funderburk and asked him if he recommended the transmission place across the street. He said they were okay, but why didn't Elbert just rebuild it himself. Elbert told him he had never done it before. Eddie said to come to his house, he had a book Elbert could use, and Elbert could do it. So Elbert did. That transmission is still running strong, today. Elbert had to borrow some special tools from Wallace Jar riel, but he got it done.

So now Elbert has a motor built, sitting in his shop ready to put in a car. He has a transmission ready to go, but still no car.

Well, Elbert was on his way to Jesup, Georgia on a back highway when out of the corner of his eye, he spotted an old car sitting in the weeds off the side of the road. Elbert couldn't tell what kind it was, but he turned around and went back. Elbert got out and walked into these weeds as high as his head. Now, he is in a suit and tie parting the weeds and watching out for a snake when he finally got to it. It was a car that he had never seen before. It was huge a four door hump back trunk, car. This is the kind of car, Al Capone, might have drove back in the 1930's. It was a 1937 Oldsmobile. The two back doors were suicide doors meaning they opened the wrong way and if you opened them going down the road the wind would jerk them open and jerk you out into the road.

Elbert happened to look up and seen an old man, watching him from off in the distance. So, he went back to his truck and drove over to talk to the old man. He asked him if that was his old car. He said no, but, it was his son's car, but he wouldn't sell it. Elbert had to ask him what kind of car was it. He said: It was a 1937 Oldsmobile. Elbert's first take on the car was, it was so ugly he liked it. The more they talked the old man told him his son was building a new house. Elbert thought to himself, yeah he will sell it. If he was building a new house he needed all the money he could find. Elbert left him his card and told him to tell his son if he wanted to sell it, to call him. When Elbert got home later that night he had already called. Elbert called him back and he said he didn't want to sell it but he could sure use the money. Elbert asked him, what he wanted for it, and he said he had to get a thousand for it. Elbert told him he would sleep on it and they hung up. When Elbert got off the phone, Poochie asked him, is that a good price? Elbert said yes he would have given him $3, 000 for it. She said, well if you want it call him back right now. So Elbert did.

The next day, Elbert asked Wallace if he would take him to get an old car, over near Lanes Bridge with his wrecker. He said sure, let's go. Well, they went within seven miles of Jesup and Wallace said you have got to be kidding me, what are you going to do with that piece of junk. I don't want that ugly thing behind my wrecker. I told him to hush Wallace, just back into that field and follow me. Elbert made sure there wasn't a hole or a stump. They hooked to it and here they came back out onto the road. They pulled it over to where the old man was and Elbert paid him. Then, they headed for home. Wallace was fussing all the way. You are never going to do anything with that junk. Elbert told him, you wait and see, one day he would drive up and take him for a ride.

It took Elbert four and a half years to build it but when he got it painted and upholstery, he drove to his shop and blew the horn until he came out and Elbert told him, to put his fat butt in, as he was taking him for a ride. He couldn't believe it, but this baby would haul buggy.

The first trip Elbert took in it was to Panama City Florida. On the way there, he broke a valve spring, but got it fixed and it run like a charm on the way back home. The next trip was to Birmingham, Alabama and he had a distributor go bad. But he got that fixed and it run fine going back home, since then, Elbert has driven it to Louisville, Kentucky twice, Knoxville, Tennessee, several times. And Pigeon Forge, Tennessee several times. At the Birmingham car show, they took an 18 by 24 inch picture of his car and framed it. He bought it and it hangs in their den today. Not many people have a picture of their car in the den.

In the past few years, Elbert has done several weddings with his car, taking the bride and groom from the church to the reception etc. He even had a couple he took to the prom and out to eat afterwards. The boy was cool now; he had on a tux, with a wide brim Fedora hat and the long key chain. If he had had a big cigar, he would have looked just like Al Capone. Both families took tons of pictures and they were on the internet, as well as in the Statesboro, Georgia newspaper.

This car is a top end car and not much from a red light. It has a Chevy V8 300 hp motor, power steering , power brakes, tilt steering wheel, wooden steering wheel, air conditioning, Crager Super Sport Wheels, reversed rims in the rear and light grey interior from a 98 Olds Braun. She is fire engine Red with tinted windows. And it rides as good as a Lincoln Town Car.

DEER AT THE BREADFAST ROOM WINDOW

One day, Poochie and Elbert were in the kitchen and he had his back to the window talking to her. All of a sudden Poochie's eyes got big and her mouth flew open and she said: turn around slowly and look at the window. There is a deer looking in the window. Elbert slowly turned and sure enough, there he was. He was not a full grown deer but he wasn't a baby either. He had nubbins for horns. They slowly started for the den door that opens to their back yard. Poochie and Elbert walked out slowly because they didn't want to scare him and cause him to fall into the pool. He slowly walked up to Poochie and rubbed on her like a cat. Pooches said: go get the cam recorder and Elbert did.

Poochie said: bring those biscuits off the stove when you come and he did. Elbert give them to Poochie and she walked up onto their deck and sat in the swing. She held out biscuit crumbs and the deer eat out of her hand. Elbert was filming the whole thing and then he went towards Elbert, and rubs against him like a cat. He then walked away dangerously close to the pool and laughingly Elbert asked Poochie how do you call a deer away from the pool, here deer, here deer? The sound on the video picked up them talking to the deer. After a few minutes the deer laid down in the shade of a tree in the back yard just like he lived there. And later that night he was still there. The next day they fed him again and he hung around all day. They saw him again a day or so later and then he was gone. He might have been shot or he just left, they don't really know.

They don't know why he even showed up. It was Easter time and the timing gave them all kinds of thoughts as to what this was. They wondered if he was a pet that had wandered off. They learned a few days later he had been down the road to Janice's sister's house. They have a big dog in the yard but the deer and the dog played with each other. One would chase the other then back and forth. This was the strangest thing. Thank goodness they filmed it and have shown it to many people. He was a spike Buck, not very big but he was pretty and it was a wonderful experience.

Several years later Elbert had run to the store and when he drove up, he could see splashing and waves in the pool, so he walked around to the pool expecting to see his niece swimming and what he saw was a little fawn deer. He got a rope from his truck and lassoed him and pulled him out. He was so tired he just lay there for a minute and it gives Elbert a chance to take the rope off. After a few minutes   he jumped up and ran off flying through the air as hard as he could run into the woods. Thank goodness, he didn't do any damage to the pool.

MOTHERS SURGERY

Mother underwent surgery to remove a section of colon that was cancerous. She got better and went home but, only for a short while. Her incision burst open and required more hospitalization and surgery. They removed even more, of her colon.

Janice and Elbert had gone to Memphis to be with her but Elbert had to leave for awhile and return to Atlanta for a few days. He intended to go back to Memphis and get Janice. A week later Janice called Elbert and told him the Doctor had given her a week to live and she wouldn't go anywhere but to their house in Cobbtown. So she would bring his mother in her Caddy and meet him in Atlanta. Elbert got them a handicap room in the motel where he was staying and waited for them to come to him. It was winter time and cold. Elbert was standing in the parking lot when they drove up. He could see Janice was crying and his mother was lying in the back seat. Elbert asked why she was crying and Janice said just help us get inside. When he opened the door the odor was terrible. But he carried his mother inside and straight into the bathroom. They stripped her down and got her in the shower as she had a colonoscopy and the bag had come loose and the stuff was everywhere and smelled terrible.

They got his mother cleaned up and a new bag applied to the opening in her stomach. She was worn out and quickly went to sleep. While Janice took a shower and got into bed Elbert went outside and gathered all the soiled blankets and put them in big garbage bags, then put them in the trunk of the car. Then he opened all four doors and left them like that all night to air out. The next morning Elbert went got them all breakfast and brought it to the room. And eventually they headed for home.

    Elbert learned later from Janice while they were on the road his mother had to use the bathroom so they pulled into a gas station. When they opened the door to go inside there stood a motorcycle gang playing pool and drinking. They showed them the bathroom and were very nice and helped them get back in the car. Then as they got to Atlanta they were paving the road at night and that was why Janice was crying when she got to the motel. The car heater was on wide open to keep his mother warm and her bag had burst and the odor was stifling and they were sitting in stopped traffic   for long periods of time.

    After a few days at their house, his mother got worse and they had to take her to the emergency room. They admitted her into the hospital and said she had a week to live at most. Two nights later she found scissors and cut the IV's and left the hospital. They called Elbert and they rushed to the hospital. They found her outside, sitting on steps leading to the building next door. The hospital said she needed to be in a nursing home. So they moved her there. A short time later, she had a problem and they took her to a Doctor friend of theirs in Augusta, Georgia that was a specialist and a surgeon, Vendee Hooks. He immediately hospitalized her in Augusta and operated on her that night. Now all of her intestines are gone but 13 inches. She was in the hospital 63 days and moved to therapy for one day and back to the hospital for 63 more days. Then back to the Metter Nursing home again.

    His mother had given Elbert power of attorney and he was paying her bills. Then she sent him to Henning, Tennessee, to sell the two houses she owned and to have a tag sale at her house. Now she has been into antiques for years and has quite a few pretty and expensive things. She had made a list and wrote down the price of everything she had. So, Janice and Elbert headed to Henning. They got it advertised and everything ready and started the sale. At the end of the day, they had sold $13,000 dollars, just for her antiques. The next few days, they sold both houses and almost everything else. Elbert called his brothers and their wives to come and help them and they were a blessing.

On the last day, they rented a truck and put what did not sell in the truck to take back home with them. They got the house cleaned up and took the key to the lady that bought the house. They then decided to go and spend the night with Elbert's dad before going back to Georgia. They had to go into Memphis where he lived and Elbert was probably driving a little fast but he had to slam on brakes and he locked up the wheels and flat spotted the tires, before coming to a stop. Elbert never hit anything but now the truck went bump, bump, bump, on those bad tires.

When they got to Elbert's dad's house it was late and Poochie went on to bed while Elbert and his dad sat up and talked. Eventually, they went to bed. When Elbert turned back the bed spread, he had not turned on the light, so it was dark in the room. But he noticed the sheet was striped. He thought to himself his dad is getting fancy in his old age. Well, the next morning, when Elbert woke up. He noticed there were no sheets on the bed at all. Poochie and Elbert both had slept on the mattress, without sheets. They got a big laugh out of that. They told his dad, they slept well and never mentioned it. They just remade the bed like it was.

They got out the phone book and called the truck rental place and told them about the tires, so they said bring it to them and they would fix it, and they did. But it put them late leaving Memphis.

When they got back home, they were going to rent a storage place for the things that didn't sell, but it was cheaper to rent an apartment. So they did. It was amazing they had everything his mother needed to set up housekeeping again so they arranged everything just like she was going to live there   and left it.

Well, three months later his mother was getting better and better so she up and checked herself out of the Nursing home and lived with them for a month or so. They took her to the apartment and all she needed was a stove and refrigerator. She insisted on moving in by herself. She wouldn't have it any other way. So, she moved in and continued to get better and better. She had a next door neighbor that she liked and she was happy there for over a year. Then she came to the house one day and said: She wanted Elbert to rent a truck she was moving back to Memphis. Elbert said what?

She said to Memphis? Where in Memphis? She told him she had bought a house already, Elbert asked her how did you do that? She said, she had bought it sight unseen she had Doris go look at it and Doris liked it. Doris was a lifelong friend of hers from before Elbert was born. And Doris lived in the neighborhood. So Elbert rented a truck, loaded all her things up. Elbert called his brothers and had them meet him to unload, when they got there.

Janice drove their car Elbert drove the truck and his mother drove her Caddy. Elbert told his mother to stay behind him and follow the big yellow truck. Well they were doing so good until they came to a weight station. Elbert had to go through the scales, and he noticed Janice was out on the expressway waiting for him to go through the scales, but where was his mother? She didn't appear to be behind him. It scared him to death and when he pulled out of the scales, he pulled over to ask Janice if she knew where his mother was. When he climbed out of the truck there was his mother. She had been behind him all the way through the scales. She had followed so close he couldn't see her in the rear view mirrors and she went through the scales with him. So he told her to not follow so close and don't go through the scales stay with Janice until came back out.

Well, they got to Memphis and found the house that she had bought sight unseen. It was a nice house and close to Doris, Elbert thought this will be great. His brothers and their wives were there and they got all her things unloaded and set up housekeeping for her, even hung pictures. They didn't spend the night though, as they all had to get back to their jobs.

Elbert's mother called them three days later and they ask her how she liked her new house? She said, it is fine she had just got nested and thought she would like this place, a lot better than the other one. Elbert didn't catch it, at first but he eventually did. Did you?

She didn't like the place they moved her into that she bought sight unseen. She didn't want them to know it and just acted like she was okay with it. So, as soon as we left she started looking for another place and found it. Then she called a moving company and had them to move her. She was calling to give us the phone number and address. Now is she something else or what?

    Elbert's mother, went on to marry for the sixth time, and went to Greece on her honeymoon. She lived four more years after that, and she always wanted to be buried in the town she was born and raised in, Macon, Tennessee. She went up there and found out, who took care of the cemetery, and arranged to be buried there, next to her brothers and sisters. She then made her funeral arrangements with Memphis Funeral Home.

    And like Paul Harvey, Elbert will tell you the rest of the story. She lived life to the fullest and stayed busy and active right up to the very end. That was his mom.

SNOW SKIING BEECH MOUNTAIN, NORTH CAROLINA

    When Elbert lived in Jacksonville, Florida, they had some neighbors down the street that become dear friends until this day. Ron and Linda Callahan, Linda's family lived in Beaufort, South Carolina and had a Construction company on Hilton head, South Carolina. The family had a Chalet on Beach Mountain and they rented it out, from time to time and loaned it to friends. One winter, the week between Christmas and New Years, they almost insisted, we take the girls and some friends and go have fun. So, the girls invited some of their friends and Janice's sister's family, all wanted to go,so they lit out. They had never been before and this was the adventure of the year for them.

    They drove and drove and had yet to see any snow and were worried that when they got there, there would not be any snow. However, when they got to Banner Elk, North Carolina and stopped at the red light. They turned left and went about a mile turning right and starting up the mountain. They are following this steep narrow road up the mountain going around some hair pin turns. When suddenly they came around a curve and there is the beginning of snow. They got so excited they pulled over and threw snow balls at each other. Then got back in the car and continued on and the snow got deeper and deeper

COTTON TOP

until when they got to the top of the mountain it looked like Alaska.

At the top the road flattened out. They seen FREDS the little country store. They pulled into the parking lot and snow and ice is everywhere. It is so cold everybody's nose turned red and they hurried inside. Inside it is packed with people and things. You could hardly walk. They started looking for gloves, and warm hats etc. They bought the things on their list like food, drinks, firewood, and kindling for the fireplace.

They loaded up and headed out to find the Chalet. They follow the directions they had and they almost missed it. They seen these steps, winding up the side of the hill and way up yonder is the Chalet, hanging off the side of the mountain. They now have to lug all their things up the steps to the top.

Elbert was going real slow and at the last minute, was able to pull over and stop. However, Joyce and Carroll were behind us. Poochie told Elbert to lower your window and wave for them to stop. He did and they waved back, as they slid on past us with their tires sliding and not turning. They slid on down the hill a ways and finally stopped in a snow bank. Elbert knew right then, they needed snow chains.

They left their car where it was for the moment. They got out and carried all their things up to the Chalet. It proved to be very nice with four or five bedrooms and a big fireplace in the living room. They turned on the power and got the electric heat going and built a fire in the fireplace and now to find the valve to cut on the water. Their instructions said to go outside in the front yard and near the trees, there is a hole with a big handle to turn on the water from the street. So, Elbert looked and looked and he finally found it. So now they are thinking, let's go exploring and see what is up here and see where everything is. But, there's a problem. We have two cars and one is in a snow bank and the other one is free, but it won't move back up the road without snow chains. Elbert is thinking, please let FRED'S, have SNOW CHAINS. And, let them be reasonably priced.

Now, to get to FRED'S, there isn't but one thing to do and that is start walking. Maybe they can hitch a ride. Carroll and Elbert start out up the road to the bigger road. As they got to the big road, a Minivan came by with it's side door open and the occupants are waving at Elbert and Carroll that are showing them their thumb, so they stop and pick them up and took them to Fred's.

Elbert found the chains that would fit his car and decided to buy a set and they will all ride in one car. And next year if they come again, they will have chains to use. They ended up costing around a hundred dollars and something. But Elbert bought them. Elbert had plans to come back to do this again, as this was fun and exciting. They caught a ride back lugging these heavy chains and put them on the car before dark in case they needed to leave for any reason.

NOTE: These chains became the criteria for the next five cars Elbert bought. Every new car had to have the same size wheels and tires, so he could use the chains over and over and over. They used them for ten years, before they finally started to come apart.

The next morning, they were off to the ski lift. This was the most fun thing they had ever had as a family. They laughed at each other falling and falling and falling again. Elbert didn't know there were over a hundred ways to fall down. They rented skis for everybody and here they went. They found the kiddy slope first and they loved that. So after a while, they moved on to the beginner slope and this is just too much fun. After all day of skiing and going in and out to eat warm up and rest. They end their first day of skiing and nobody got hurt. Now, they all got in the car, a Ford LTD four doors and headed back to the Chalet. Did he mention there are ten of them? And they all have on these bulky clothes, jackets plus five sets of ski's and ski boots and poles. You should have seen them. They looked like modern day Beverly Hill Billy's. Five sit in the back and two lay across them then three rode in the front seat.

They made it back to the Chalet and everybody is showering and putting on warm clothes. Some wanted to wash and dry some of their clothes so that is going on and Elbert is in the process of changing clothes and down to nothing but my jockey shorts, when all of a sudden: BAAMMMNN   WHOOOOOOSH.

Water is spraying everywhere the hose on the washer busted and Elbert needed to turn off the water fast. So, he ran to the front door with nothing on but his jockey shorts and tried to run in waist deep snow to the water cut off. He had almost made it when he stepped in a hole almost over his head. He climbed out of that clawing at the snow and ice and he cut his hands and feet but he got the water cut off. Then he went back inside to put some clothes on and then found the problem a busted hose. Elbert cut the water off to the washer and then had to go back outside and turn the water back on again, he came in bleeding from the scrapes and his lips are blue and his teeth are chattering as he headed for a hot shower to warm up and get into some warm clothes .

    The next morning, after a big breakfast everybody struggled into their ski clothes and they piled into the car again and here they went. Elbert checked at Fred's, but he didn't have a new hose. So, they headed off to go skiing. They got there and got their ski tickets and they are all looking at the ski lift taking people up the mountain and hoping nobody says let's do that now. Well, that was too much to hope for. So here they go and they are riding to the first place you can get off the ski lift and ski back down the hill. Well, they learned it is harder to get off the lift than to get on it. It never stops, so you have to get ready and ski out of the way of the chair, or it will knock you down. After it knocks you down a few times, you learn and you remember.

    So after watching a hundred people, well maybe not a hundred people, as just they head on down the hill, like it was easy as pie. They just did the same thing. The only thing was, those other people went on down the hill and they all fell forty times all along the way.

    After getting down to the bottom, Elbert started looking for Poochie. There she was way up the hill, walking along, with her skis in her hand. So, Elbert walked up to her and helped her get back down. When they got back down, they decided to watch everybody for awhile. They seen Leigh fall and was talking to somebody. Elbert took off and decided to just head for the bottom. Everything is working pretty well and he is going faster and faster and he is almost to the bottom. Then he realized he didn't know how to stop. Elbert started yelling for people to get out of the way, saying he don't know how to stop.

    Well Elbert missed the people and went right through this opening in the fence, and into the ski shop where you rent skis. The doors were open, thank God. When he stopped, he leaned on the counter and this guy looked at him like he was crazy, and Elbert said: Thank goodness those doors were open.

Elbert took off his skis and walked back out there to wait on everybody else. Elbert was talking to this little old lady when he heard somebody yelling they can't stop. The old lady was taking a picture of her grand kid, and when she looked up, Leigh nailed her doing about fifty miles an hour. They both lay on the snow and the lady said: she just got out of the hospital with back surgery. Elbert thought, oh no, Leigh has killed her. But she was okay. She got up laughing.

They were watching the little kids they ski and don't even use ski poles. It seems they are closer to the snow and don't need them. This has been a terrific trip so far and hopefully the first of many. Elbert ask Leigh, what did that guy tell you coming down from the ski lift? Leigh smiled, he said, don't try to be so careful, or you will fall forty times. Just head for the bottom and let it rip. You might fall, but it will be only one time, not forty times. That was what she was doing when she plowed into that lady.

THE EVERGREEN BUNCH

Elbert's family had been snow skiing several times and they had run into several friends up there before, like Pat and Kay and Don and Faye Kennedy and their family. Then their friends in the evergreen community had heard their stories of the fun they were having. They suggested they all get together and plan a trip. So, the week between Christmas and New Years that year, they all went. There was Joan and Wendell and their bunch, Robert and Becky West and their bunch, Jerry and Melba Caldwell and their bunch, Howard West and his bunch, and Elbert and Janice and their bunch. They had a pure Convoy going up there on the highway. Wendell led the way and drove so fast, Robert and Becky were bringing up the rear, having to drive 95 miles per hour to stay up with everybody else. Then Wendell wanted to take the Blue Ridge parkway and while it was fun for many, Becky got car sick and turned the color of grass. Elbert felt so sorry for her, she was really car sick.

They had pulled into a state park that had a pretty little lake, so they spent several hours walking around to let Becky rest and get better. They were only half way there. It was funny in one respect, but certainly not funny for Becky. As usual some wanted to go one way, some another, but we ended up staying together.

They eventually made it to Beach Mountain, and got nested. Becky eventually got her color back. Everybody had heard about the Boone Inn in Boone, North Carolina, so they all had to go there for breakfast the next morning. Elbert never saw a man eat so many ham biscuits as Jerry Caldwell did. It sure was good.

After they were full, they went back to Beach Mountain to ski, and they all went skiing and they all had a ball. Everything is cool and it's time to head back to the cabins, they had rented. So they spread the word to everybody and started leaving. Well, the cabin Elbert and Janice were staying in faced the ski slope and Elbert got him a coffee and he is watching the skiers when he seen the emergency people going up the slope and then another, then another and another. Well he is trying to figure out what they are doing, when here they come back down, hauling skier after skier on their little sleds. About that time, some of our crowd came in and they are laughing, and Elbert told them what he had just seen.

After awhile, somebody started cooking supper as they all were going to eat together that night at Elbert's place. Well, all of a sudden, they missed Jerry and Melba. Somebody went looking for them and they were nowhere to be found. Well, everybody waited and waited, they figured they might not have got the word that everybody was leaving and going back to the cabins. But surely they did.

Well, everybody started eating without them and about an hour later, somebody finally seen them drive up to the cabin. They got out of the car and was walking okay, so they knew it wasn't them being hauled off hurt. They come in and told everybody their story. Melba, had rode the ski lift up to the first place to get off and was coming down out of control and had no idea how to stop. Well, there was a ski instructor talking to a class and she had them all lined up in a row in front of her talking to them, when here come Melba, like a bowling ball and she got a strike. She plowed into them and broke the leg of the only lady in the crowd that could drive. Now they didn't even have a driver for their vehicle. And several of them ended up in the hospital.

Melba, feeling guilty and sorry for them, went to the hospital with them. And this was before cell phones and she didn't have any idea, how to call anybody and let us know, where they were.

Years earlier, Elbert had found a Rolex watch, when they lived in Jacksonville, and he happened to be wearing it. A young boy had just walked up to him and asked what time was it and Elbert told him. A few minutes later, Elbert looked again to see what time it was and it was gone. Elbert had just lost that watch and it was nowhere to be found. It was in the snow somewhere close but he never did find it. Elbert said he guessed it was easy come, easy go. Then Leigh came up and she had lost her camera she had just bought. The next day, they went to lost and found and there was her camera, but Elbert never did find his watch. When the snow melted, somebody found them, a very good watch just like he did.

RETIREMENT

Retirement become the Buzz word around Xerox , as far back as 1993, Elbert wasn't old enough and nobody really bothered him about it and he was really busy with other things, he didn't give it much thought.

Then in 1994, he started hearing about bridges to retirement, for those people not old enough to retire, but he was still not interested. Shortly after that, he got an early out offer. But he said thank you, but no thanks.

Well, now here came another offer. It is very attractive, but he is still not interested. Elbert is making really good money and enjoying the benefits of this hard earned income. Now, he didn't get to where he was, by being stupid. He knew from prior years, that there was something going on and as yet to be disclosed. Elbert knew the Southern Region was carrying the whole company at the time. And the rest of the U.S. was having it rough. But Elbert really didn't put a lot of thought to it and started asking questions but, he didn't like the answers he was getting.

Then, there was the third offer of early retirement with

outstanding benefits to take it. He didn't want to, but something told him, you better take it. So he did. Elbert retired at 54 years old and went home with his retirement. The next eight years were very rewarding and the stock market was rewarding to the extent, he had more money than he started with and he had withdrawn quite a bit through the years.

Well, now he started to get his real education. He ended up on the Tattnall County Chamber of Commerce Board of Directors. And shortly after that, he was asked to serve on the Tattnall County Development Authority board of Directors, then, the Tattnall County Department of Family and Children Services Board of Directors.

This is when he started learning what was and had been going on within our country, state, and even county government. He never thought much about it, as he was so involved with his work and the company he worked for. He just assumed, our politicians were taking care of business and all was well. He soon learned, there was mixed opinions on that. And depending on whom you talk to, some were happy and some were not. Now to learn what is and what is not. Who is part of the problem and who is part of the solution? Then, where do we get the money, to right the wrongs, and build on the future.

He learned, there were people in this world that wanted to run everything, and would fight you to the death to get their way. He is talking about serious desires that they would run over you to get their way. Then, he found out there are people that don't want the lime light, but they are wanting their way bad enough to lie, steal and cheat. Then he found, there are people out there that are sheep. They will follow along with whatever, only because they want to be associated with others and be on the winning side. Whoever wins, they are the ones that voted for him or her. They might not like the person or what he stands for, but they will tell you he is the man. He learned we have a country in turmoil and basically, it is because for forty years our government has not done its job. They have put self interest ahead of what they were elected for. And second to that is the Greed of Major Corporations for maximum profits.

MISSION TRIP TO CHESTER, WEST VIRGINIA

With the approval of his church, Janice and Elbert volunteered to join others from other association and meet up in Charleston, West Virginia on the night of the day they left. They packed their things and Elbert loaded his truck and tool box with all the tools he thought he might need to remodel the Parsonage of the Baptist Church in Chester, West Virginia. The ladies and the teenagers were to cook all our meals and to conduct Vacation Bible School.

It was summer time and the roads were crowded with travelers going and coming from vacation, but a lot of the trip was on two lane back roads. The further north they went, they got into the hills and mountains they seen. They had never been this way before, so everything they seen were for the first time and really exciting. They stopped for lunch and visited a welcome station and wouldn't you know it, they ran into some of the people from back home, by chance. They came around a curve and lo and behold, there was a toll booth and a tunnel, demanding a cool $1.25 thank you. They went through the tunnel and out the other side of the mountain. They had just about forgotten about toll booths when they came up on another one, another $1.25 thank you. Well, it looks like they found a way to pay for their roads. They met up with their crowd at the motel where they had reservations. They all got a good night rest and left out early the next morning in a convoy. Now it was follow the leader that knew the way and where we were going. Well, they had no sooner got going again and wouldn't you know it, yet another toll booth, another $1.25 thank you.

They traveled on a highway running parallel to the Ohio River. Every so often there would be a red light and a bridge to cross the Ohio River. One of these red lights they stopped at had a sign that said Steubenville, Ohio, Home of Dean Martin. Now let me tell you, this was a very small town in Ohio.

The next town of any size was Wheeling, West Virginia. The highway went right through the middle of a giant Steel Mill. The town was basically long and narrows with several side streets. All through this town as they headed North, on the left side of the street was Bar, a Bar, a Bar, a Bar, Elbert had never seen so many bars. It was Bar Row.

Each had a different name and they learned the majority of the people there, worked in the steel mill. When their shift ended the men went straight to their favor bar to have a drink with the boys and talk about everything under the sun. On the other side of the street were houses and one lone Catholic and one Methodist Church.

As they traveled on northward they came to the town of their destination Chester, West Virginia. They came to a red light and if you went west one mile you would be in Ohio. If you went north one mile you would be in Ohio. And if you went east one mile you would be in Pennsylvania.

They went to the right and followed a winding road that went straight to the Baptist Church. The Church was built into and on top of a hill, a very pretty small Church with Sunday school rooms and a social hall down stairs and the Church at ground level. Pretty close to the Church was the Parsonage. A very nice five bedroom brick house with a basement. The pastor that had recently left had several big dogs, a German Shepherd and a Collie dog, that were kept in the basement. They had done some terrible damage in the basement. Elbert replaced sheet rock and door trim. They painted the Parsonage inside and outside. They installed storm doors on all exterior doors and painted the deck also. When they were through it was beautiful if they did say so themselves. Elbert was amazed at two of the older ladies, as they did something that he couldn't do, and still can't. They painted the baseboards in that whole house and closets, getting up and down a million times. Elbert might have been able to get down once and back up once but they were amazing. They did that for four days. They had to have had the Lords help.

The Ladies and the teen agers held Vacation Bible School and the people that came said they had never had such a good time and thanked the visitors over and over again. There were two ladies that did all the cooking, Elbert's wife Janice and the pastor's wife from Reidsville Baptist Church. They cooked three meals a day for everyone and did snacks for Bible School and never complained, not once.

At the end of the week, they said their goodbye's to their new friends and headed out for home. Everybody went their separate ways to travel home and sight see, as they wished. Elbert and Janice had never seen the Amish Country, so they crossed the Ohio River, into Ohio and there they were in traffic behind a horse drawn cart and witnessed the way they traveled around their community running errands just like we do, but not in an automobile, but a horse and buggy. Up ahead they noticed a large grocery store and there was a pay phone on the wall outside of the building. Janice wanted to call home and talk to the girls so as she talked on the phone, Elbert noticed a long shelter all across the front of the store. He noticed a horse and buggy entered it and went to the door. A boy helped a lady load the buggy and they then drove out and started up the road. As Elbert was watching all this he noticed a man and a woman walking fast to their horse and buggy, tied to a hitching rail, across the parking lot. As they got to their buggy, it started pouring down rain and they had no top. The lady pulled out an umbrella and held the groceries in her lap as they headed up the road.

    Then Elbert came to the realization, he had moved away from Janice so he could see everything and she didn't know where he was. She got wet, running to the truck. She had been watching all that Elbert had seen also and said since it looked like the rain was to set in for some time, let's head on home. They did and drove straight through and paid toll after toll. People live a different life in many ways up north, than we do down south. That is just the way it is, I guess. One is not really, better than the other, it's all in what you are used too and how you were raised. Elbert noticed we don't talk funny though, they do. They seem to think we talk funny.

    CARPENTER WORK

    The whole thirty years Elbert worked for Xerox, he also worked on weekends, holidays, and vacations, helping his father in law. He says worked. He was more a gopher than anything for a long time. Then Elbert started to use what he had learned. He followed Odis around and over time, Odis trusted Elbert to do certain things. When Odis passed away, and Elbert had retired, Elbert started getting calls to come fix this and that. Then it was to change out a window or door, small jobs.

    Then it got to be bigger things like Decks. Some were small at first then they got bigger, fancier, and more elaborate different levels etc. Elbert must have built over a hundred decks. The largest was a 140 foot long twelve feet wide with three exits, and a roof over 300 square feet and a 400 square foot screened in room. That was 1700 square feet total. He then built a 1200 square foot deck that was three levels.

Then it was Jim Walter homes. Elbert helped build two, two story 3200 square foot homes,   then a 3000 square foot single level home. Then it was a Pond house for sister in law. Elbert remodeled several homes. He built several carports, some for one car and some for three cars. He built a lot of things for the City Recreation Department and helped design and built a large Pavilion in town. It is 4000 square feet and is totally built out of Cypress, rough cut and shingles on the roof and sides. That was $27,000 dollars worth of Cypress, paid for by a Grant from the state.

Now for the next two years, Elbert helped build most of the buildings at Beaver Creek Plantation, in Cobbtown. He met the owners at lunch one day when he was working on the pavilion in town and they wanted him to come help them, as soon as he was finished, so he did.

Beaver Creek Plantation was owned by three brothers and Elbert got to know them very well and they are the best of friends today. Their main business is and remains Trucking. They run somewhere up to as high as 40 trucks, and haul any and everything. Elbert went out to the Plantation   and they were already into building the Lodge, so he started an addition to the existing building and helped them finish the building.

One night at about eight o'clock, Elbert went to wash up and Jack said, let's put the tile floor in this room down, before we go. Elbert told him, we have been at it for 12 hours and he was ready to go home and eat supper. Elbert went to wash up and when he came back, Jack is on his knees spreading the mud to lay 12 inch tile for the floor. Elbert couldn't leave him so they worked till midnight and got it done. That is the way Jack is and he pulled that stunt, many more times. Later on, Elbert and Jack laid the entire tile floor and the pavers on the front porch also. They became a team and what Jack didn't know, Elbert did and what Elbert didn't know, Jack did. Together, they have built a lot of pretty things at Beaver Creek.

After the Lodge was finished, they rented an off road six wheel drive articulating dump truck. Jack and Elbert met the truck delivering it and the man unloaded it and left. Elbert looked at Jack and Jack looked at Elbert and Jack said Drive it to the lake so it would be there in the morning. Elbert said, how do you start that thing? Jack said, I don't know. But they figured it out and Elbert drove it to the lake.

This lake had been dry for forty years at least. The dam broke and it had never been repaired. It was just left alone and Pine trees had grown up everywhere, and if you didn't know it you couldn't tell it had ever been a lake. Well, they had just bought a new Excavator and they had an older one, so jack says one day, for Elbert to get on the old one and Jack would run the new one, and they would pull up all the trees, stack them and burn them. The idea was to clean out the lake of trees. Elbert had always wanted to run a bull dozer, and an excavator and Elbert spent four months running whatever he needed to be on. Jack and Elbert cleaned out that lake of trees until they couldn't get any more due to quicksand and soft peat moss in vast areas.

Most all of the boggy area's were on jack 'side of the creek in the middle of the lake and Jack would bury his excavator every day, just as they were ready to go home. Then, they would spend another hour or two, pulling Jack out. Elbert and the other guys could have killed him some time. This stuff was like quicksand. One day they had set fire to a pile of trees and they went home. The next morning when they drove up to the lake, that fire had burned out but about a hundred feet away, smoke was coming out of the ground at the edge of the peat moss. What had happened was, the fire went underground and it burned for three months or until we closed the gate in the dam and water put it out.

Jack had an engineer come out to talk about what kind of spillway to build, where and how big etc. Jack and he talked for two hours and Elbert just listened until Elbert had to say something. Elbert took the pencil and drew the spillway. The engineer looked at Elbert and Elbert had used what Mr. Vinson had taught him when he took a course in concrete design, at the University of Memphis years ago. The engineer redrew it and said this would work and that is what they built, or something close to it.

Then Jack started digging a trench in the middle of the damn to deposit clay from a mile away to core the dam. That is when Elbert started running the big articulating dump truck, hauling clay from the clay pit. They had told Elbert to always be on level ground when he went to dump a load, or it might turn over. Elbert ask what should he do if he thinks it is going to turn over. They said brace yourself. Well on the second load Elbert brought to the dam, he raised the bed, to dump the load and he seen it starting to tip over. So, he braced himself, and he heard it go WHOOMP. The back end turned over, but the cab did not turn over. Elbert thought, oh no he has twisted this thing into. Elbert got out and looked and it was made to pivot in the middle he had not even hurt it. Jack was on the bull dozer, and Elbert looked at Jack and raised his arms as to say, what the hell do I do now? Jack smiled and did the same, like, what do I know? Jack then came over there and with the bulldozer, he stood it back up and he said: Go get another Load!

After the lake was finished, Jack and Elbert built a cabin at their trucking company and hauled it to Beaver Creek. Then they built another for a total of two.

Elbert went to work for them for a while doing a little of everything, but eventually went back to his building his own things. Elbert started going to Auctions with Jack to buy trucks and trailers as their business expanded. And Elbert learned a lot about the trucking business. But they had forgotten more than Elbert ever learned. But it was interesting and Elbert has been able to help some real nice people.

After going back to answering the calls he was getting, to build this and that, Elbert really got busy for a while and their church had needed a new larger Social hall. Elbert took on a 6500 square foot two story Social Hall for his church. It took him a year to finish it but he was really proud of it. Then jack wanted Elbert to help them build a log, two bedroom cabin. I helped them but he wasn't in a very good mood at the time. This is when Lynn died and he liked to have never got over that. And it showed in his work.

After that, he remodeled several houses and two Funeral homes. Then one day, Jack called and asked if he wanted to ride to Savannah with him to buy some mattresses, for a new Building he had built at Beaver Creek. Elbert met him in Metter and rode with him. They ended up only going to Statesboro, but they found what Jack wanted and took them to the building where they were needed. They got them all unloaded and installed then they went to lunch and ate barbecue. When Jack took Elbert to his truck, Elbert was hurting but he didn't say anything. Elbert asked Jack if he had heartburn from that barbecue, but he said no. When Jack drove off, Elbert sat in his truck a minute and decided to go to the drug store and check his blood pressure.

HEART ATTACK

Elbert went in the drug store and used one of those chair blood pressure reading things. It was 203 over 188, and he knew he was in trouble. He headed for the doctor's office next door to the hospital and he asked the lady there to look at what he had written down for blood pressure readings. Elbert asked did he need to see a doctor or go on to the emergency room. She looked up at him and said you need the emergency room now. Elbert just turned and walked out, heading for the emergency room. Then he realized he had forgot his truck so he walked back to get it and drove next door to the emergency room. When he got inside, he handed the paper with blood pressure reading on it to the nurse, as he could not talk by then. They put him in a wheel chair and took him to a room and stripped him down and started doing all kinds of things. After awhile they determined he had already had a heart attack and there was damage and he needed to be rushed to Savannah for catheterization to see what blockages he might have. He was told if a stent would solve his problems, they would do it right then, but if he needed by pass, it would be done in the operating room scheduled later that night or the next morning. Elbert ended up with two stents and he is fine now, to a certain degree.

It took several months and doubling his medicine to get his blood pressure down to normal, but they did it. Elbert stayed on Plavix, a blood thinner, for a year and after getting off of it, he got some of his energy back, but not all of it

COMENTARY, LISTEN AND HEAR YOUR HEART

You know, it dawned on Elbert one day, that there is a lot of wisdom in the words of his life. He has to wonder sometimes, when will people ever learn? There are those that blunder through life, not remembering their past. Not remembering their mistakes or their accomplishments. You have to ask sometimes when they will ever learn to accept the wisdom and pay attention to those that have gone on before them. Read, listen and contemplate where, how, and why did they go where they went? Look and listen to the excitement and the fun they had. Eagerly look where their next adventure took them. Learn to walk a mile in another man's shoes as they have. Have empathy for the down trodden. Never, I mean Never, push another out of the way, stop and pick him up and carry him with you. Never except credit where credit is not due. Trust in your instincts, for they are the foundation your parents taught you. And when you work for a man, then for heaven's sake, work for the man. Hush and be quiet and give your task the attention it deserves.

When we were young, we were full of life. We were curious of everything before us and excited to see and touch and smell the moment before us. We were so excited about what later in the day had in store for us that we didn't stop to smell the roses as we ran everywhere. Elbert has said it a thousand times and never realized he knew the answer all the time. The question was, in regards to running everywhere, never walking. Why doesn't children slow down, they are going to fall down or knock over something over or knock somebody else down running like that. The answer is, they can't wait to get to the next stage of their life. They run here and there so they can get on to the next fun and exciting thing to do right now.

Elbert has lived every moment he has been given. His dreams have been fulfilled. He has experienced everything he wanted to touch and feel. He has been places that were like in the movies and the books he has read. Elbert has seen happiness, those that were lonely, and those that were sad. He has known the rich and the super rich. He is reminded of the words of his brother Wayne, when he came home from Basic training in the Air Force. He was talking to their mother and he said, about the world he had just seen. There are people and there are people and there are people. He was talking about the Good, the Bad and the Ugly. He had never been around minorities or foreign people. He had never been even been around Yankees.

We come into this world, then we live it, then we leave it. Elbert lived the life he seen and he participated. He did all the things he wanted to do and now as he enters those years of paying for all the fun he had. He finds there were other things that he was suppose to have done and at least done better than he did. He should have been more available to his wife, his children, his friends and family. He should have spent more time with them. He should have spent more time acknowledging what they wanted and what they did. He should have listened to them more. He should have had more availability. He wished he had been around more to hold them when they were sad, when they wanted to talk, or show him something. He missed out on a lot of these things as he was so involved with his work that he let it rob him of thousands of moments, he could be remembering and they could be remembering also. He got on a train that he couldn't get off of.

He wished he had studied the bible more than he did. The answers to a lot of life's questions lie there waiting to be read. He wished he had spent more time in Sunday school and Church. Not only would he have understood more about life. He would have had more answers to a lot of things.

Elbert's life has not been totally controlled by himself. There has been a time the lord has walked with me. He has talked with me and given me encouragement. He has given me many gifts. His life was one of those gifts. His children were gifts. His wife was a gift. His success has been a gift. His friends and relatives and those he lived and work around are gifts. And you know what? They are the very ones he should have been more of an example to. His life is not without purpose. He is here by the grace of God and he has had responsibilities of which, some have been fulfilled and he can see now,   some that he has yet to fulfill.

Elbert believes we will all stand before god in Judgment one day. It's a shame, he has not been more conscience of that, all during his life, but he hasn't. He believes he will go to heaven and be with the

Lord. He doesn't believe he is worthy. He doesn't believe his rewards will be as great as others. But he is comfortable with that. There are people that have given their life for the Lord. They deserve to sit on the right hand of God. There have been people to give their future and what they might have done or accomplished to the Lord. They are more deserving than Elbert. What Elbert does know is he has walked with him and talked with him and he is his own. Elbert doesn't know how he could love him or why he does, but Elbert knows he does.

You might say, just how does he know that? Look back on Elbert's life and count the times Elbert put himself in harm's way and he walked away clean, unbroken and alive until this day. Look at the wonderful life Elbert has had in this world. And he will tell you a story that happened on Sunday in Jacksonville, Florida years ago. It dawned on him later, what had just happened. Elbert had done the right thing and trusted the lord would provide and he did. You might not be impressed with what Elbert just told you, but Elbert is proud to say, that was just the first time, that he recognized, what had just happened. There have been several other times, not quite the same but close enough, to clearly make him aware, that the lord had just provided again and again for him and his family. He did it again just last week. In your darkest hour, do what is right and have faith, and he will provide.

I LOVE EVERYTHING THAT IS OLD

That includes, People, Places and things, of past times. The biggest apology, Elbert owes a High School Teacher is, to a history Teacher, Mr. Wicker. At the time, Elbert thought that was the most boring subject known to man. His real problem was, with dates and names, Elbert remembered the events, but couldn't remember the dates or their name. Elbert had a 1930 model A Ford for 31 years. He now has, a 1937 Oldsmobile. He now loves old things. Elbert and Janice just returned from visiting another antique shop. Their home is full of antique treasures they have accumulated through the years.

They went to London, England and immediately were in awe of the dates on buildings. Elbert thought he had seen some old things in America, but he quickly learned they have nothing older than 200 years. They visited places that were 1200 years old and older. He has farming tools that were used to gather wheat, shell corn, and many other uses, a hundred years ago and more. He has teeth from the Mammoth and the Mastodon Elephants in America. He has camel teeth found in Florida. He has shark teeth found in rivers, that don't run all the way to the ocean, 150 miles from the ocean. At one time the whole state of Florida was covered by water. When the water receded, the sharks, and whales were trapped in rivers, there to die and leave their teeth to be found sometime in 1970.

There was a time when there were more camels in the state of Florida, than there is in the world today. All this, he learned scuba diving in rivers and studying paleontology. Elbert thinks Mr. Wicker would be impressed with him now.

At times, as Elbert has grown up, he wished he had lived in the past times. He wanted to live in the cowboy and Indian days. Then he wanted to live in the Victorian era. He wanted to sail the sailing ships. He especially loves old people. He loves to sit and listen to them tell of years past, and some of the outstanding people, long gone now. On their farm, still stands the house his wife's mother was born and raised in. The cemetery holds the people who settled the community they live in. Elbert is lucky to have met and loved many of the old folks in the community his wife grew up in.

Elbert was raised in an era where children were to speak when spoken to and was to be seen and not heard. Therefore, he would sit in the presence of the old folks and listen to them talk. He used to be interested in what they were talking about. Not the everyday things, but the stories about when they were growing up. Some of it was unbelievable at the time. It still amazes him, there were secrets they didn't want children to hear, but they would forget they were sitting there listening to every word. That is when they would send children outside to sit on the porch until they were ready to leave. So they wouldn't hear what they were talking about.

You knew when you heard something you shouldn't have, because when you repeated it and you were asked, where did you hear that? Who told you that? And he was told, don't you ever repeat that. You know what, so and so got drunk and had a wreck. Did you hear about so and so? Her black eye comes from the next door neighbor. He learned, you don't ask questions about anything you heard, because some of it, you were not suppose to know it, ever. Like so and so is in jail for a year. No, don't tell me, not Uncle so and so. And, thank goodness it wasn't for twenty years.

I better stop here for now. Who knows, there might be more to tell one day. Elbert hopes you have enjoyed these stories. Elbert wished more of his relatives had written down the past. Life is so interesting and it all amazes him.

NEW CAREER

Back in 2006 after Elbert had a heart attack, he began seriously reading books by author's Stuart Woods and Sandra brown. These were adventure mysteries and Elbert really got into these books. Elbert decided to one day in 2010 to write his memoirs for his children and grandchildren, called Cotton Top, Remember me. Then he wrote a novel about his adventures scuba diving called Cay Sal, the discovery. Then he wrote a sequel to that called Old Gold and another sequel called Diamonds and Gold. Then he wrote a novel called Red Bull about his military days in the Air Force. Then he wrote a Romantic action thriller called Chasing Second Chances. In 2013 RED BULL was published in paperback and on Kindle, electronic publishing. So now Elbert is known as a writer and author.

MORE HEALTH PROBLEMS

Elbert all of a sudden got weak and weaker and finally went to the doctor. Elbert was diagnosed as diabetic. While in the hospital, it was discovered Elbert had a tumor on his left kidney and it had to be removed. He was admitted again and the bottom one third of his left kidney was removed. This was in 2012. Today in 2013 one year later, all is well and totally gone.

So, until another time in the life of Elbert, we will ask you to keep the faith and reach for the stars, as we are not promised tomorrow. God Love you all.